MRYA

THE HULK WILL ALWAYS BE A PART OF DR. BRUCE BANNER, BUT BANNER WANTS TO BE REMEMBERED FOR HIS CONTRIBUTIONS TO SCIENCE AND NOT FOR TURNING INTO A BIG, GREEN FORCE OF RAGE AND DESTRUCTION. TO ACHIEVE THAT GOAL, BANNER HAS STRUCK A MUTUALLY BENEFICIAL DEAL WITH MARIA HILL, THE DIRECTOR OF S.H.I.E.L.D. SHE PROVIDES BANNER WITH A LAB, STAFF AND ALL OF THE RESOURCES HE NEEDS TO BETTER MANKIND, AND BANNER PROVIDES S.H.I.E.L.D. WITH THE HULK FOR ANY MISSIONS THAT MIGHT NEED EXTRA MUSCLE.

D1299192

INDESTRUCTIBLE HULK

GODS AND MONSTER

VOLUME 02

INDESTRUCTIBLE HULK VOL. 2: GODS AND MONSTER. Contains material originally published in magazine form as INDESTRUCTIBLE HULK #6-10. First printing 2014. ISBN# 978-0-7851-6648-1. Published by MARVEL WORLDWIDE, INC., a subsidiary of MARVEL ENTERTAINMENT, LLC. OFFICE OF PUBLICATION: 135 West 50th Street, New York, NY 10020. Copyright © 2013 and 2014 Marvel Characters, Inc. All rights reserved. All characters featured in this issue and the distinctive names and likenesses thereof, and all related indicia are trademarks of Marvel Characters, Inc. No similarity between any of the names, characters, persons, and/or institutions in this magazine with those of any living or dead person or institution is intended, and any such similarity which may exist is purely coincidental. **Printed in the U.S.A.** ALAN FINE, EVP - Office of the President, Marvel Worldwide, Inc. and EVP & CMO Marvel Characters B.V.; DAN BUCKLEY, Publisher & President - Print, Animation & Digital Divisions; JOE QUESADA, Chief Creative Officer; TOM BREVOORT, SVP of Publishing; DAVID BOGART, SVP of Operations & Procurement, Publishing; C.B. CEBULSKI, SVP of Creator & Content Development; DAVID GABRIEL, SVP Print, Sales & Marketing; JIM O'KEEFE, VP of Operations & Logistics; DAN CARR, Executive Director of Publishing Technology; SUSAN CRESPI, Editorial Operations Manager; ALEX MORALES, Publishing Operations Manager; STAN LEE, Chairman Emeritus. For information regarding advertising in Marvel Comics or on Marvel.com, please contact Niza Disla, Director of Marvel Partnerships, at ndisla@marvel.com. For Marvel subscription inquiries, please call 800-217-9158. **Manufactured between 3/14/2014 and 4/21/2014** by R.R. DONNELLEY, INC., SALEM, VA, USA.

10 9 8 7 6 5 4 3 2 1

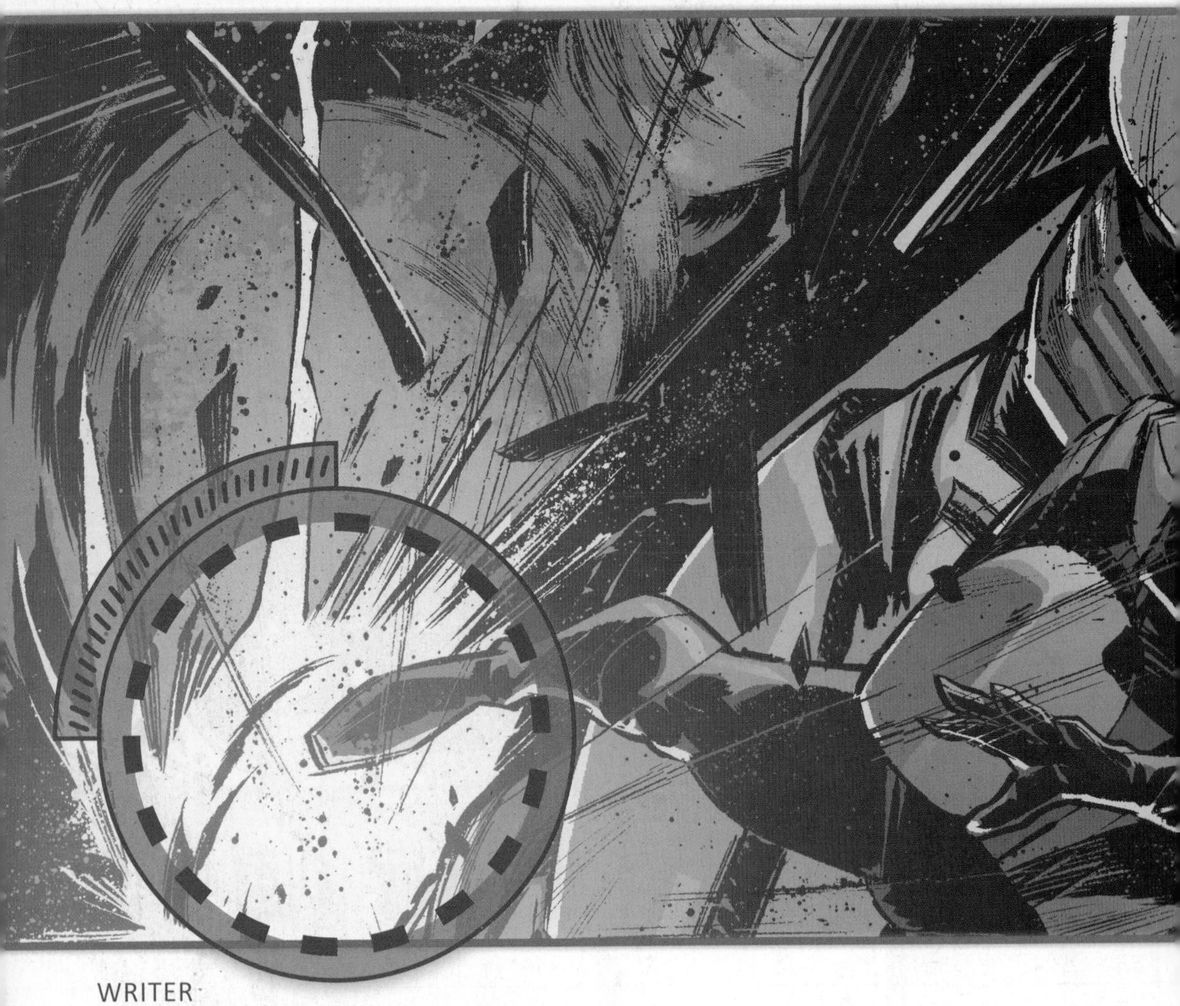

WRITER
MARK WAID
ARTISTS
WALTER SIMONSON (#6-8)
& **MATTEO SCALERA** (#9-10)
INK ASSISTS (#7-8) **BOB WIACEK**
COLOR ARTISTS
ANDRES MOSSA (#6-7), **JIM CHARALAMPIDIS** (#8)
& **VAL STAPLES** (#9-10)
LETTERER
CHRIS ELIOPOULOS
COVER ART
WALTER SIMONSON & **LAURA MARTIN** (#6-8)
& **PAOLO RIVERA** (#9-10)
ASSISTANT EDITOR
JON MOISAN
EDITOR
MARK PANICCIA

COLLECTION EDITOR
MARK D. BEAZLEY
ASSOCIATE MANAGING EDITOR
ALEX STARBUCK
EDITOR, SPECIAL PROJECTS
JENNIFER GRÜNWALD

SENIOR EDITOR,
SPECIAL PROJECTS
JEFF YOUNGQUIST
SVP PRINT, SALES & MARKETING
DAVID GABRIEL

EDITOR IN CHIEF
AXEL ALONSO
CHIEF CREATIVE OFFICER
JOE QUESADA
PUBLISHER
DAN BUCKLEY
EXECUTIVE PRODUCER
ALAN FINE

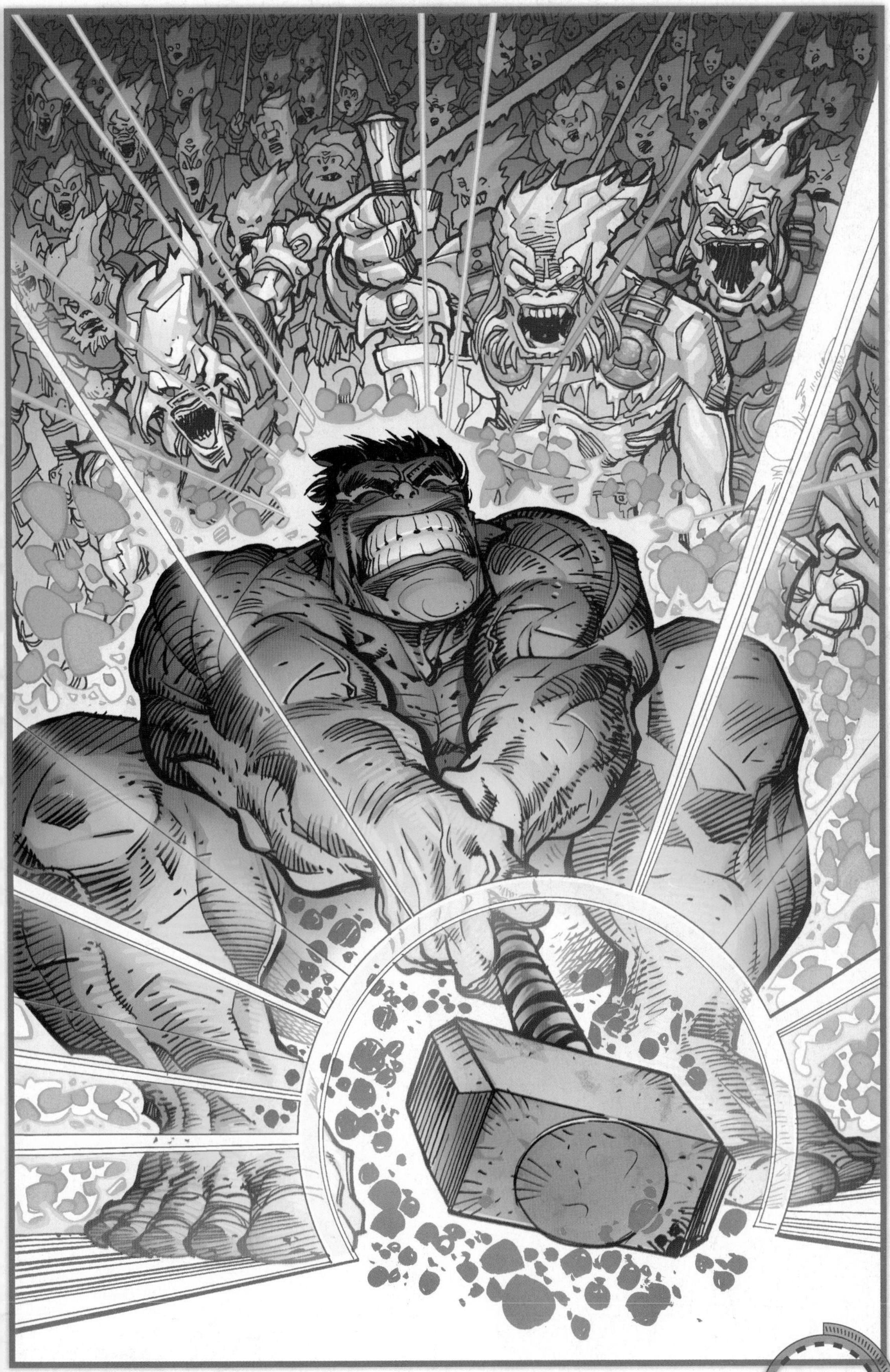

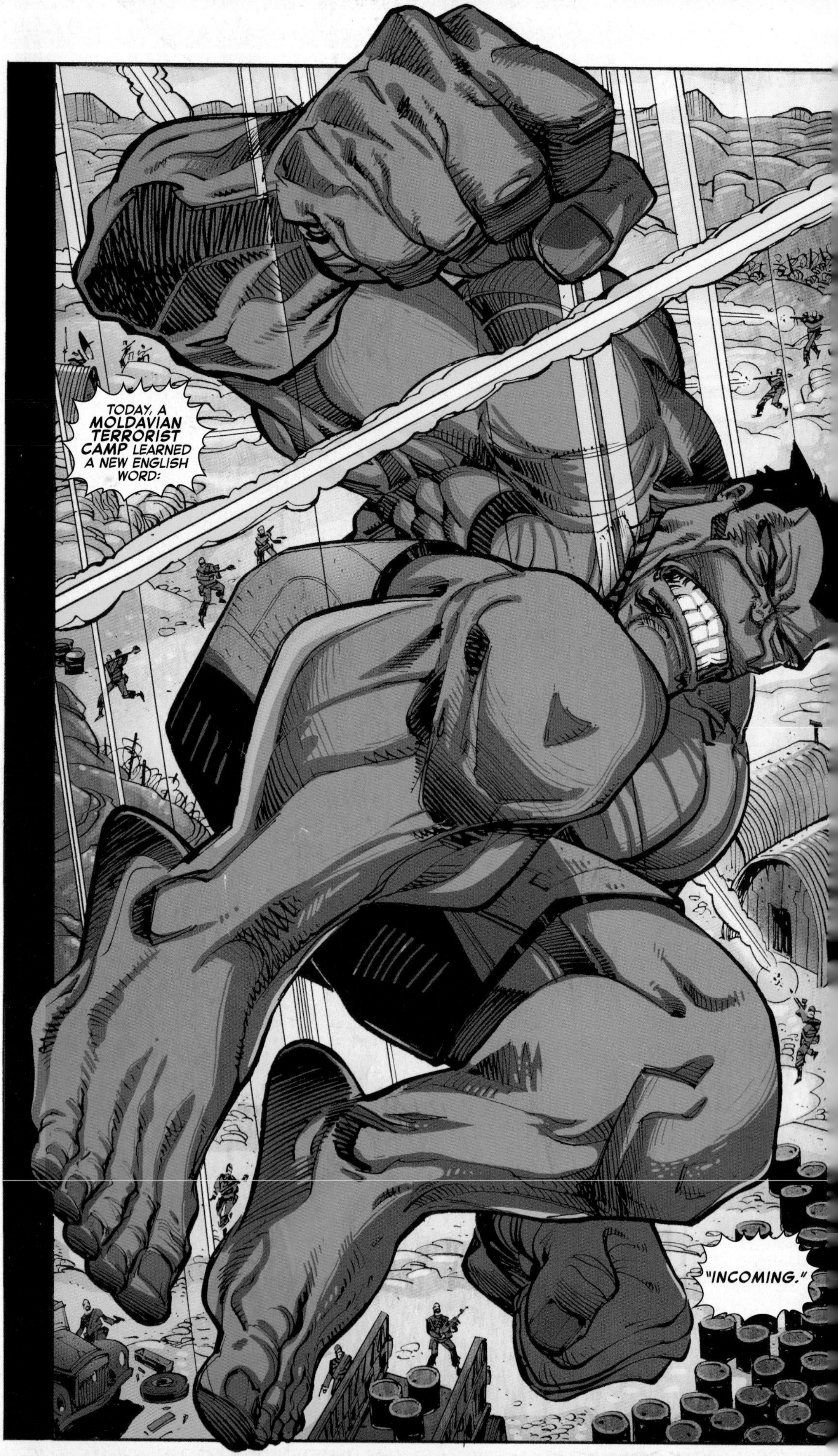
TODAY, A MOLDAVIAN TERRORIST CAMP LEARNED A NEW ENGLISH WORD:
"INCOMING."

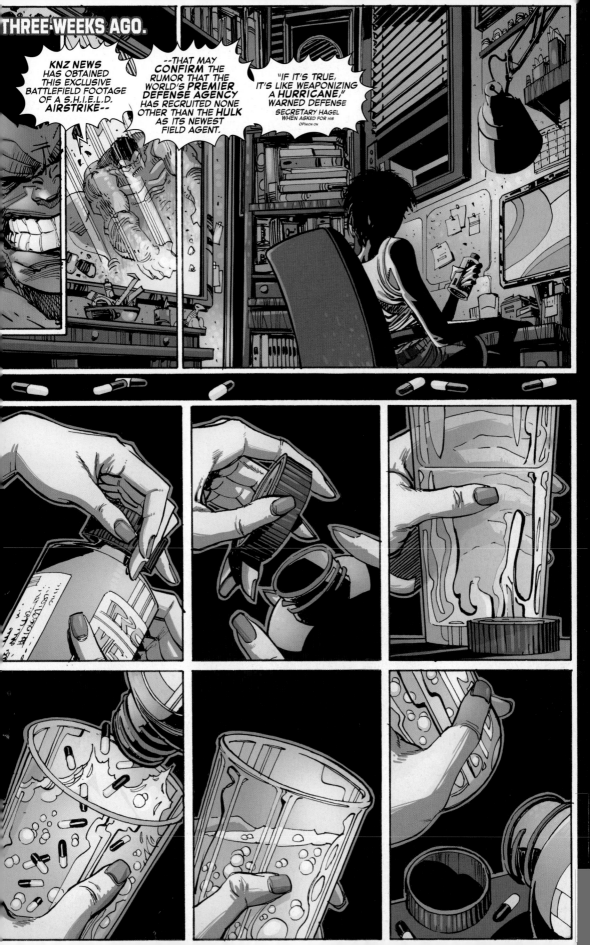

KNZ NEWS HAS OBTAINED THIS EXCLUSIVE BATTLEFIELD FOOTAGE OF A S.H.I.E.L.D. AIRSTRIKE--

--THAT MAY CONFIRM THE RUMOR THAT THE WORLD'S PREMIER DEFENSE AGENCY HAS RECRUITED NONE OTHER THAN THE HULK AS ITS NEWEST FIELD AGENT.

"IF IT'S TRUE, IT'S LIKE WEAPONIZING A HURRICANE," WARNED DEFENSE SECRETARY HAGEL WHEN ASKED FOR HIS OPINION ON

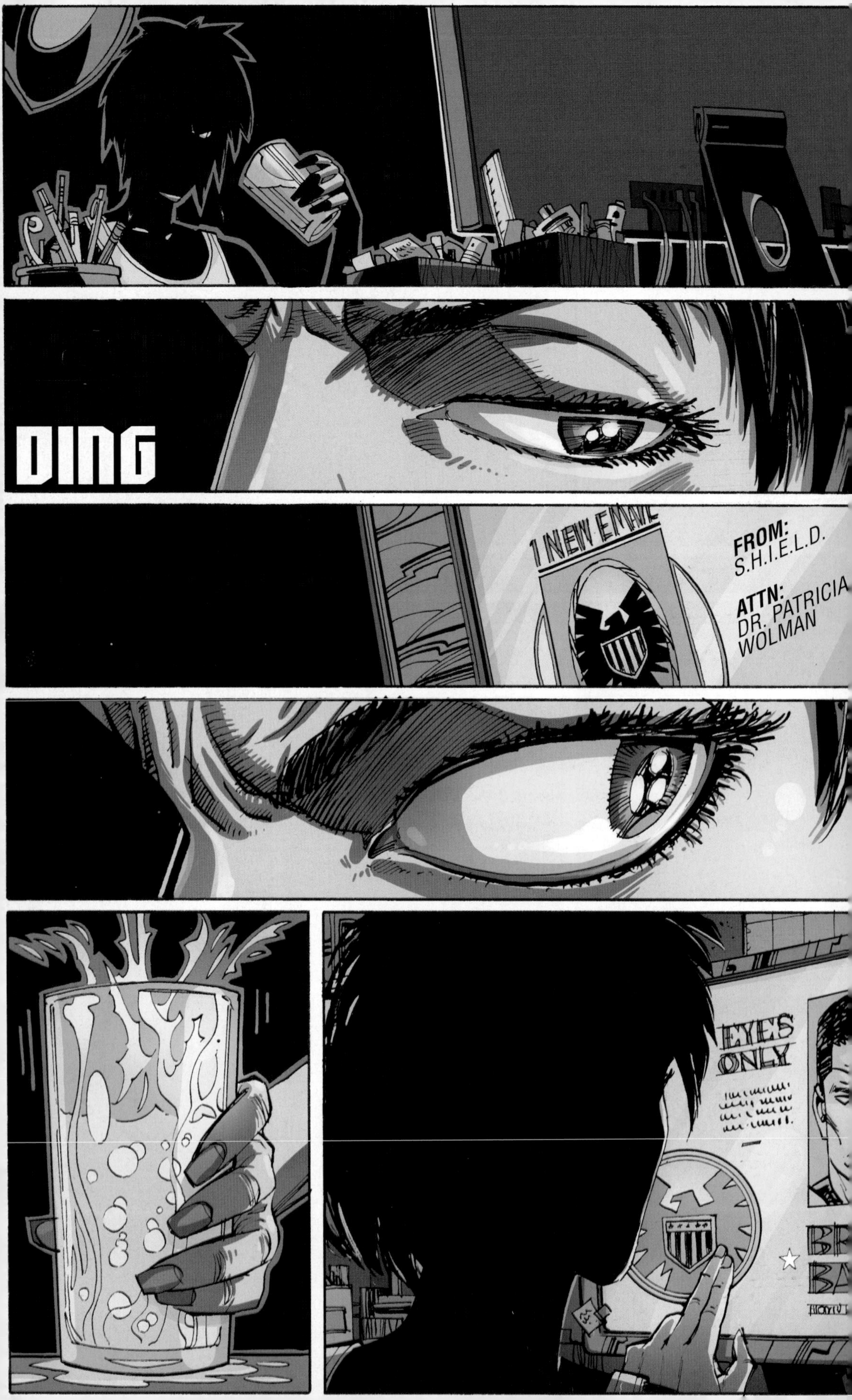
DING
1 NEW EMAIL
FROM: S.H.I.E.L.D.
ATTN: DR. PATRICIA WOLMAN
EYES ONLY

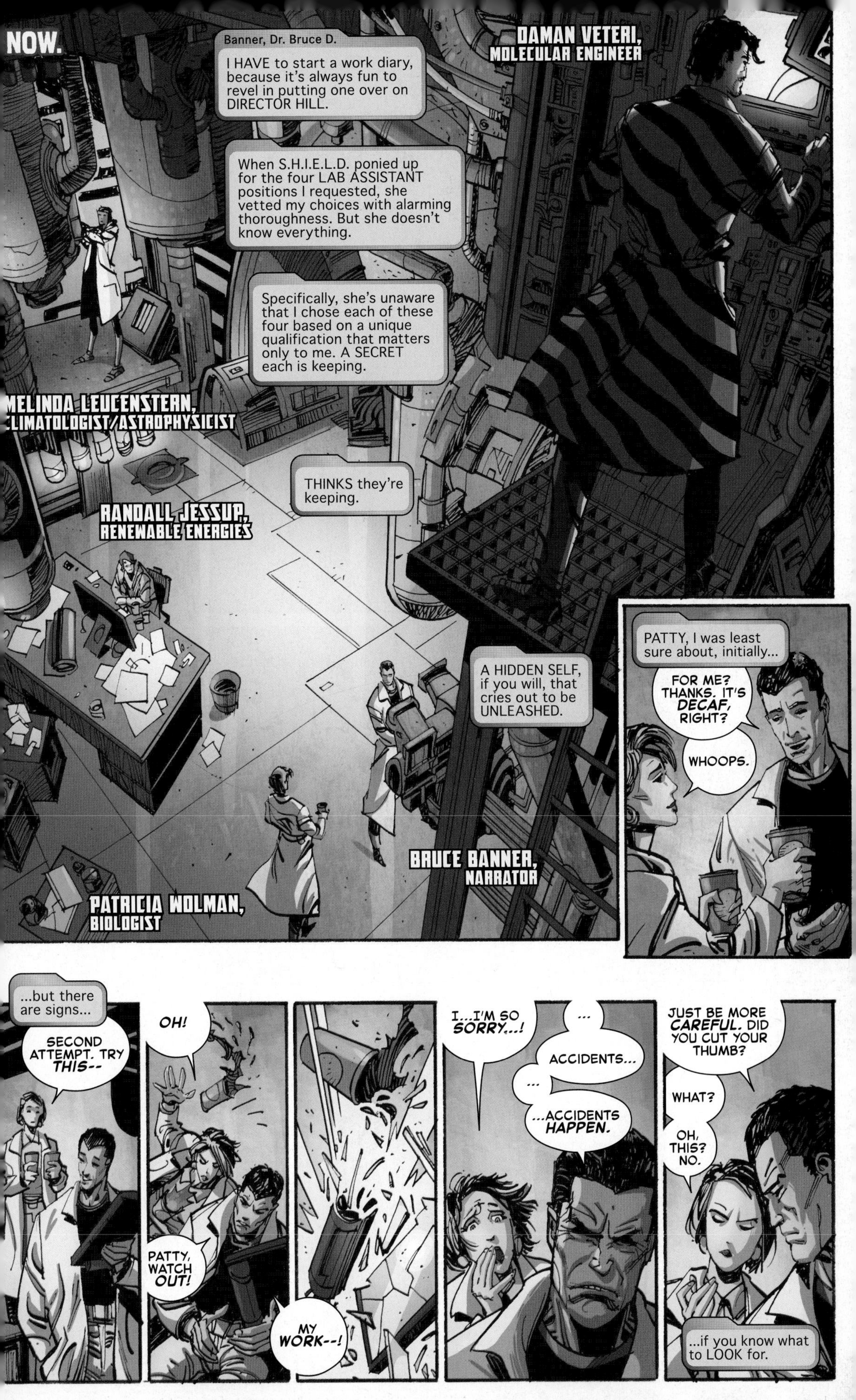
NOW.
Banner, Dr. Bruce D.
I HAVE to start a work diary, because it's always fun to revel in putting one over on DIRECTOR HILL.
DAMAN VETERI, MOLECULAR ENGINEER
When S.H.I.E.L.D. ponied up for the four LAB ASSISTANT positions I requested, she vetted my choices with alarming thoroughness. But she doesn't know everything.
Specifically, she's unaware that I chose each of these four based on a unique qualification that matters only to me. A SECRET each is keeping.
MELINDA LEUCENSTERN, CLIMATOLOGIST/ASTROPHYSICIST
THINKS they're keeping.
RANDALL JESSUP, RENEWABLE ENERGIES
A HIDDEN SELF, if you will, that cries out to be UNLEASHED.
BRUCE BANNER, NARRATOR
PATRICIA WOLMAN, BIOLOGIST
PATTY, I was least sure about, initially...
FOR ME? THANKS. IT'S DECAF, RIGHT?
WHOOPS.
...but there are signs...
SECOND ATTEMPT. TRY THIS--
OH!
PATTY, WATCH OUT!
MY WORK--!
I...I'M SO SORRY...!
...
ACCIDENTS...
...
...ACCIDENTS HAPPEN.
JUST BE MORE CAREFUL. DID YOU CUT YOUR THUMB?
WHAT?
OH, THIS? NO.
...if you know what to LOOK for.

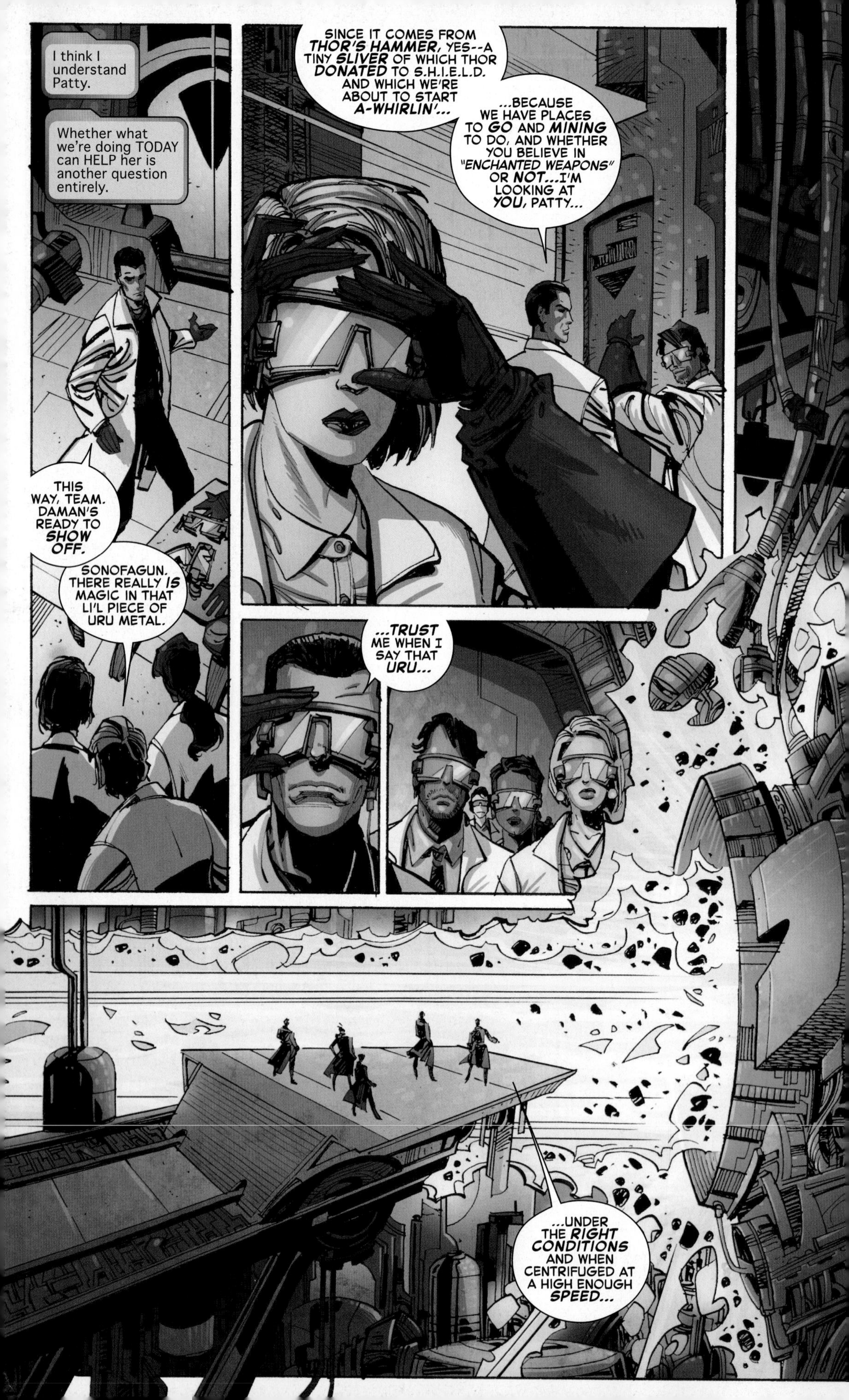
I think I understand Patty.
Whether what we're doing TODAY can HELP her is another question entirely.
SINCE IT COMES FROM THOR'S HAMMER, YES--A TINY SLIVER OF WHICH THOR DONATED TO S.H.I.E.L.D. AND WHICH WE'RE ABOUT TO START A-WHIRLIN'...
...BECAUSE WE HAVE PLACES TO GO AND MINING TO DO, AND WHETHER YOU BELIEVE IN "ENCHANTED WEAPONS" OR NOT...I'M LOOKING AT YOU, PATTY...
THIS WAY, TEAM. DAMAN'S READY TO SHOW OFF.
SONOFAGUN. THERE REALLY IS MAGIC IN THAT LI'L PIECE OF URU METAL.
...TRUST ME WHEN I SAY THAT URU...
...UNDER THE RIGHT CONDITIONS AND WHEN CENTRIFUGED AT A HIGH ENOUGH SPEED...

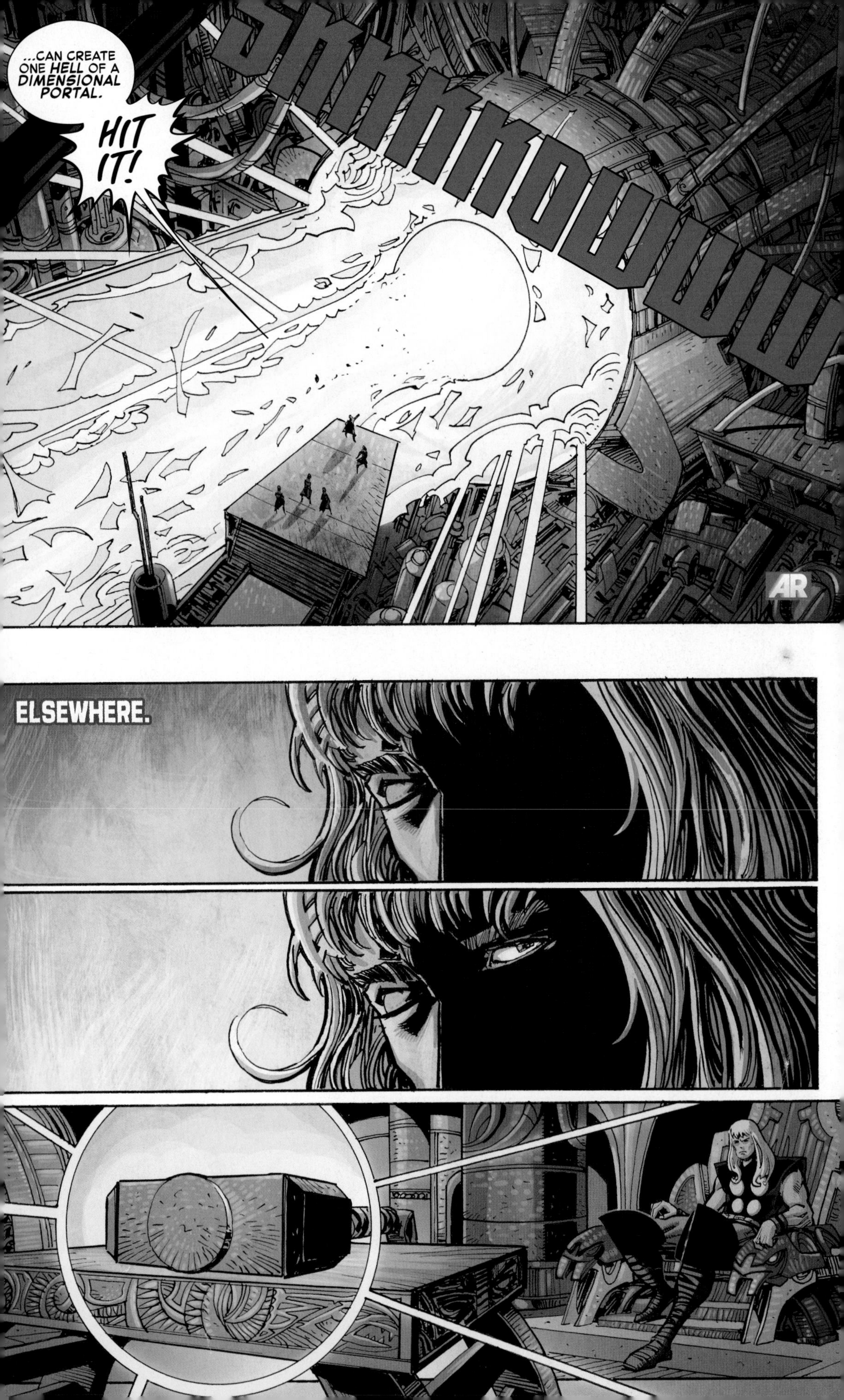
...CAN CREATE ONE HELL OF A DIMENSIONAL PORTAL.
HIT IT!
ELSEWHERE.

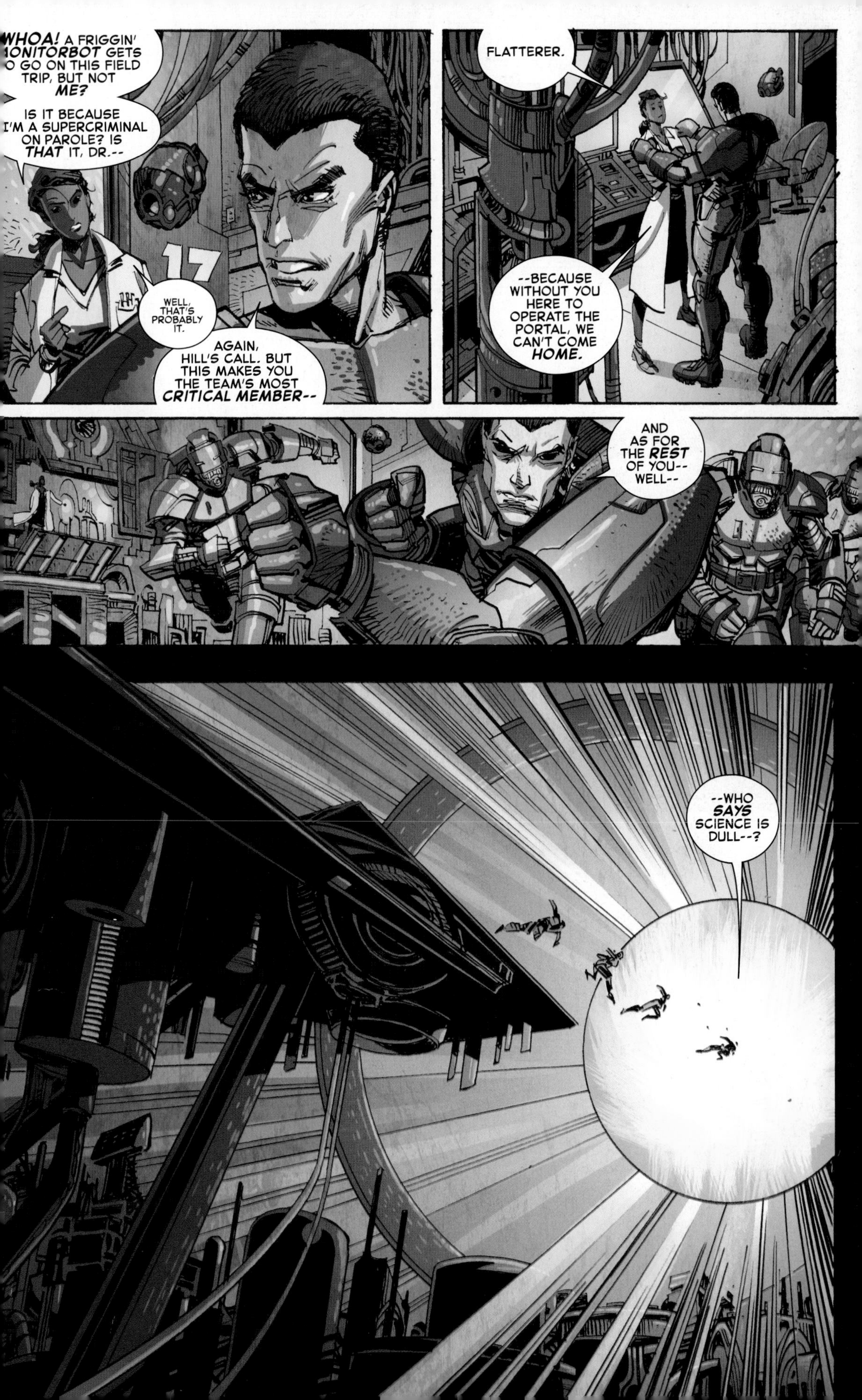
WHOA! A FRIGGIN' MONITORBOT GETS TO GO ON THIS FIELD TRIP, BUT NOT ME?
IS IT BECAUSE I'M A SUPERCRIMINAL ON PAROLE? IS THAT IT, DR.--
WELL, THAT'S PROBABLY IT.
AGAIN, HILL'S CALL. BUT THIS MAKES YOU THE TEAM'S MOST CRITICAL MEMBER--
FLATTERER.
--BECAUSE WITHOUT YOU HERE TO OPERATE THE PORTAL, WE CAN'T COME HOME.
AND AS FOR THE REST OF YOU-- WELL--
--WHO SAYS SCIENCE IS DULL--?

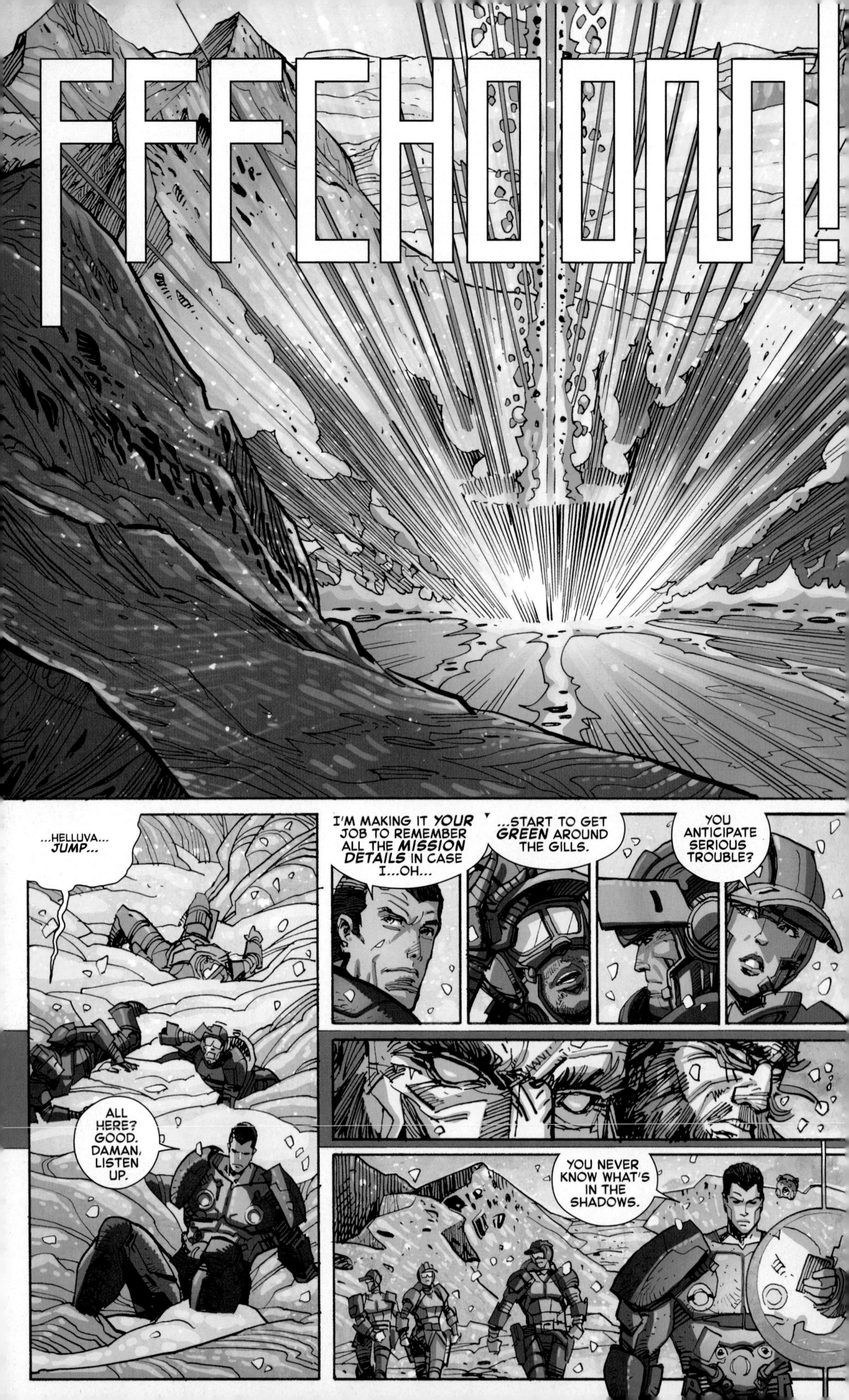
FFFCHOOM!
...HELLUVA... JUMP...
ALL HERE? GOOD. DAMAN, LISTEN UP.
I'M MAKING IT YOUR JOB TO REMEMBER ALL THE MISSION DETAILS IN CASE I...OH...
...START TO GET GREEN AROUND THE GILLS.
YOU ANTICIPATE SERIOUS TROUBLE?
YOU NEVER KNOW WHAT'S IN THE SHADOWS.

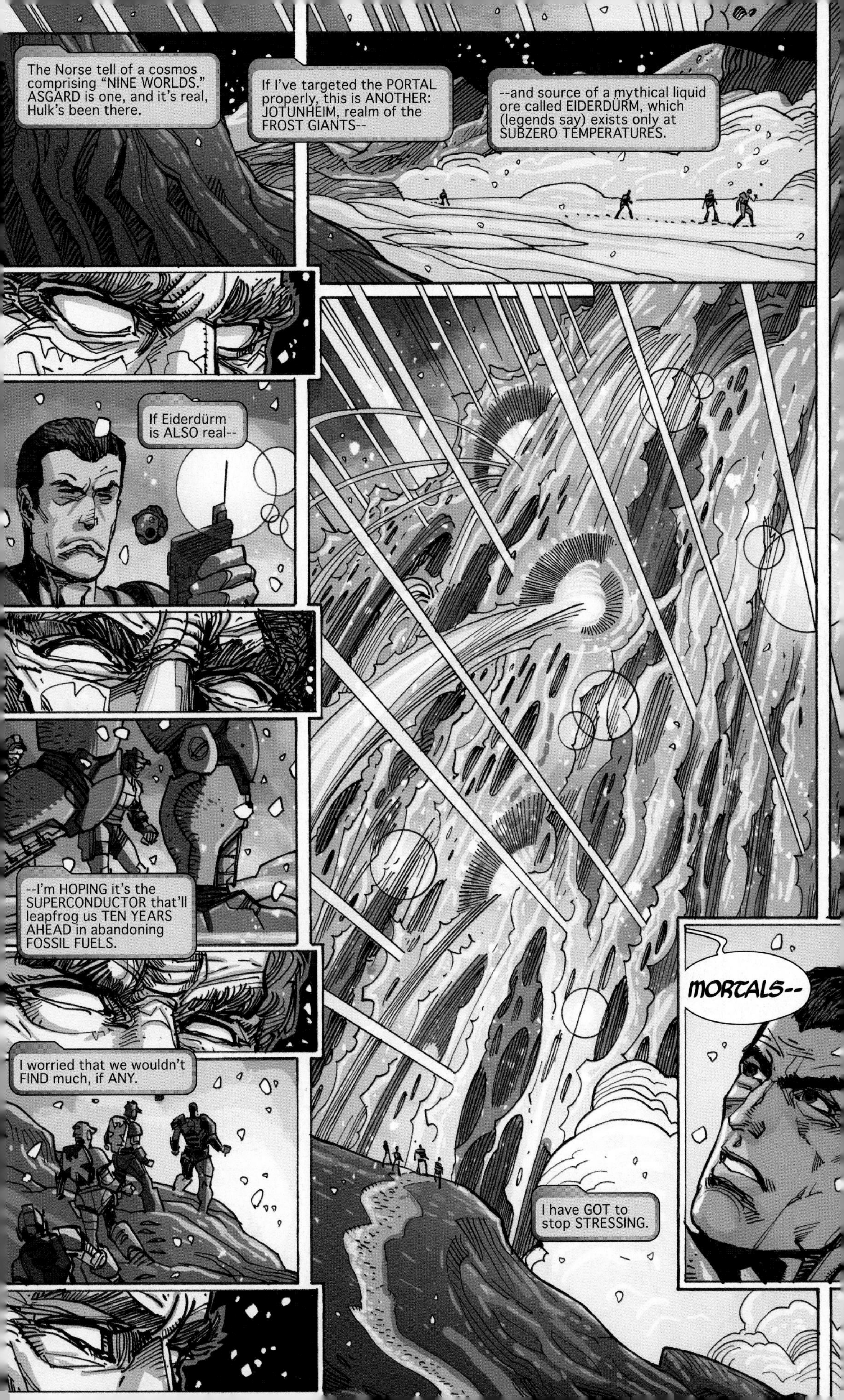
The Norse tell of a cosmos comprising "NINE WORLDS." ASGARD is one, and it's real, Hulk's been there.
If I've targeted the PORTAL properly, this is ANOTHER: JOTUNHEIM, realm of the FROST GIANTS--
--and source of a mythical liquid ore called EIDERDÜRM, which (legends say) exists only at SUBZERO TEMPERATURES.
If Eiderdürm is ALSO real--
--I'm HOPING it's the SUPERCONDUCTOR that'll leapfrog us TEN YEARS AHEAD in abandoning FOSSIL FUELS.
I worried that we wouldn't FIND much, if ANY.
I have GOT to stop STRESSING.
MORTALS--

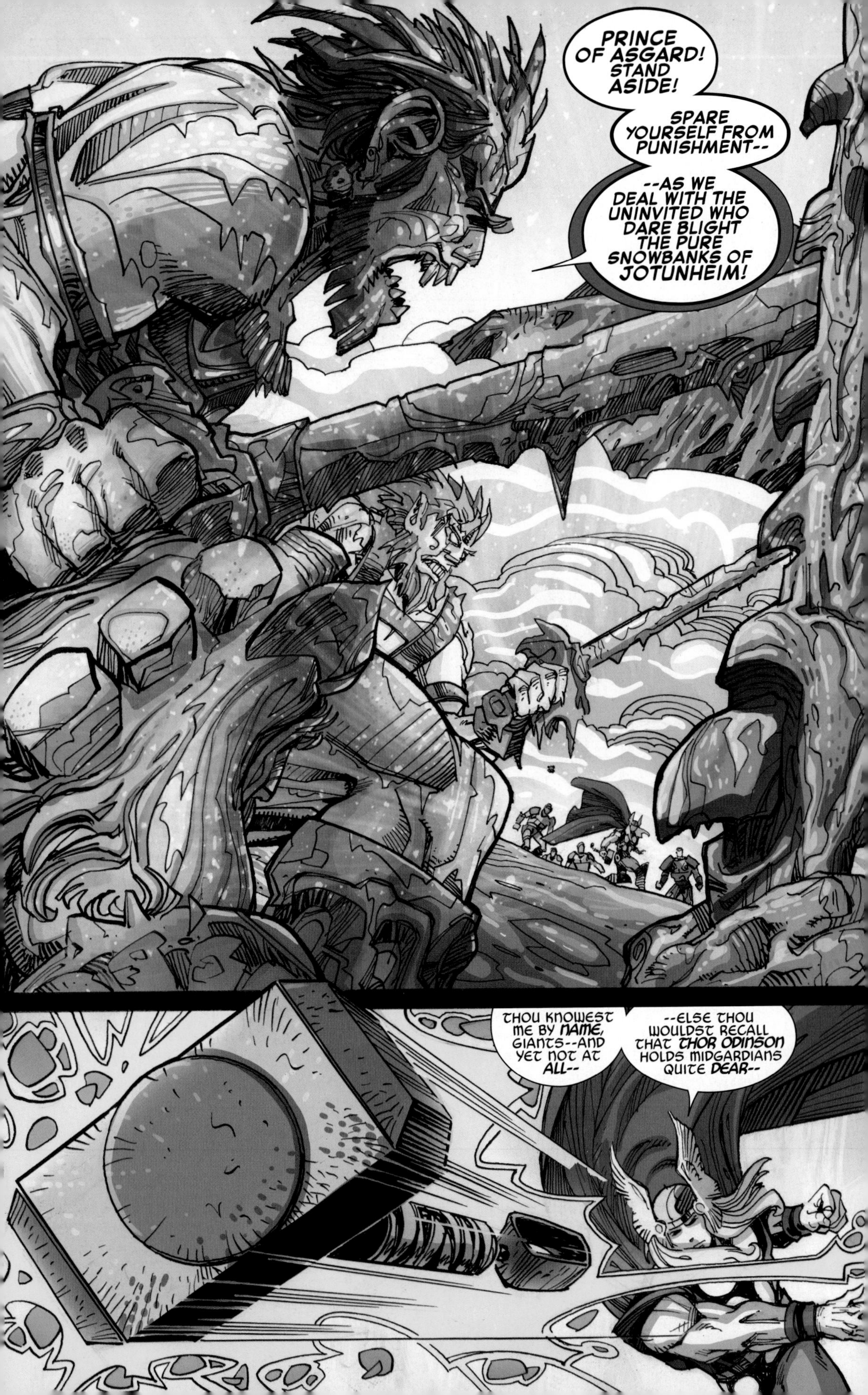
PRINCE OF ASGARD! STAND ASIDE!
SPARE YOURSELF FROM PUNISHMENT--
--AS WE DEAL WITH THE UNINVITED WHO DARE BLIGHT THE PURE SNOWBANKS OF JOTUNHEIM!
THOU KNOWEST ME BY NAME, GIANTS--AND YET NOT AT ALL--
--ELSE THOU WOULDST RECALL THAT THOR ODINSON HOLDS MIDGARDIANS QUITE DEAR--

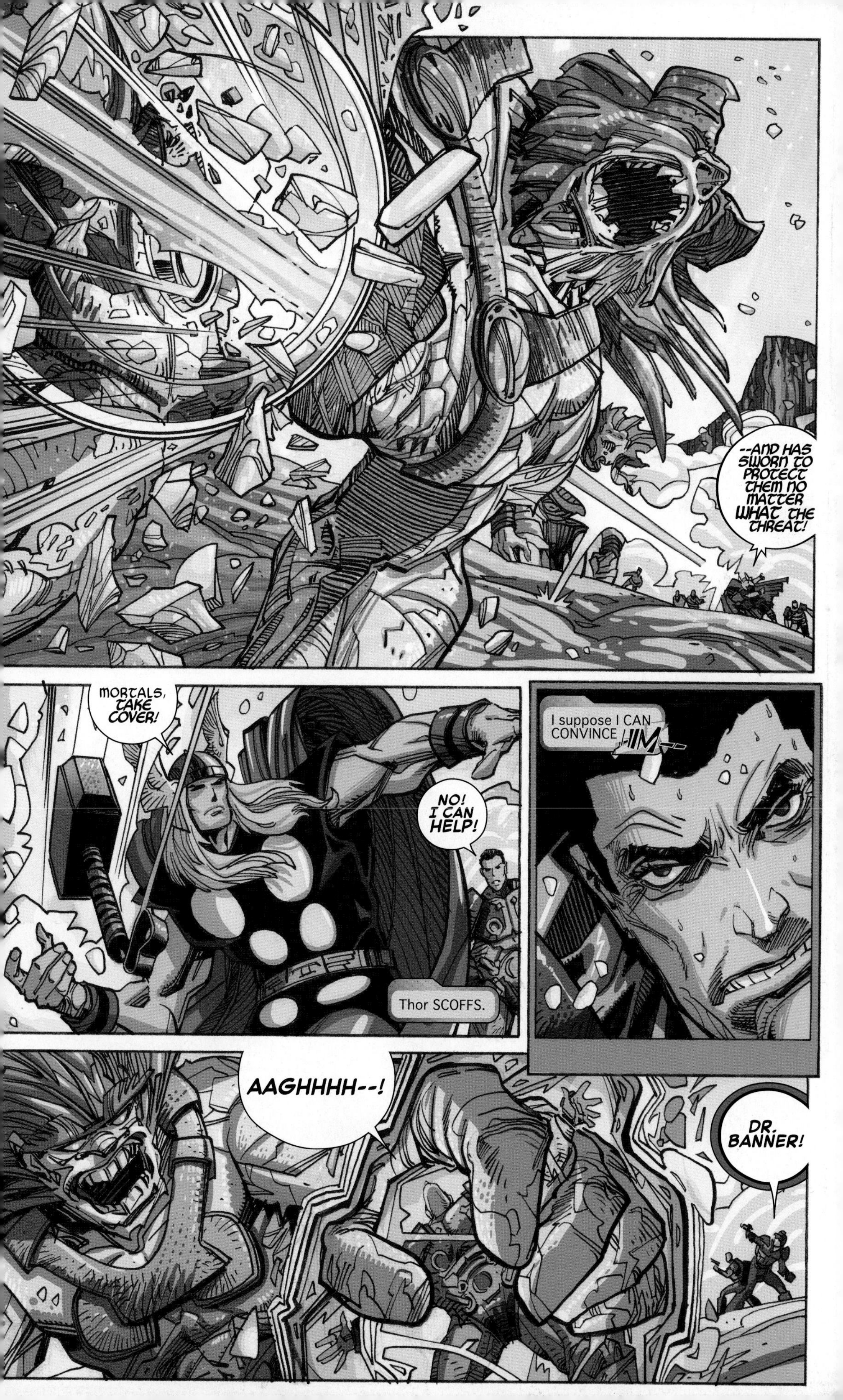
--AND HAS SWORN TO PROTECT THEM NO MATTER WHAT THE THREAT!
MORTALS, TAKE COVER!
NO! I CAN HELP!
Thor SCOFFS.
I suppose I CAN CONVINCE HIM--
AAGHHHH--!
DR. BANNER!

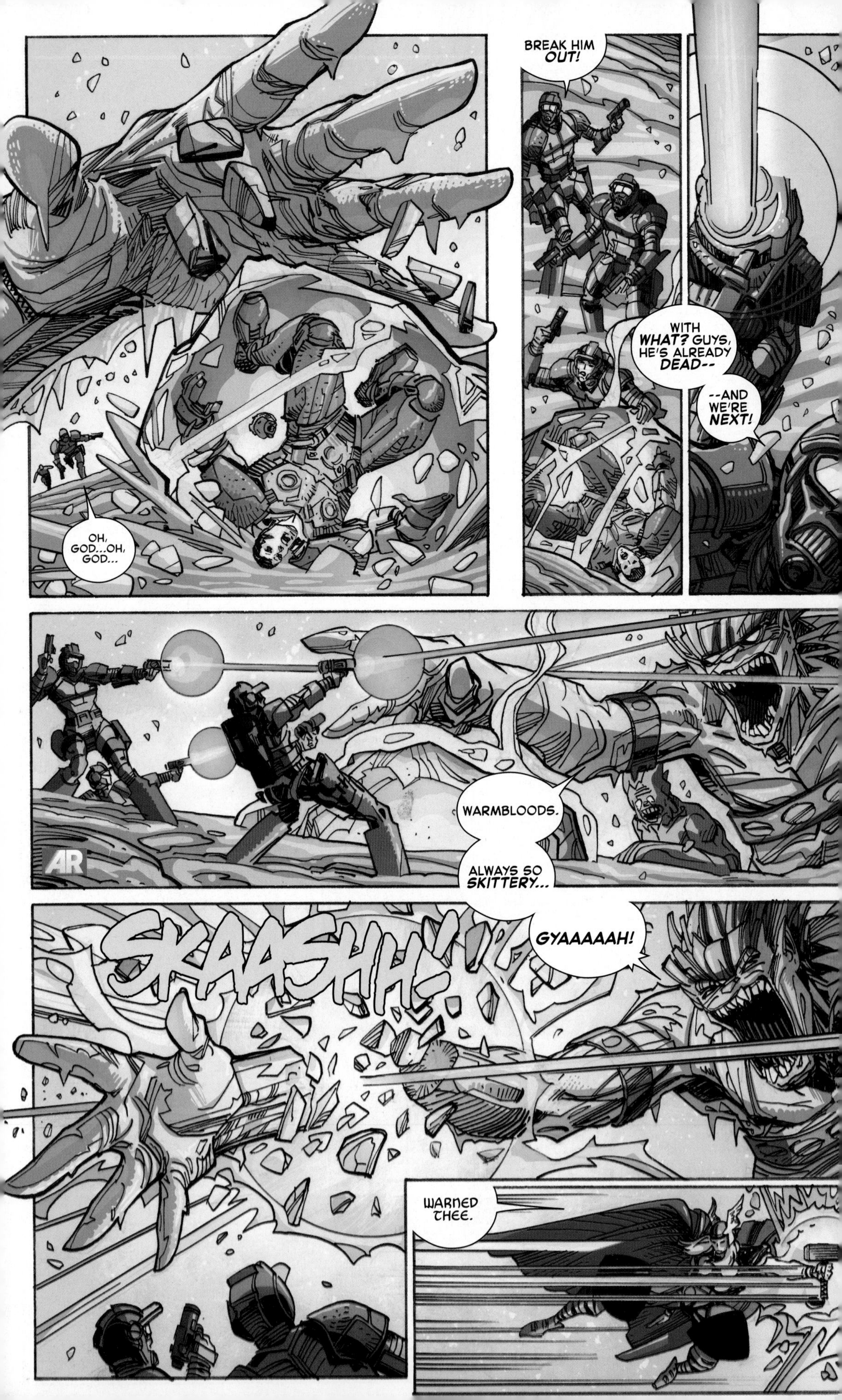

OH, GOD...OH, GOD...
BREAK HIM OUT!
WITH WHAT? GUYS, HE'S ALREADY DEAD--
--AND WE'RE NEXT!
WARMBLOODS.
ALWAYS SO SKITTERY...
SKAASHH!
GYAAAAAH!
WARNED THEE.

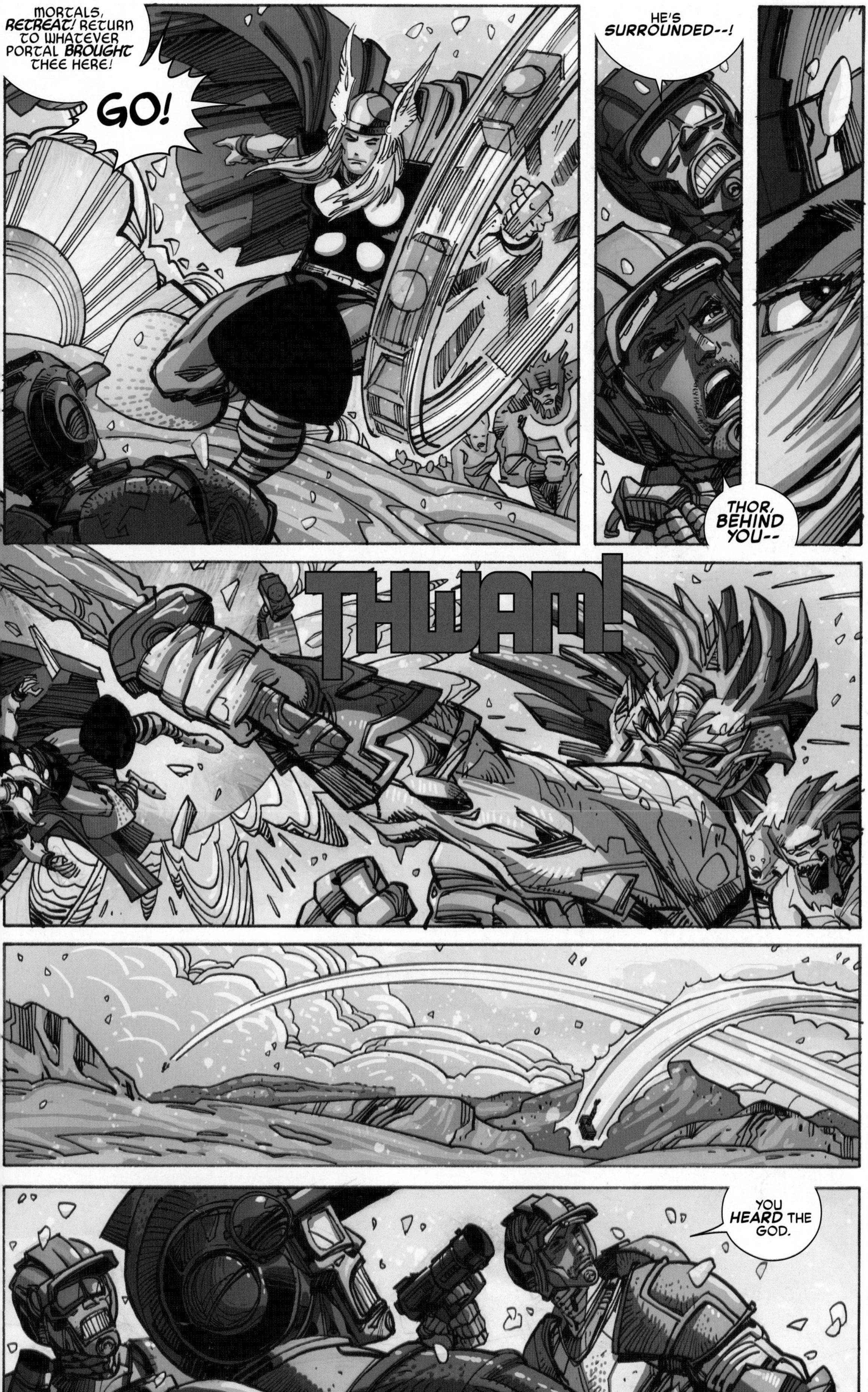
MORTALS, RETREAT! RETURN TO WHATEVER PORTAL BROUGHT THEE HERE!
GO!
HE'S SURROUNDED--!
THOR, BEHIND YOU--
THWAM!
YOU HEARD THE GOD.

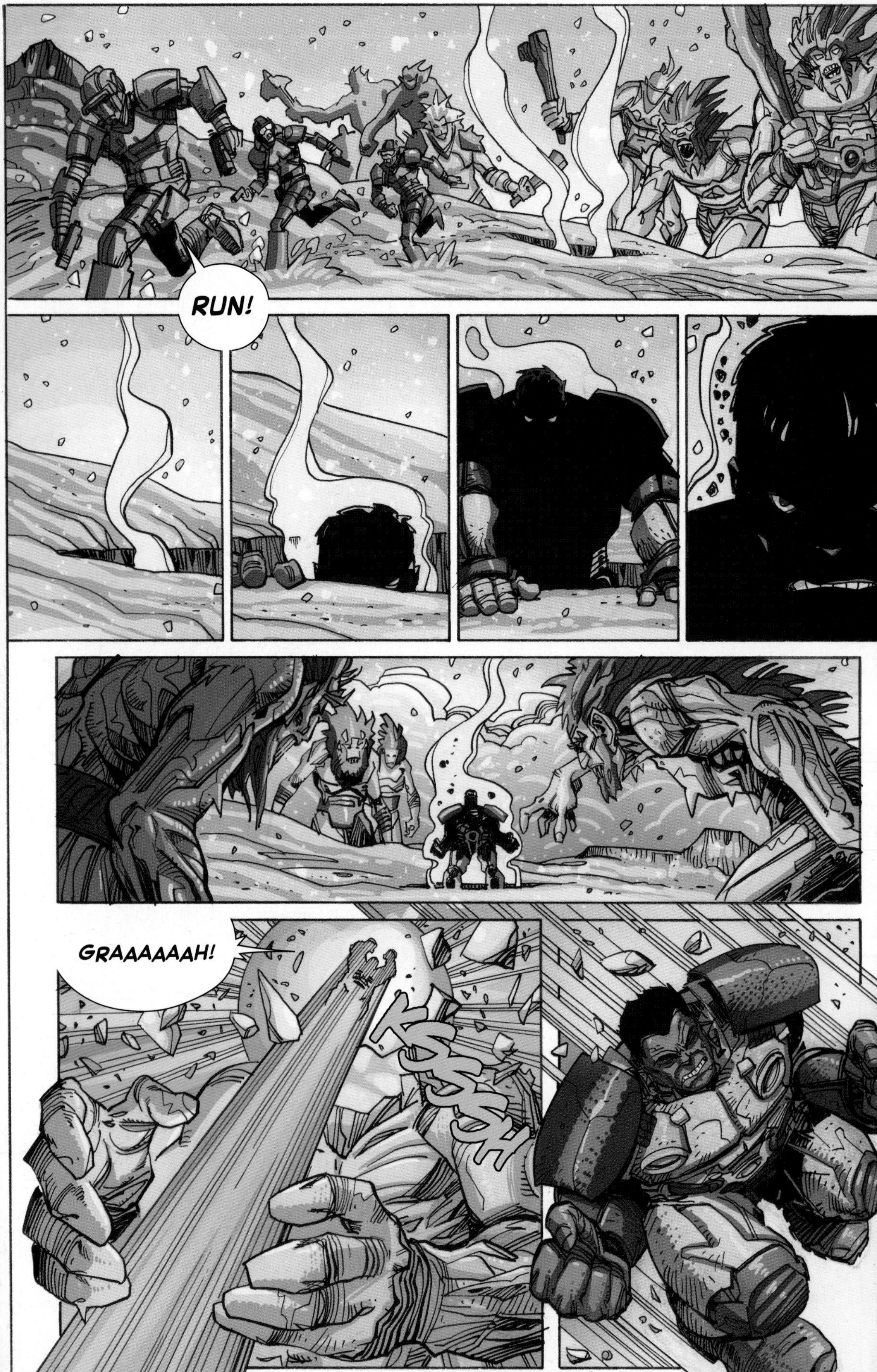
RUN!
GRAAAAAAH!

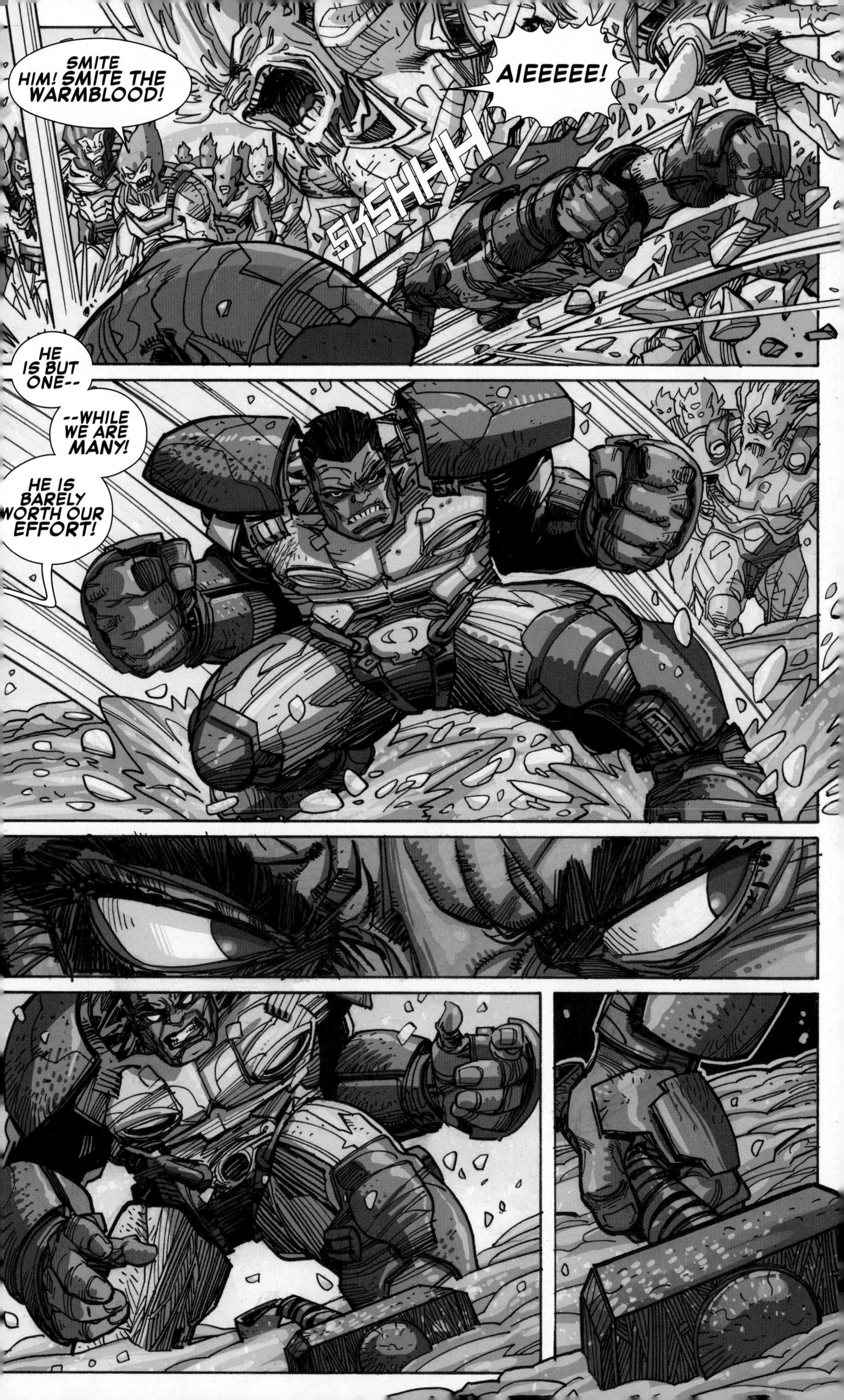
SMITE HIM! SMITE THE WARMBLOOD!
AIEEEEE!
SKSHHH
HE IS BUT ONE--
--WHILE WE ARE MANY!
HE IS BARELY WORTH OUR EFFORT!

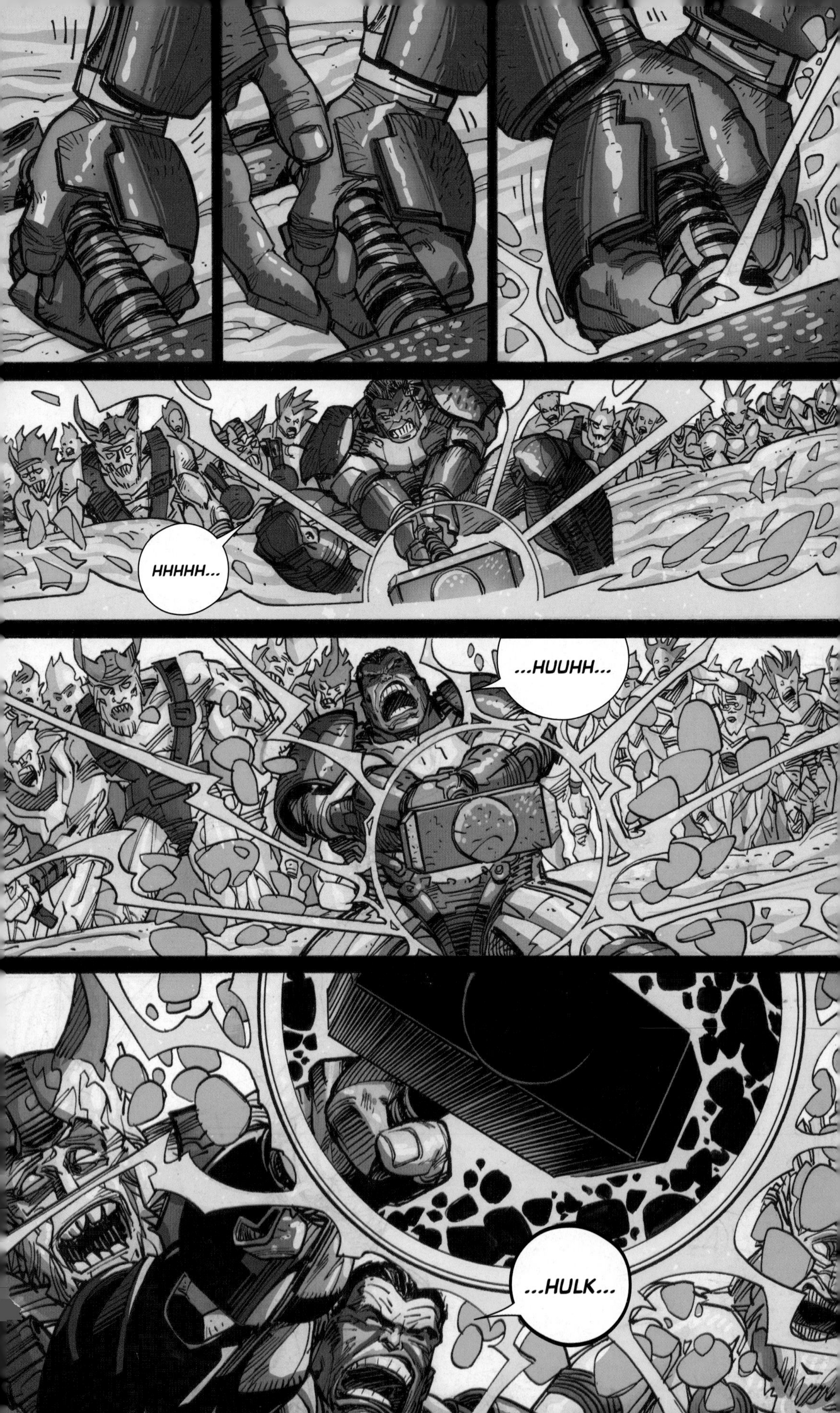
HHHHH...
...HUUHH...
...HULK...

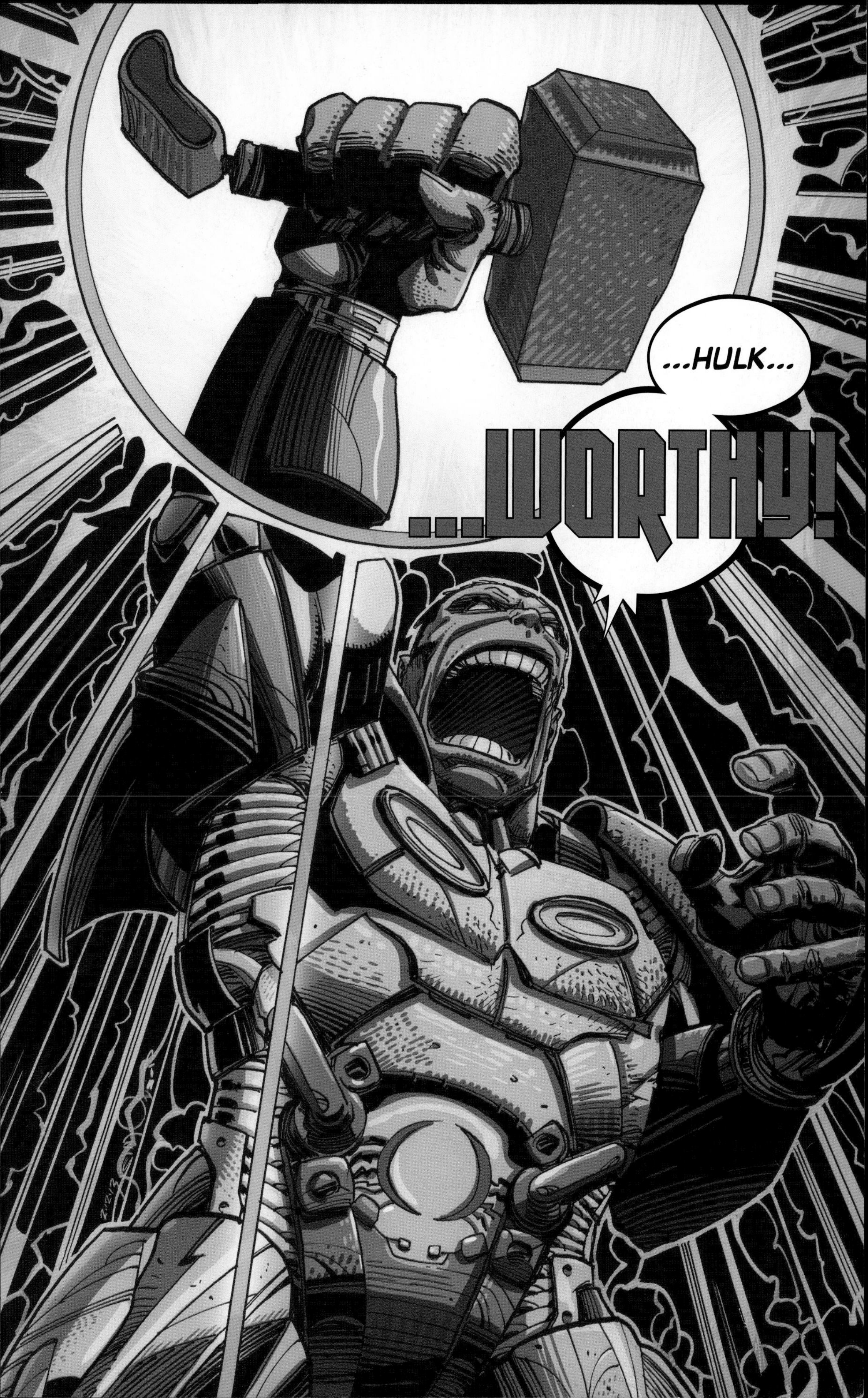
...HULK...
...WORTHY!

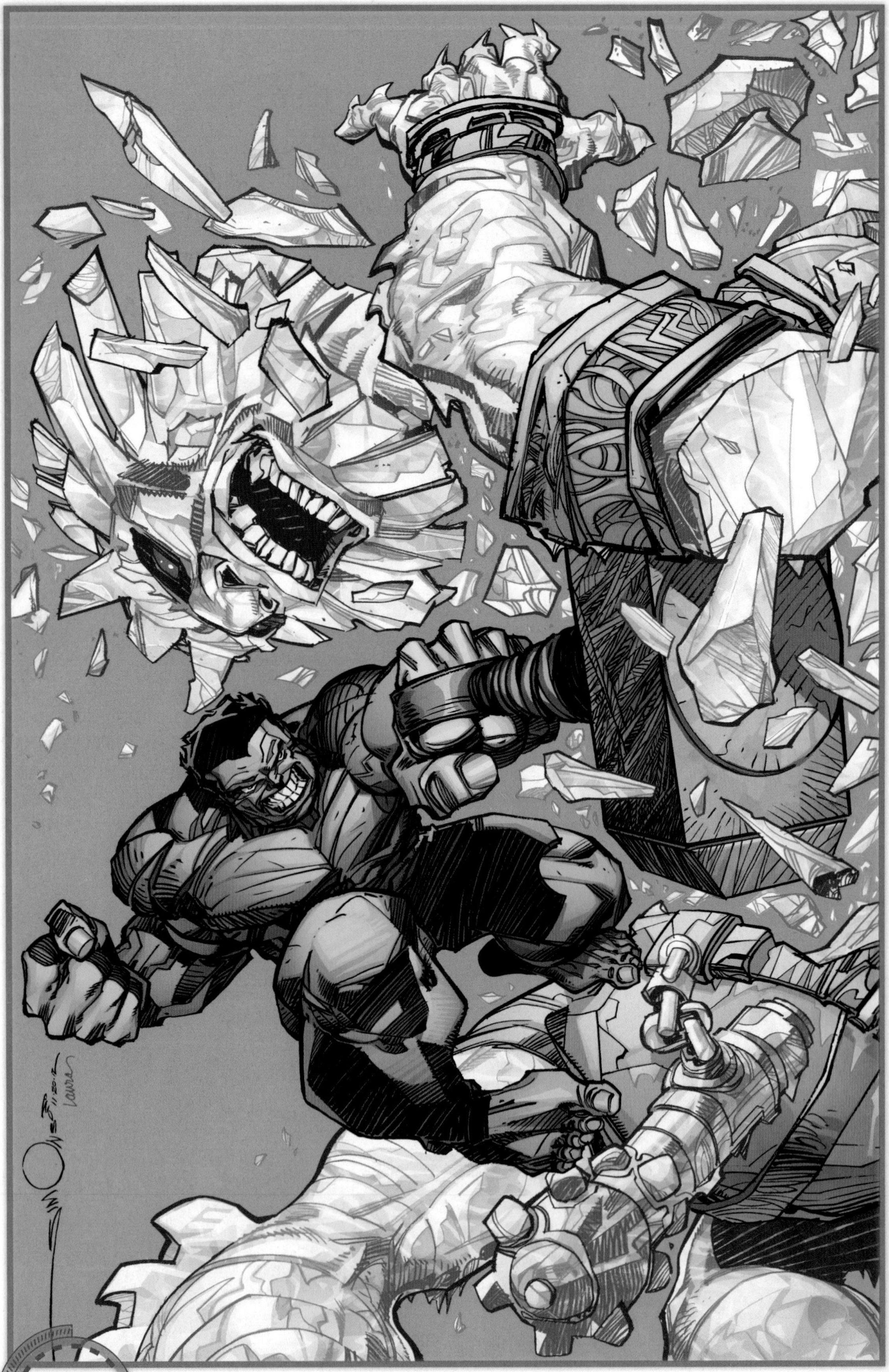

07

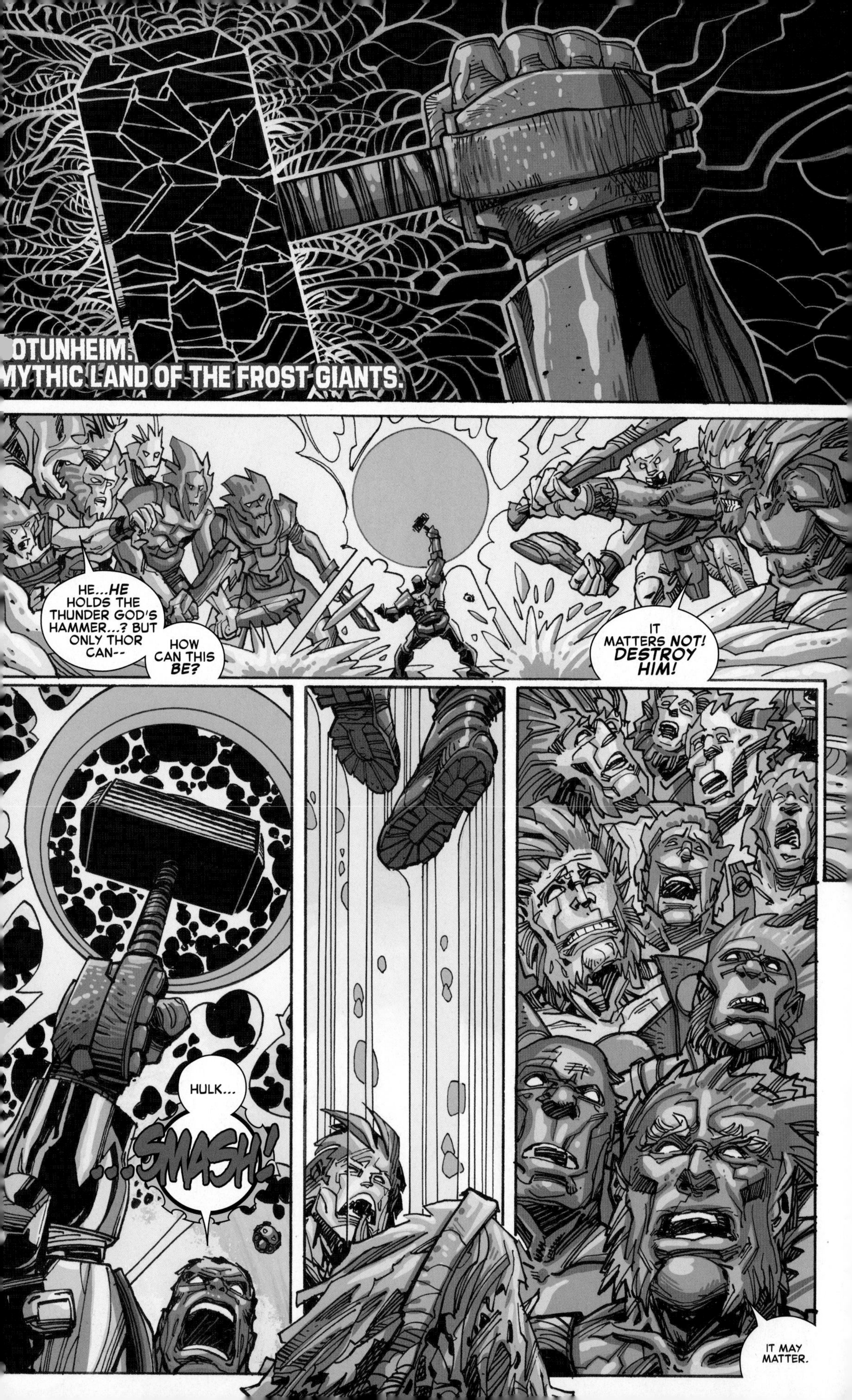
OTUNHEIM.
MYTHIC LAND OF THE FROST GIANTS.
HE...HE HOLDS THE THUNDER GOD'S HAMMER...? BUT ONLY THOR CAN--
HOW CAN THIS BE?
IT MATTERS NOT! DESTROY HIM!
HULK...
...SMASH!
IT MAY MATTER.

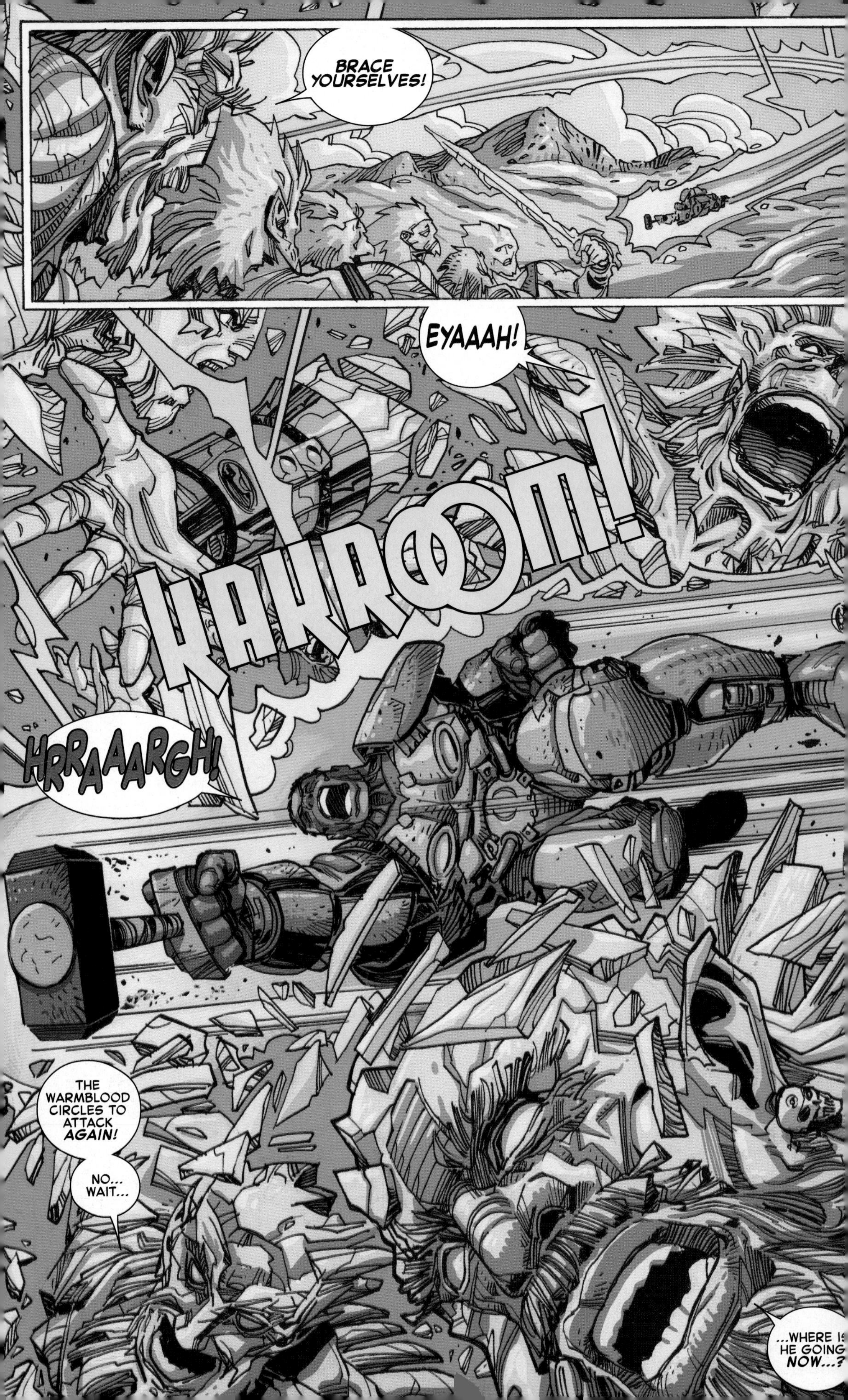
BRACE YOURSELVES!
EYAAAH!
KAKROOM!
HRRAAAARGH!
THE WARMBLOOD CIRCLES TO ATTACK AGAIN!
NO... WAIT...
...WHERE IS HE GOING NOW...?

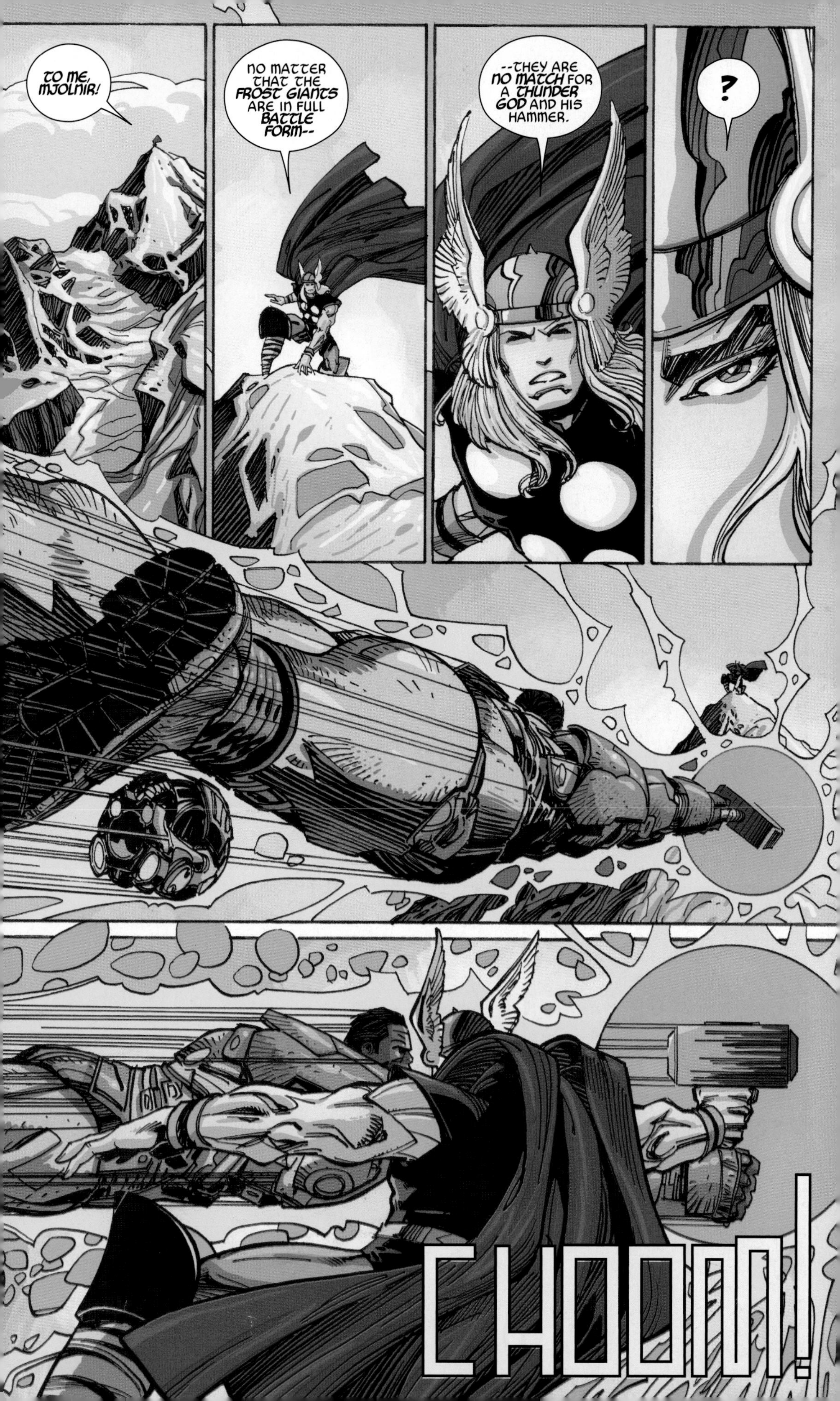
TO ME, MJOLNIR!
NO MATTER THAT THE FROST GIANTS ARE IN FULL BATTLE FORM--
--THEY ARE NO MATCH FOR A THUNDER GOD AND HIS HAMMER.
?
CHOOM!

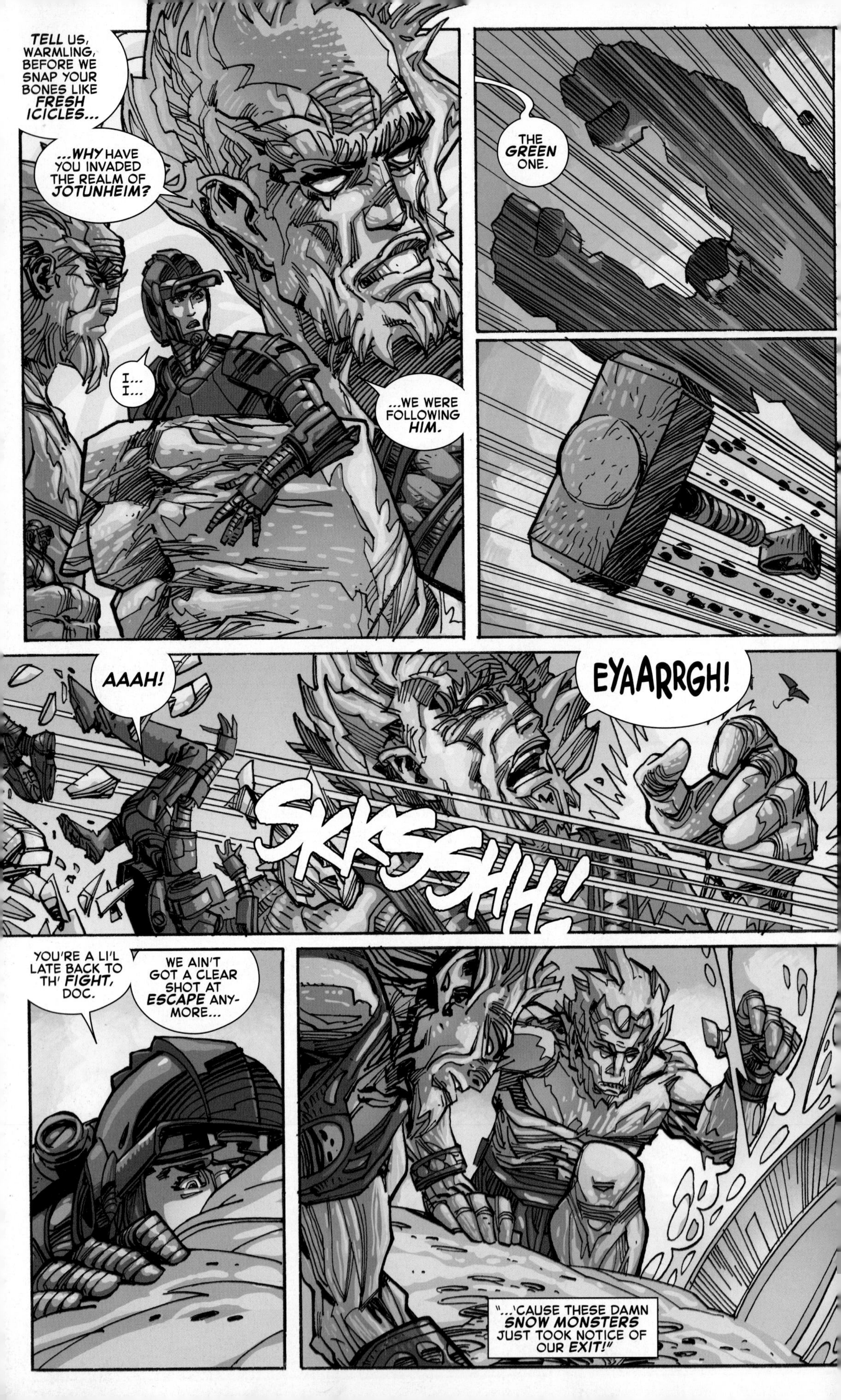
TELL US, WARMLING, BEFORE WE SNAP YOUR BONES LIKE FRESH ICICLES...
...WHY HAVE YOU INVADED THE REALM OF JOTUNHEIM?
I... I...
...WE WERE FOLLOWING HIM.
THE GREEN ONE.
AAAH!
EYAARRGH!
SKKSSHH!
YOU'RE A LI'L LATE BACK TO TH' FIGHT, DOC.
WE AIN'T GOT A CLEAR SHOT AT ESCAPE ANY-MORE...
"...'CAUSE THESE DAMN SNOW MONSTERS JUST TOOK NOTICE OF OUR EXIT!"

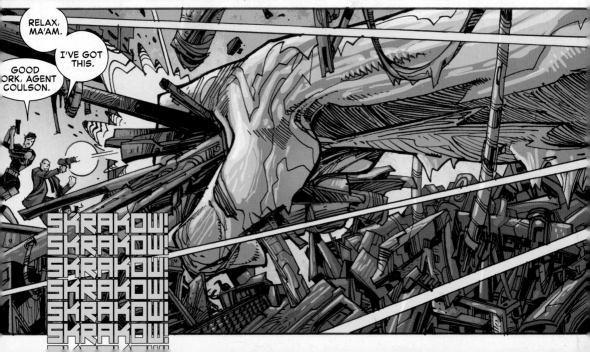

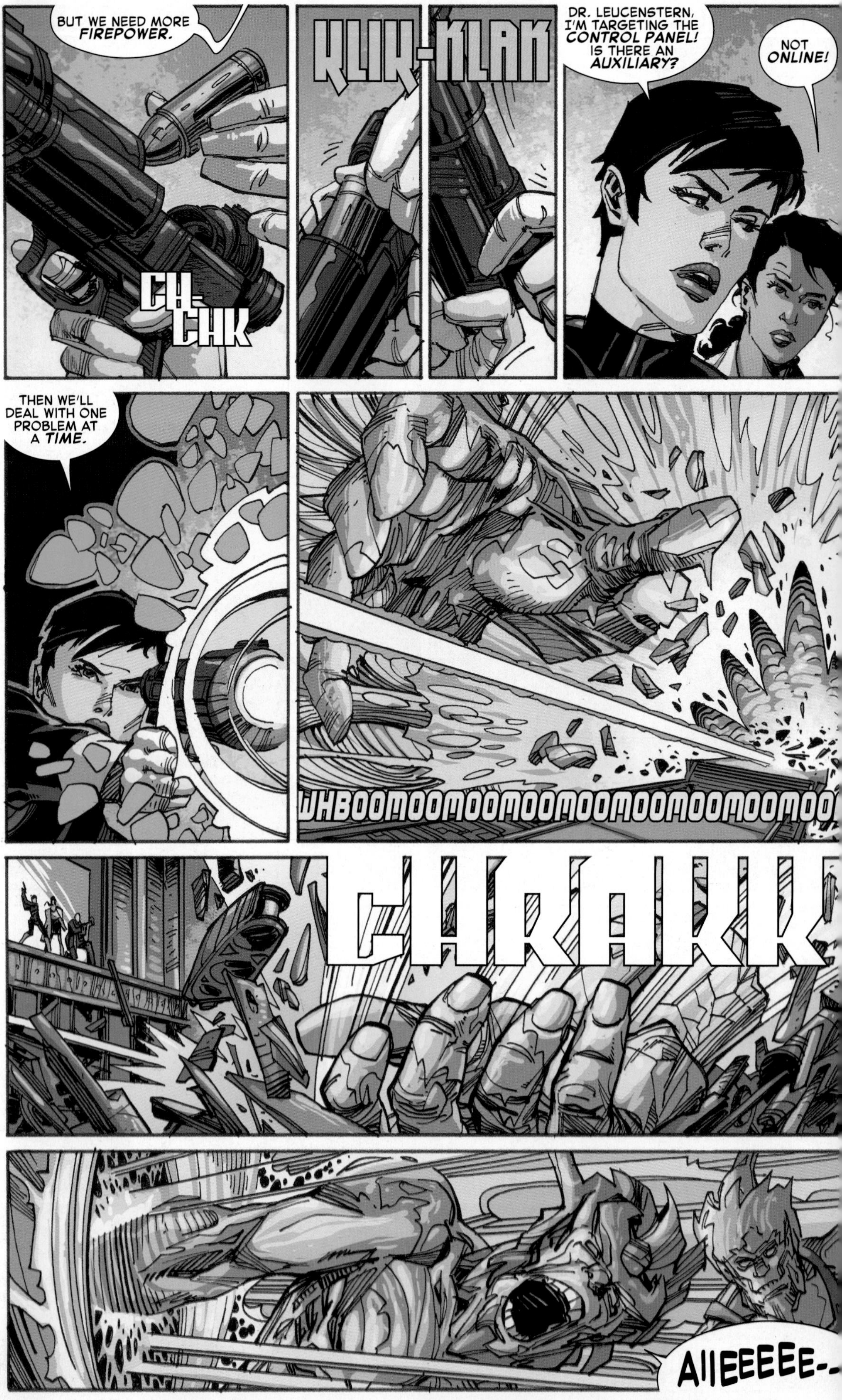
BUT WE NEED MORE FIREPOWER.
CH-CHK
KLIK-KLAK
DR. LEUCENSTERN, I'M TARGETING THE CONTROL PANEL! IS THERE AN AUXILIARY?
NOT ONLINE!
THEN WE'LL DEAL WITH ONE PROBLEM AT A TIME.
WHBOOMOOMOOMOOMOOMOOMOOMOOMOO
CRAKK
AIIEEEEE--

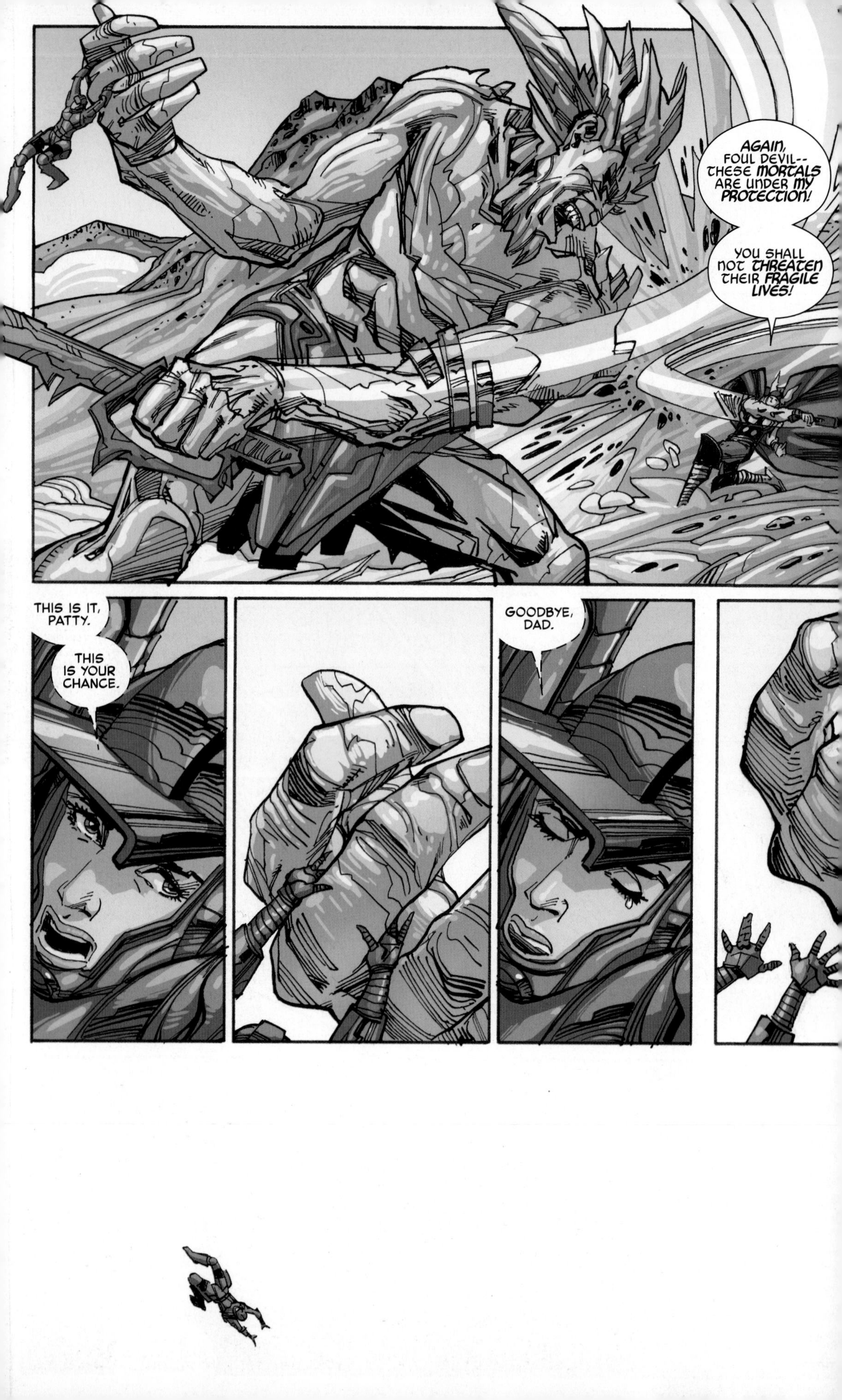
AGAIN, FOUL DEVIL-- THESE MORTALS ARE UNDER MY PROTECTION!
YOU SHALL NOT THREATEN THEIR FRAGILE LIVES!
THIS IS IT, PATTY.
THIS IS YOUR CHANCE.
GOODBYE, DAD.

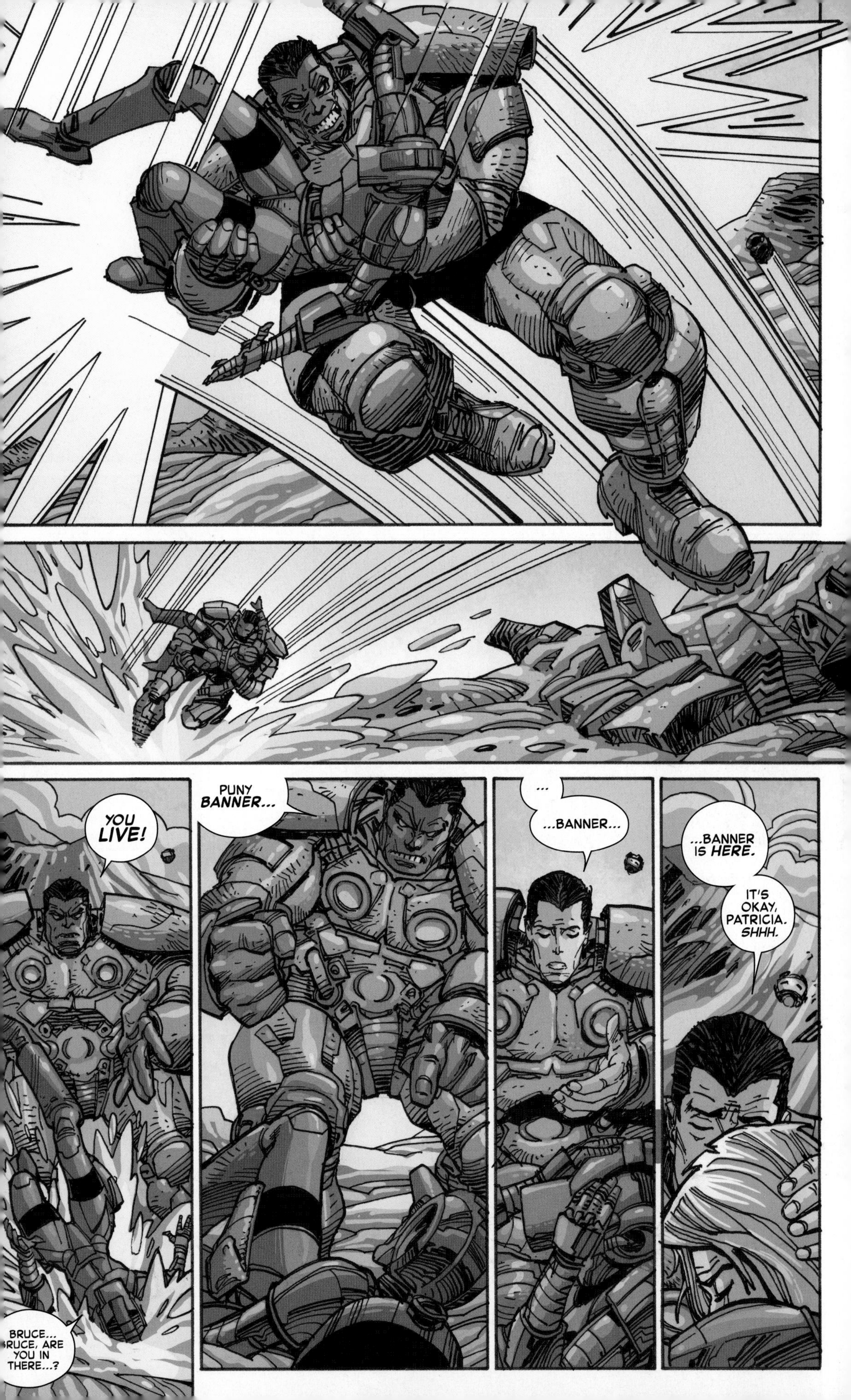
YOU LIVE!
PUNY BANNER...
...
...BANNER...
...BANNER IS HERE.
IT'S OKAY, PATRICIA. SHHH.
BRUCE... BRUCE, ARE YOU IN THERE...?

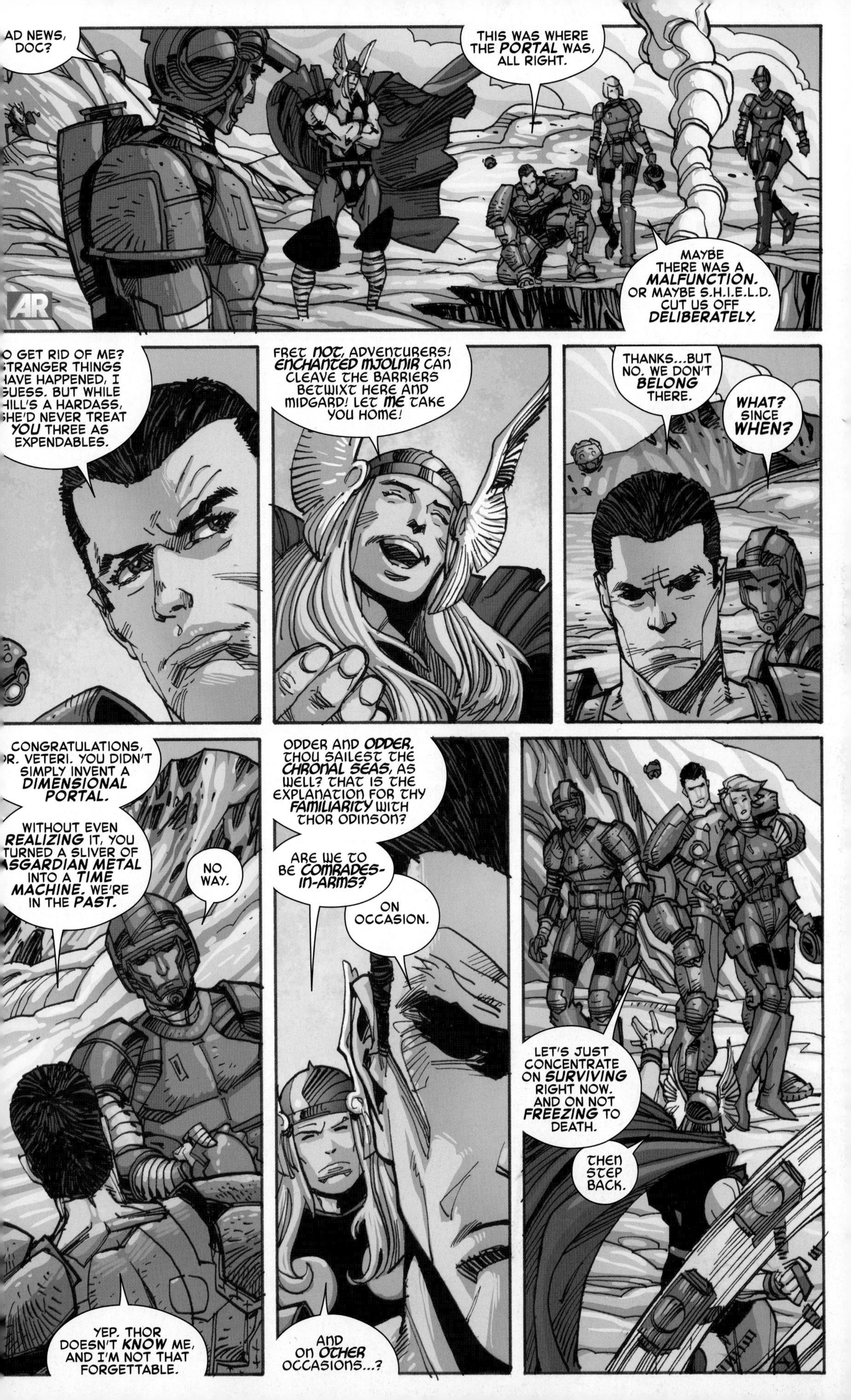

AD NEWS, DOC?
THIS WAS WHERE THE PORTAL WAS, ALL RIGHT.
MAYBE THERE WAS A MALFUNCTION. OR MAYBE S.H.I.E.L.D. CUT US OFF DELIBERATELY.
O GET RID OF ME? STRANGER THINGS HAVE HAPPENED, I GUESS. BUT WHILE HILL'S A HARDASS, SHE'D NEVER TREAT YOU THREE AS EXPENDABLES.
FRET NOT, ADVENTURERS! ENCHANTED MJOLNIR CAN CLEAVE THE BARRIERS BETWIXT HERE AND MIDGARD! LET ME TAKE YOU HOME!
THANKS...BUT NO. WE DON'T BELONG THERE.
WHAT? SINCE WHEN?
CONGRATULATIONS, R. VETERI. YOU DIDN'T SIMPLY INVENT A DIMENSIONAL PORTAL.
WITHOUT EVEN REALIZING IT, YOU TURNED A SLIVER OF ASGARDIAN METAL INTO A TIME MACHINE. WE'RE IN THE PAST.
NO WAY.
YEP. THOR DOESN'T KNOW ME, AND I'M NOT THAT FORGETTABLE.
ODDER AND ODDER. THOU SAILEST THE CHRONAL SEAS, AS WELL? THAT IS THE EXPLANATION FOR THY FAMILIARITY WITH THOR ODINSON?
ARE WE TO BE COMRADES-IN-ARMS?
ON OCCASION.
AND ON OTHER OCCASIONS...?
LET'S JUST CONCENTRATE ON SURVIVING RIGHT NOW. AND ON NOT FREEZING TO DEATH.
THEN STEP BACK.

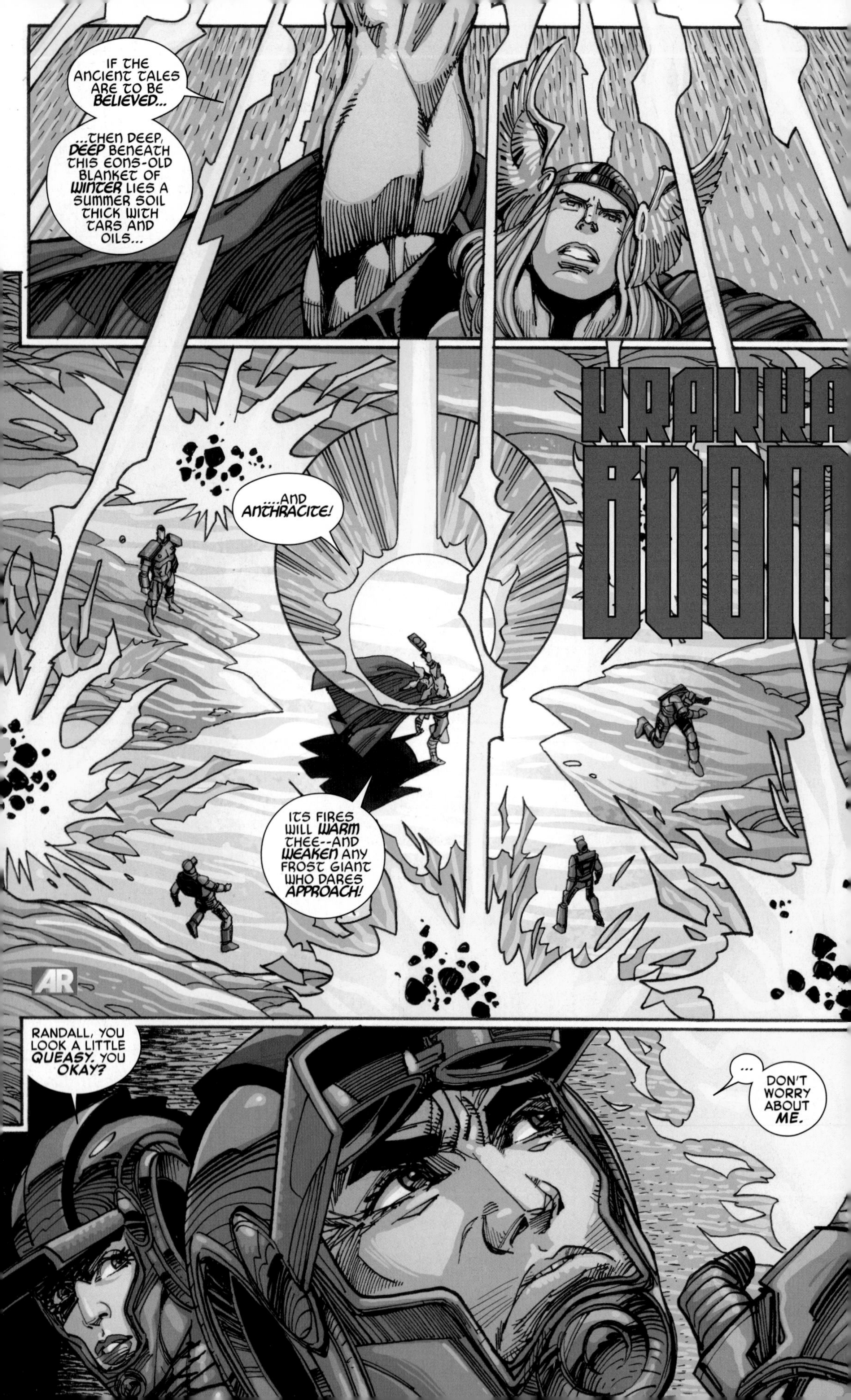
IF THE ANCIENT TALES ARE TO BE BELIEVED...
...THEN DEEP, DEEP BENEATH THIS EONS-OLD BLANKET OF WINTER LIES A SUMMER SOIL THICK WITH TARS AND OILS...
KRAKKA BOOM
....AND ANTHRACITE!
ITS FIRES WILL WARM THEE--AND WEAKEN ANY FROST GIANT WHO DARES APPROACH!
RANDALL, YOU LOOK A LITTLE QUEASY. YOU OKAY?
... DON'T WORRY ABOUT ME.

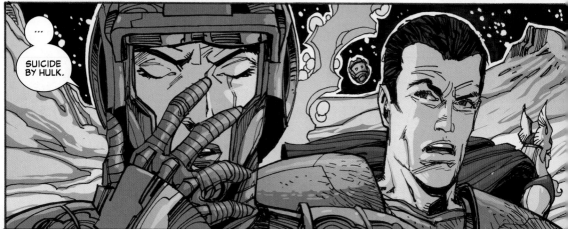

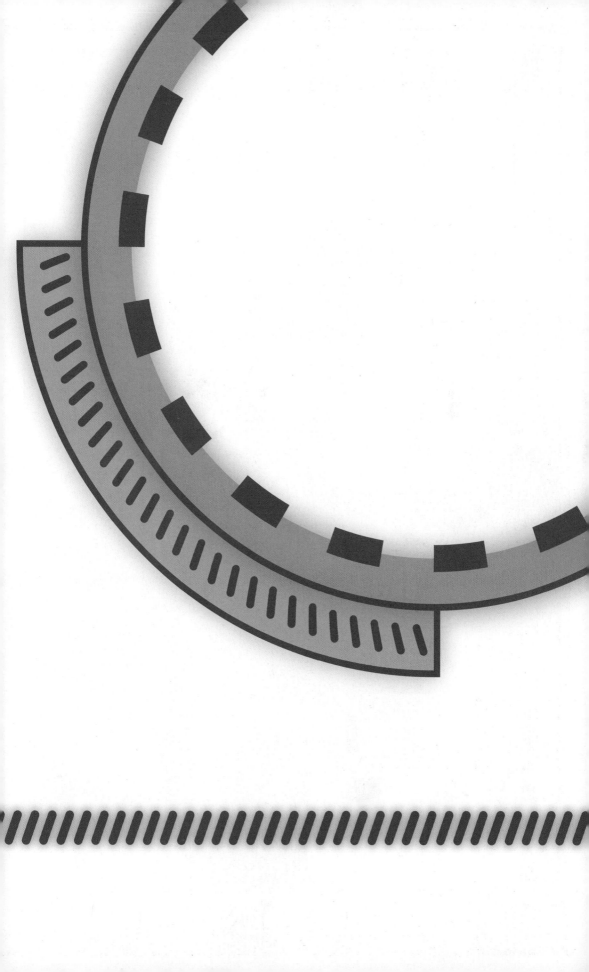

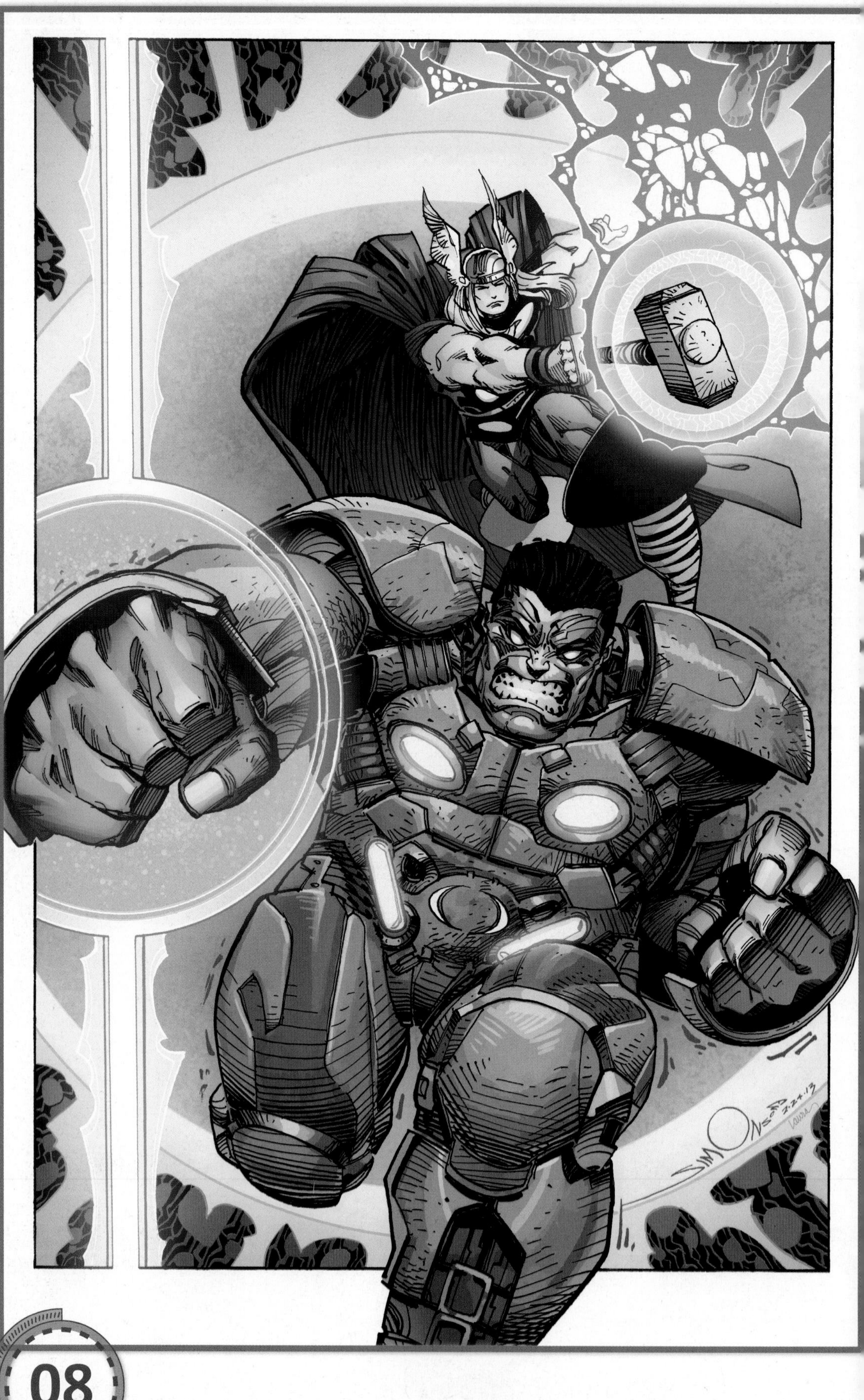

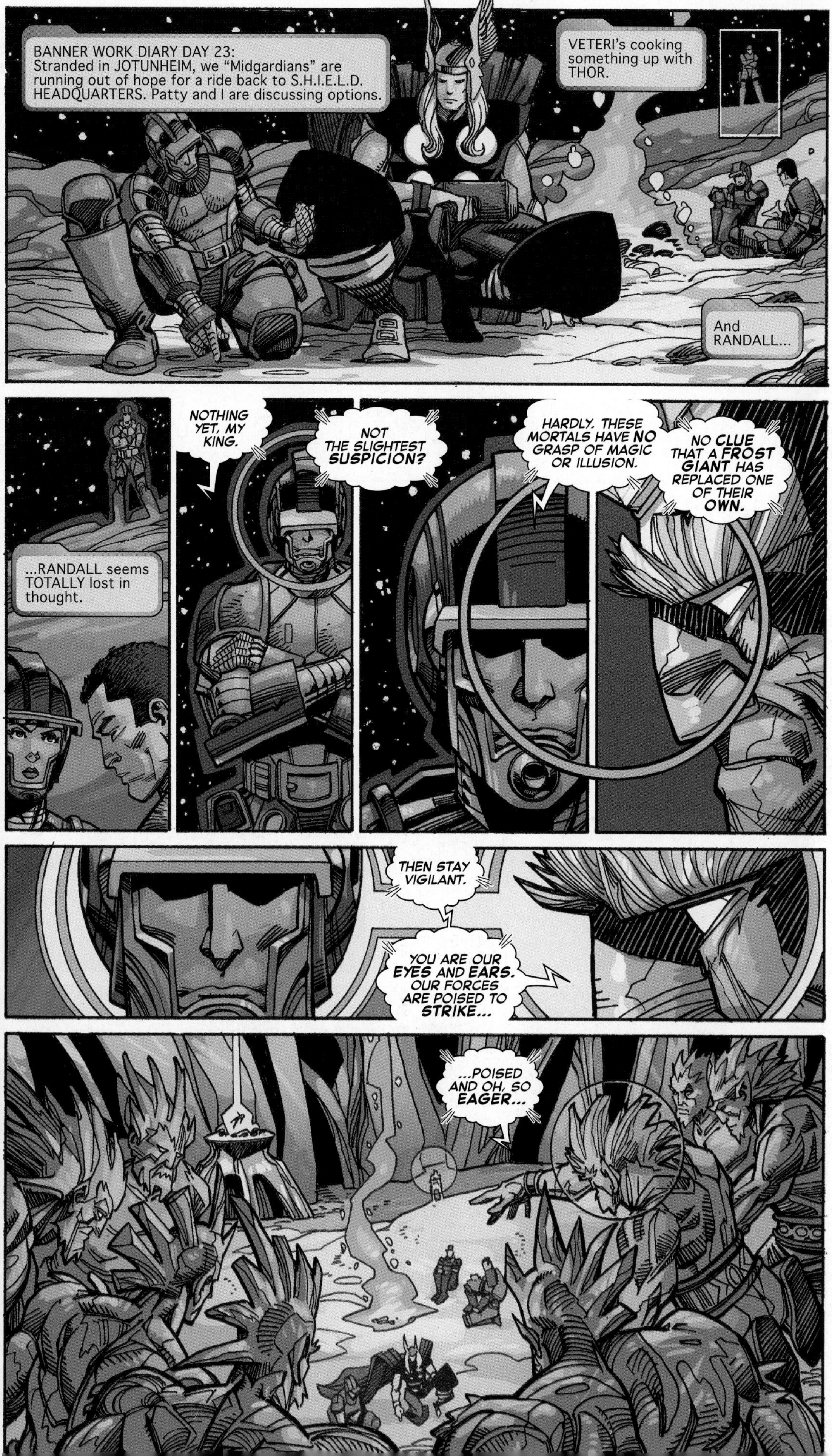
BANNER WORK DIARY DAY 23:
Stranded in JOTUNHEIM, we "Midgardians" are running out of hope for a ride back to S.H.I.E.L.D. HEADQUARTERS. Patty and I are discussing options.
VETERI's cooking something up with THOR.
And RANDALL...
...RANDALL seems TOTALLY lost in thought.
NOTHING YET, MY KING.
NOT THE SLIGHTEST SUSPICION?
HARDLY. THESE MORTALS HAVE NO GRASP OF MAGIC OR ILLUSION.
NO CLUE THAT A FROST GIANT HAS REPLACED ONE OF THEIR OWN.
THEN STAY VIGILANT.
YOU ARE OUR EYES AND EARS. OUR FORCES ARE POISED TO STRIKE...
...POISED AND OH, SO EAGER...

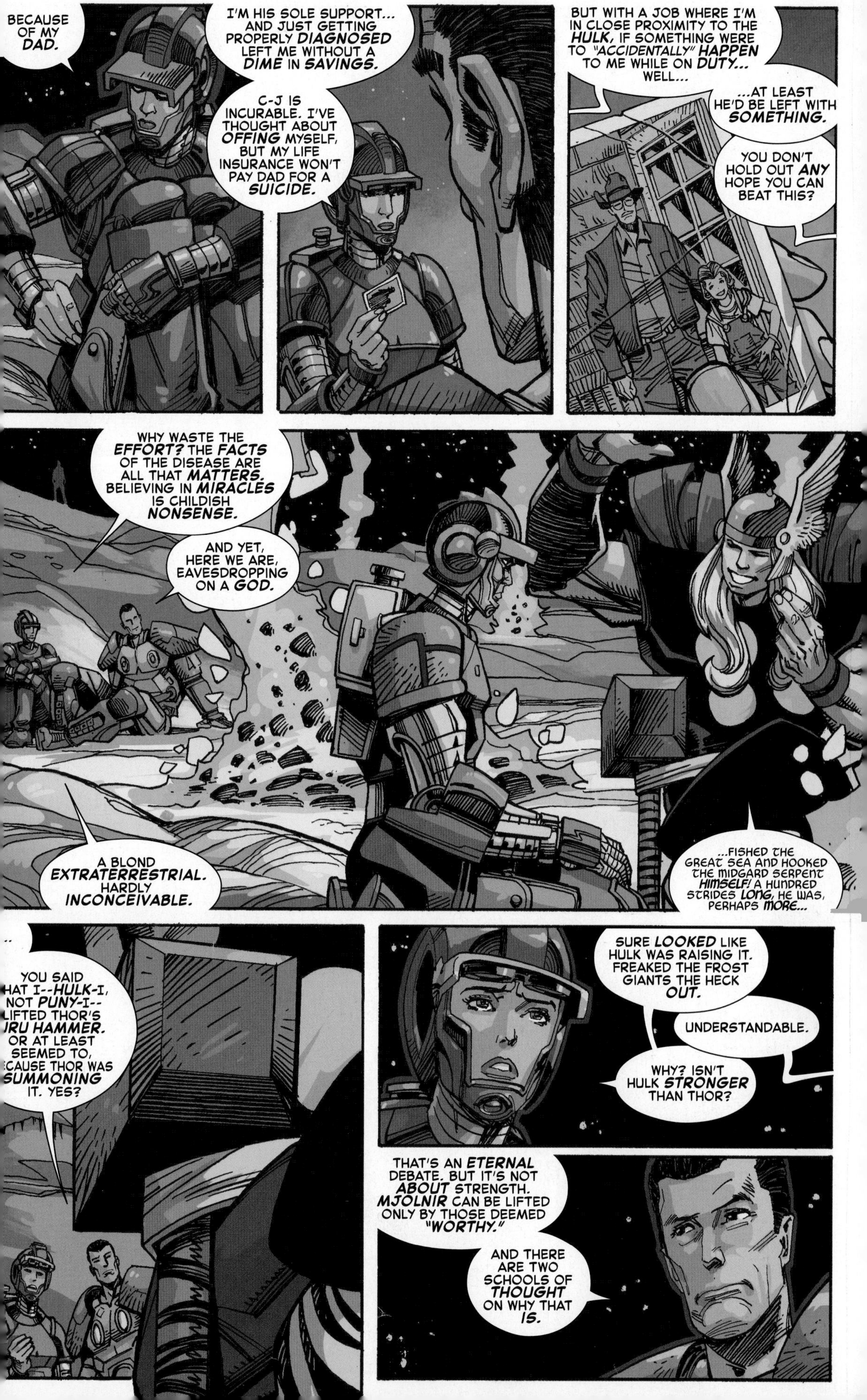
BECAUSE OF MY DAD.
I'M HIS SOLE SUPPORT... AND JUST GETTING PROPERLY DIAGNOSED LEFT ME WITHOUT A DIME IN SAVINGS.
C-J IS INCURABLE. I'VE THOUGHT ABOUT OFFING MYSELF, BUT MY LIFE INSURANCE WON'T PAY DAD FOR A SUICIDE.
BUT WITH A JOB WHERE I'M IN CLOSE PROXIMITY TO THE HULK, IF SOMETHING WERE TO "ACCIDENTALLY" HAPPEN TO ME WHILE ON DUTY... WELL...
...AT LEAST HE'D BE LEFT WITH SOMETHING.
YOU DON'T HOLD OUT ANY HOPE YOU CAN BEAT THIS?
WHY WASTE THE EFFORT? THE FACTS OF THE DISEASE ARE ALL THAT MATTERS. BELIEVING IN MIRACLES IS CHILDISH NONSENSE.
AND YET, HERE WE ARE, EAVESDROPPING ON A GOD.
A BLOND EXTRATERRESTRIAL. HARDLY INCONCEIVABLE.
...FISHED THE GREAT SEA AND HOOKED THE MIDGARD SERPENT HIMSELF! A HUNDRED STRIDES LONG, HE WAS, PERHAPS MORE...
YOU SAID HAT I--HULK-I, NOT PUNY-I-- LIFTED THOR'S IRU HAMMER. OR AT LEAST SEEMED TO, ECAUSE THOR WAS SUMMONING IT. YES?
SURE LOOKED LIKE HULK WAS RAISING IT. FREAKED THE FROST GIANTS THE HECK OUT.
UNDERSTANDABLE.
WHY? ISN'T HULK STRONGER THAN THOR?
THAT'S AN ETERNAL DEBATE. BUT IT'S NOT ABOUT STRENGTH. MJOLNIR CAN BE LIFTED ONLY BY THOSE DEEMED "WORTHY."
AND THERE ARE TWO SCHOOLS OF THOUGHT ON WHY THAT IS.

"PHYSICIST *JAMES KAKALIOS* ADVANCED MY FAVORITE *SCIENCE-BASED* THEORY:

"THAT *URU* METAL, FORGED UNIQUELY BY THE DWARF *EITRI*, CAN EMIT *GRAVITON PARTICLES*--

"--MOST LIKELY IN RESPONSE TO AN EXTERNAL STIMULUS PROVIDED BY SOMETHING WITHIN THE HAMMER AKIN TO OUR *NANOTECHNOLOGY*.

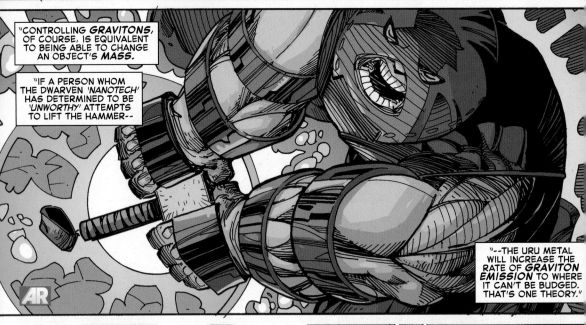

"CONTROLLING *GRAVITONS*, OF COURSE, IS EQUIVALENT TO BEING ABLE TO CHANGE AN OBJECT'S *MASS*.

"IF A PERSON WHOM THE DWARVEN *'NANOTECH'* HAS DETERMINED TO BE *'UNWORTHY'* ATTEMPTS TO LIFT THE HAMMER--

"--THE URU METAL WILL INCREASE THE RATE OF *GRAVITON EMISSION* TO WHERE IT CAN'T BE BUDGED. THAT'S ONE THEORY."

WHAT'S THE *OTHER*?

THAT IT'S JUST FLAT-OUT *MAGIC*.

THE KIND THAT'S ALL *AROUND* US IF WE LET OURSELVES *SEE* IT.

"MAGIC," HUH? CAN IT *CURE* ME?

THAT'S NOT WHAT I'M *SUGGESTING*--

THEN DON'T WASTE MY *TIME*.

THE LIQUID ORE *EIDERDÜRM* IS A *SUPERCONDUCTOR*, RIGHT?

SO HERE'S WHAT I PROPOSE.

SEEING YOU COMMAND *LIGHTNING* GAVE ME THE *IDEA*.

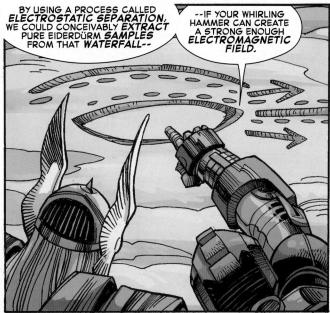

BY USING A PROCESS CALLED *ELECTROSTATIC SEPARATION*, WE COULD CONCEIVABLY *EXTRACT* PURE EIDERDÜRM *SAMPLES* FROM THAT *WATERFALL*--

--IF YOUR *WHIRLING* HAMMER CAN CREATE A STRONG ENOUGH *ELECTROMAGNETIC FIELD*.

THOU DOST REALIZE THAT SHOULD THE EIDERDÜRM *TOUCH* THEE, THOU SHALT REMAIN HERE IN JOTUNHEIM *FOREVER*, A FROZEN *STATUE*?

I...DID *NOT* KNOW THAT.

BUT I ALWAYS *SAY:* [LI]VE FAST, DIE YOUNG, AND LEAVE A GOOD-LOOKING *CORPSE*.

HA! WHAT A *MAGNIFICENT SENTIMENT!* AN ALCHEMIST *AND* A *POET*, THOU ART! *WELL-SAID!* I SHALL *QUOTE* THEE!

I...DIDN'T REALLY *COIN* THE...

WHATEVER. OKAY, I'M A GENIUS.

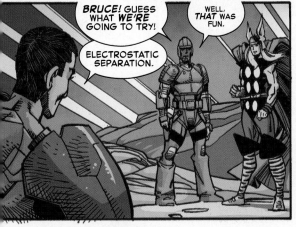

BRUCE! GUESS WHAT *WE'RE* GOING TO TRY!

WELL, *THAT* WAS FUN.

ELECTROSTATIC SEPARATION.

PERHAPS AN ENDEAVOR OF THIS MAGNITUDE CALLS FOR THE MIGHT OF THE *JADE GIANT!* CAREST THOU TO *TRANSFORM?*

LET'S CALL THAT *PLAN "B."*

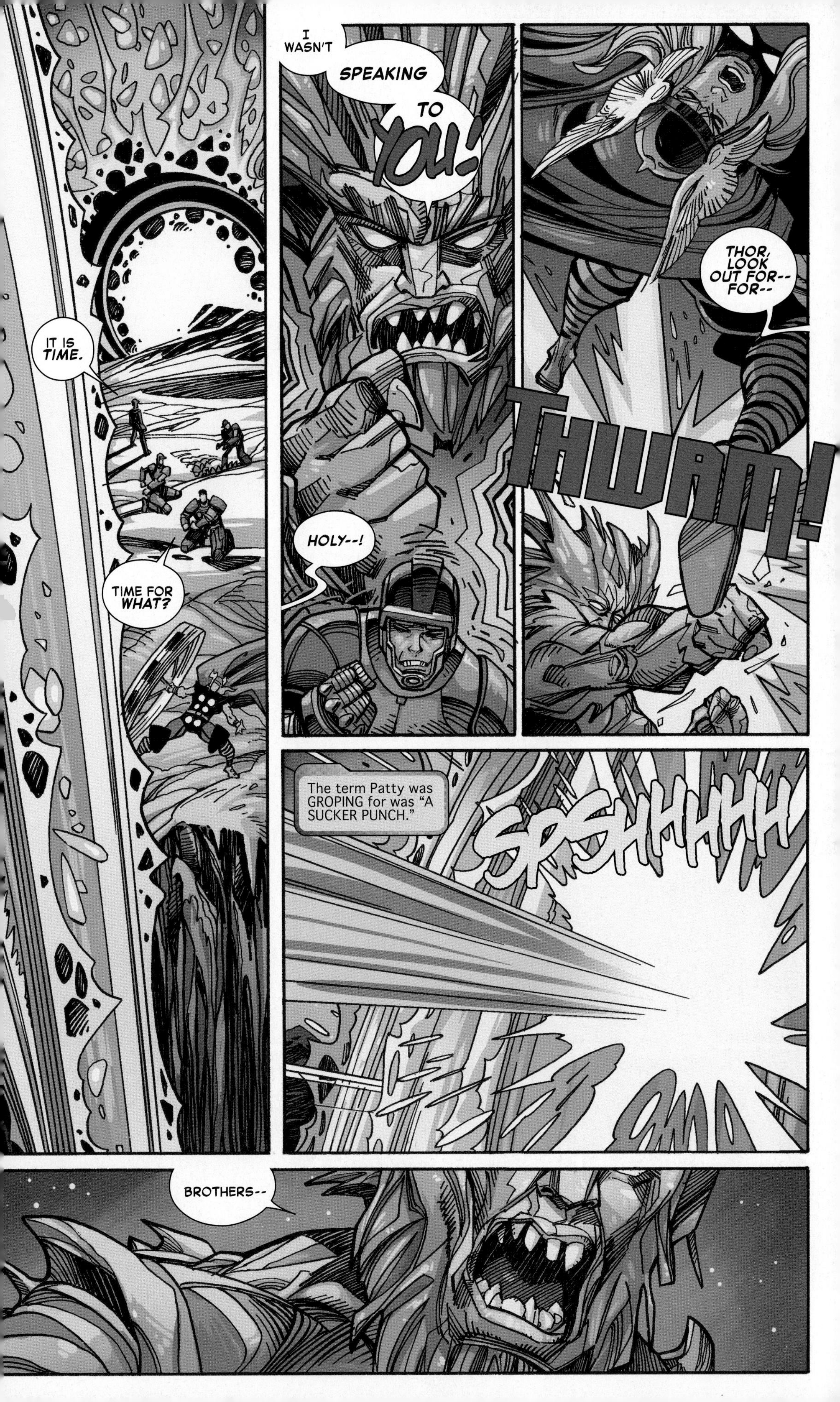
IT IS TIME.
TIME FOR WHAT?
I WASN'T SPEAKING TO YOU!
HOLY--!
THOR, LOOK OUT FOR-- FOR--
THWAM!
The term Patty was GROPING for was "A SUCKER PUNCH."
SPSHHHHH
BROTHERS--

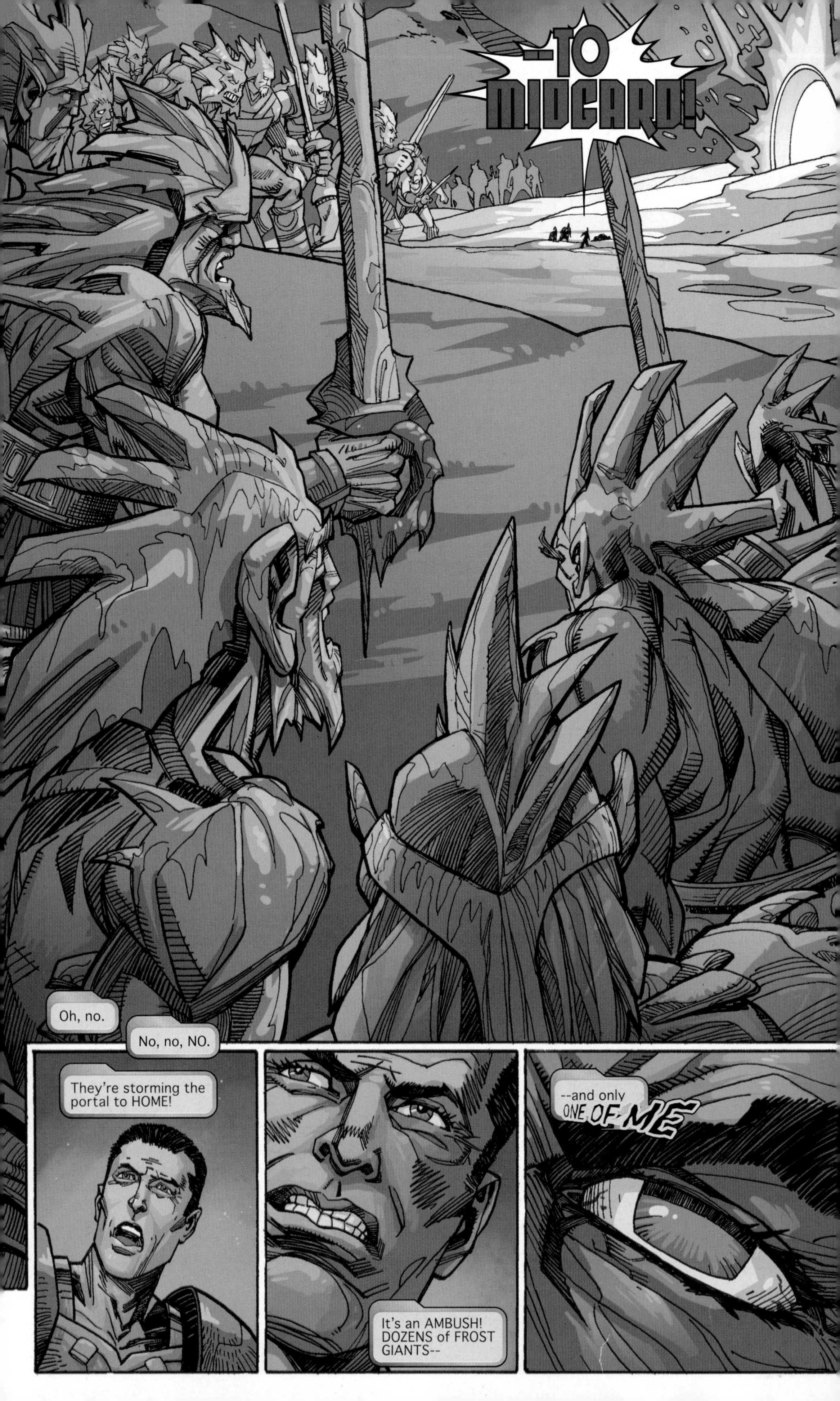
--TO MIDGARD!
Oh, no.
No, no, NO.
They're storming the portal to HOME!
It's an AMBUSH! DOZENS of FROST GIANTS--
--and only ONE OF ME

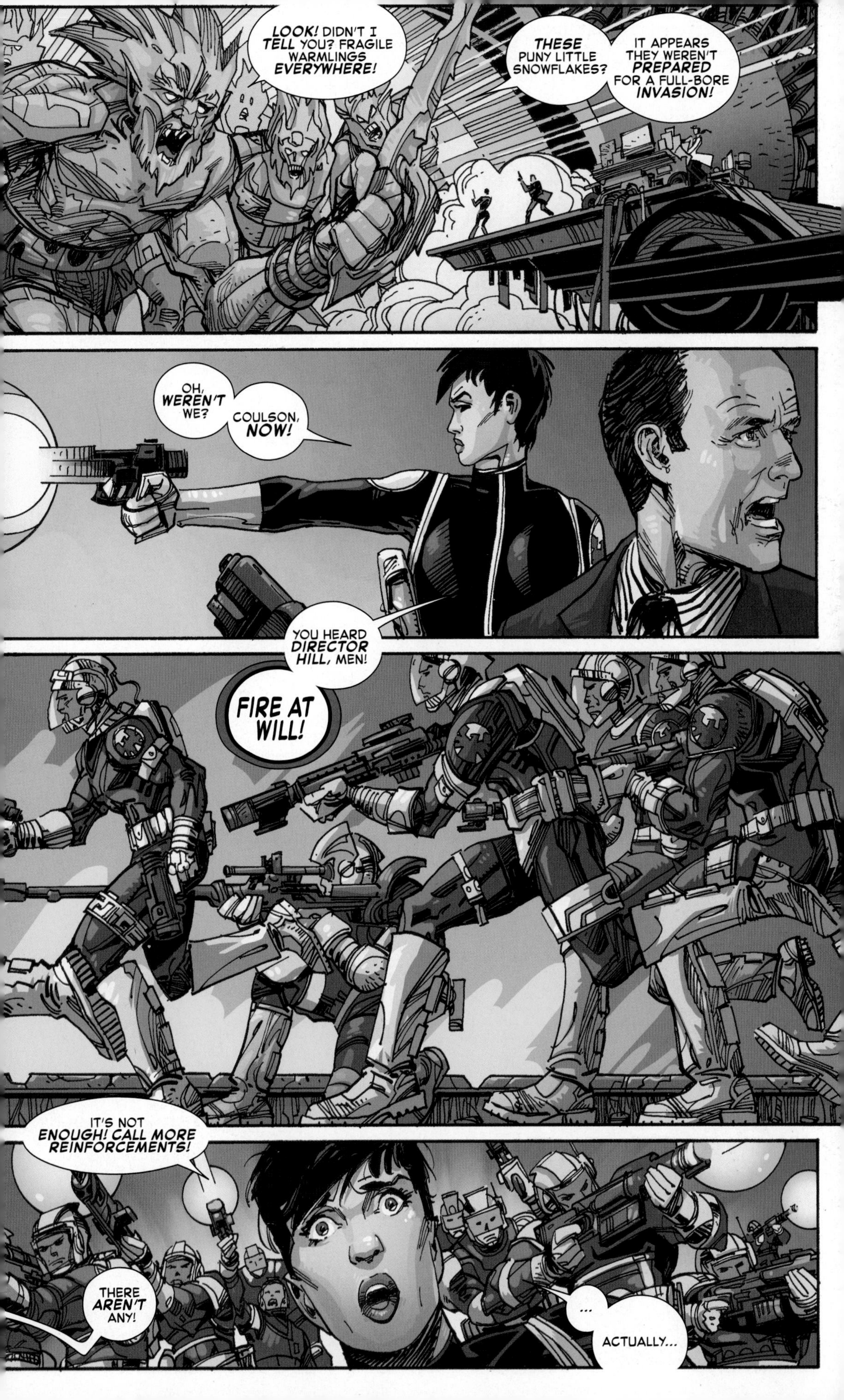
LOOK! DIDN'T I TELL YOU? FRAGILE WARMLINGS EVERYWHERE!
THESE PUNY LITTLE SNOWFLAKES?
IT APPEARS THEY WEREN'T PREPARED FOR A FULL-BORE INVASION!
OH, WEREN'T WE?
COULSON, NOW!
YOU HEARD DIRECTOR HILL, MEN!
FIRE AT WILL!
IT'S NOT ENOUGH! CALL MORE REINFORCEMENTS!
THERE AREN'T ANY!
...
ACTUALLY...

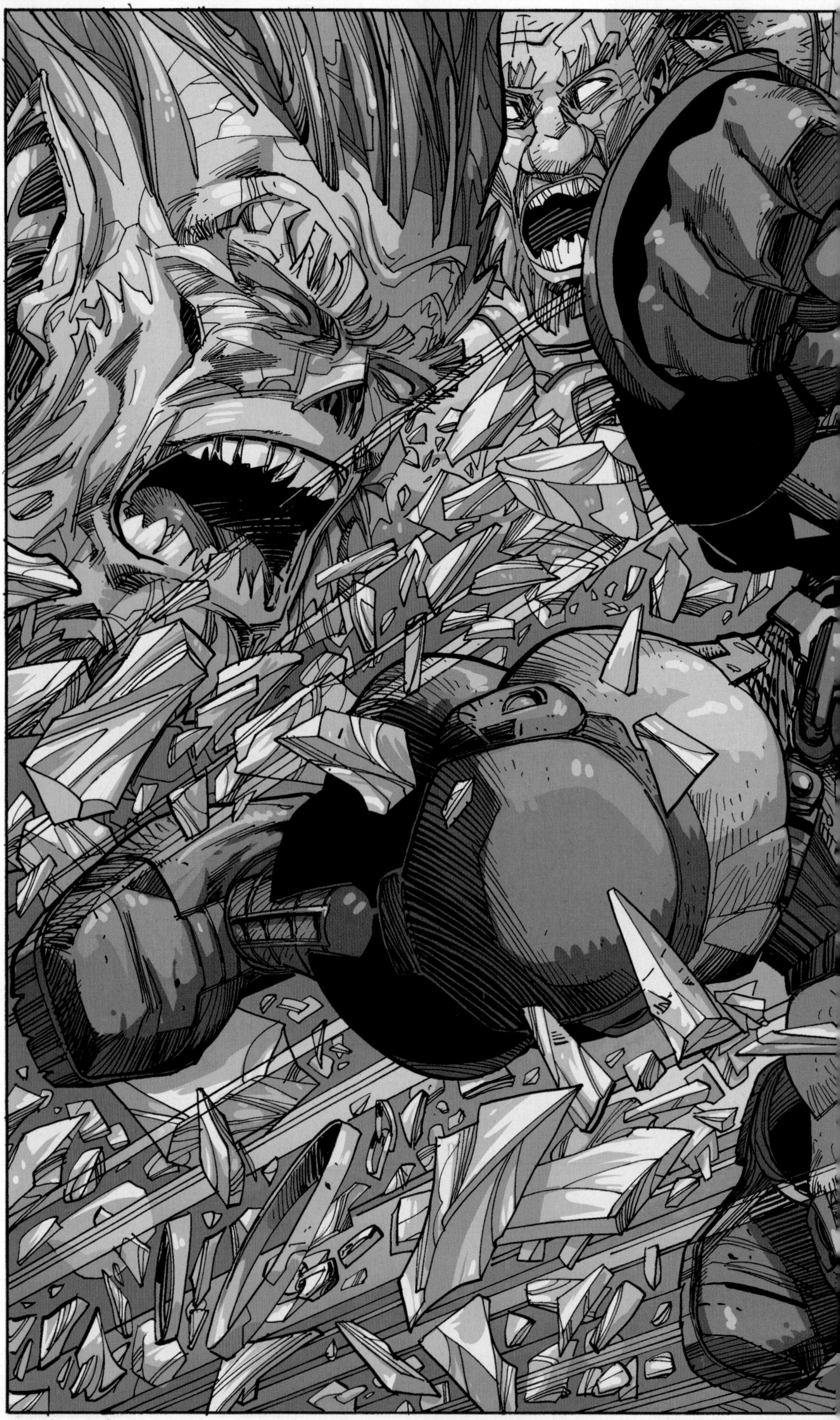

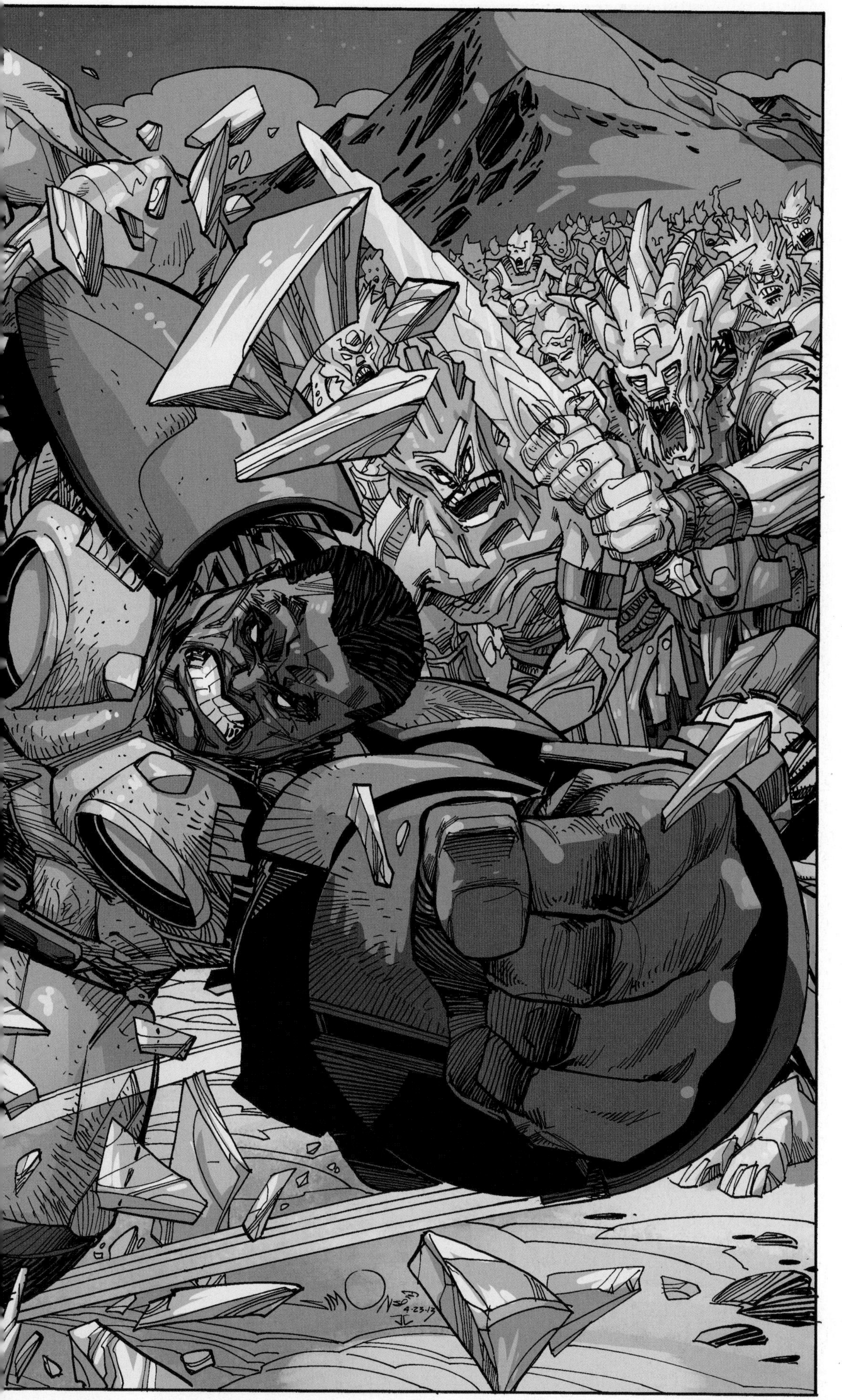

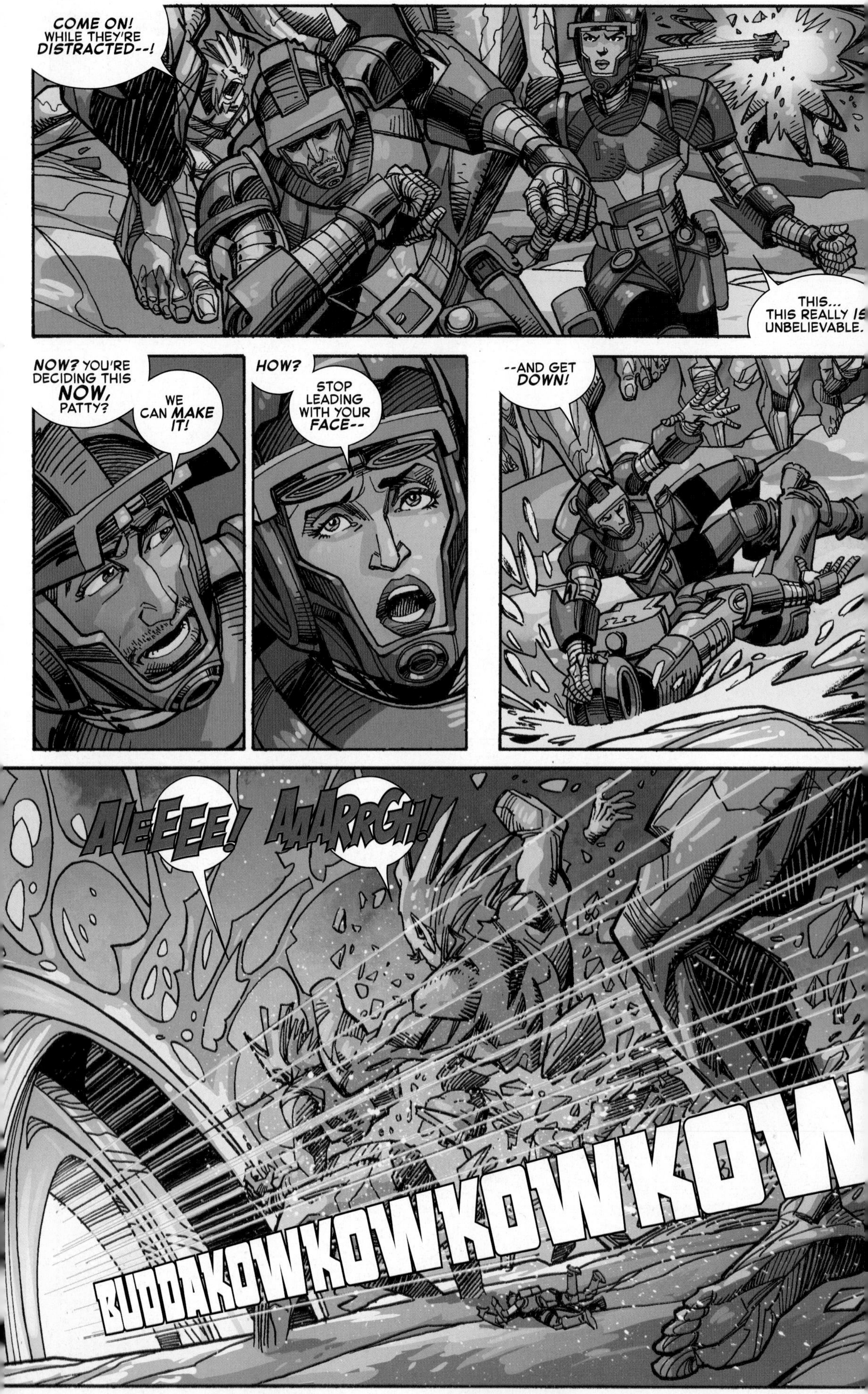
COME ON! WHILE THEY'RE DISTRACTED--!
THIS... THIS REALLY IS UNBELIEVABLE.
NOW? YOU'RE DECIDING THIS NOW, PATTY?
WE CAN MAKE IT!
HOW?
STOP LEADING WITH YOUR FACE--
--AND GET DOWN!
AIEEEE!
AAARRGH!
BUDDAKOWKOWKOWKOW

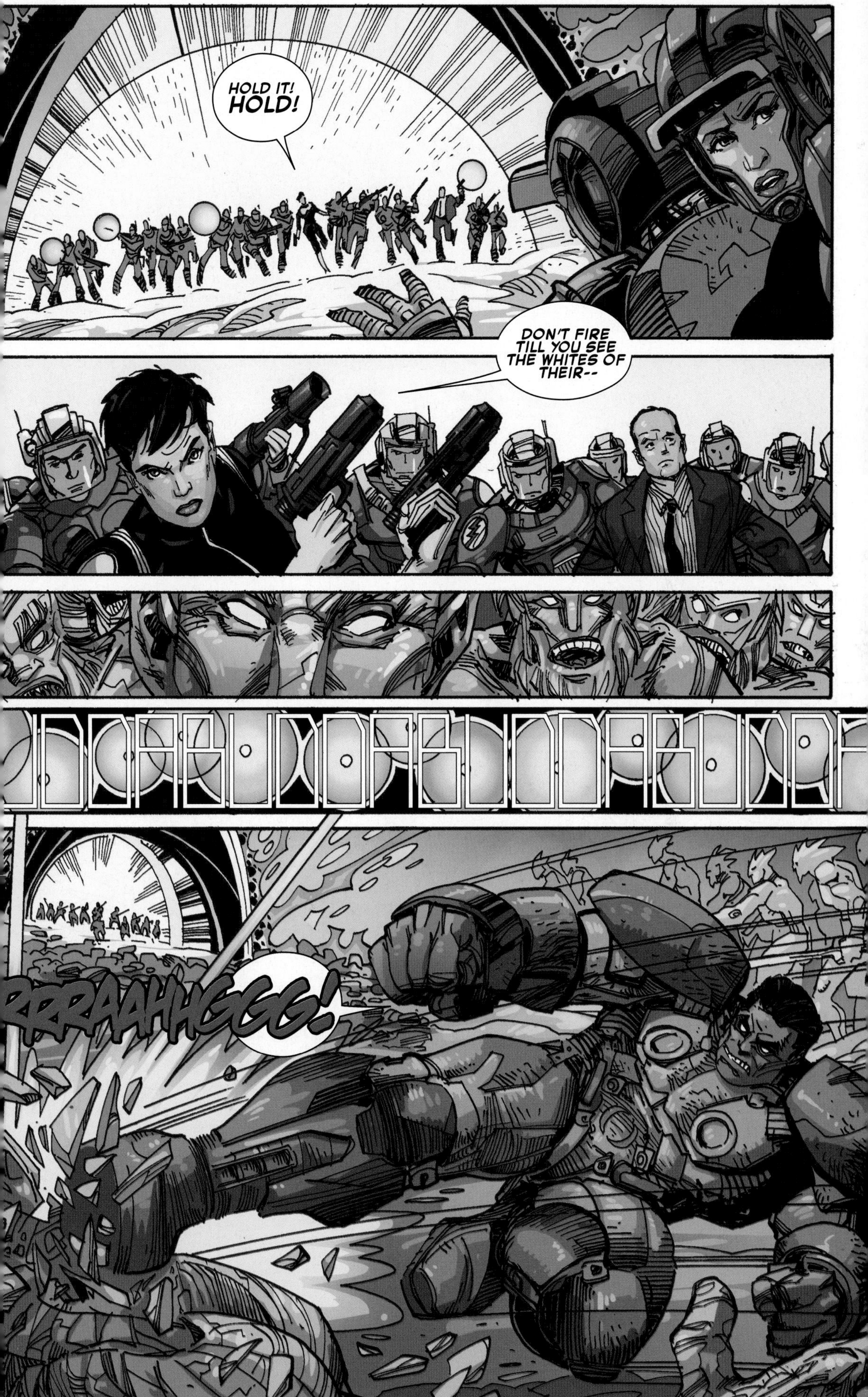
HOLD IT! HOLD!
DON'T FIRE TILL YOU SEE THE WHITES OF THEIR--
RRRAAHHGGG!

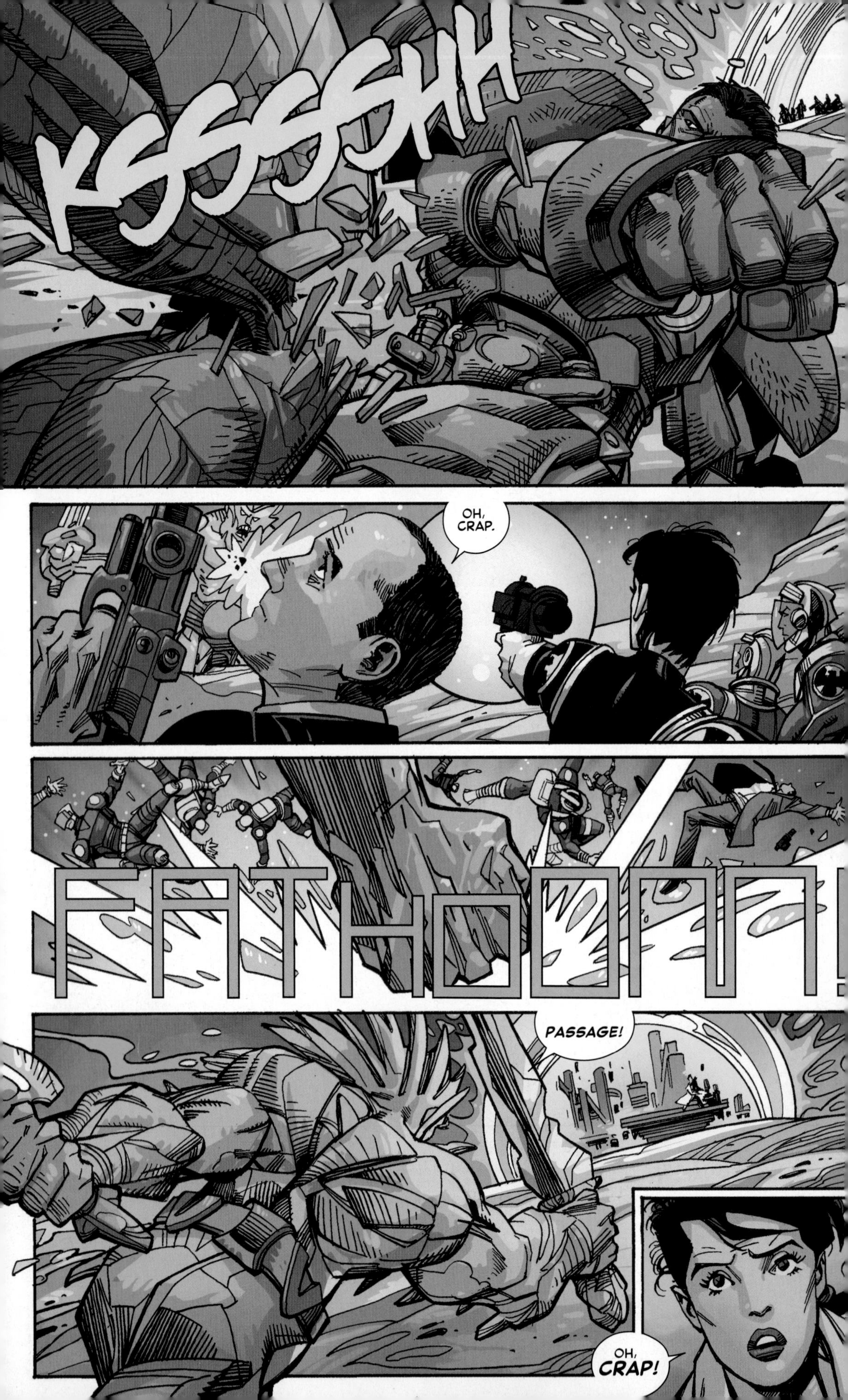
KSSSSHH
OH, CRAP.
FATHOOM!
PASSAGE!
OH, CRAP!

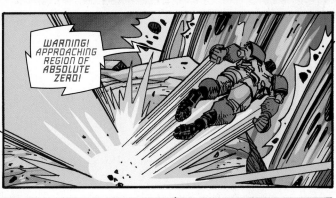

WARNING! APPROACHING REGION OF ABSOLUTE ZERO!

ARMOR THERMAL UNIT TO FULL RADIANT POWER--

SPSHHH

SKSHHHH!

...nnnnnnhh...

--REPEAT-- THERMALS ON FULL--

YOU MAY...PUT ME DOWN, FRIEND HULKSMASH. THANKS TO THEE, I ONCE MORE AWAKEN.

MY GRATITUDE IS THINE.

NOW...LET US THRASH GIANTS.

PUNY GIANTS.

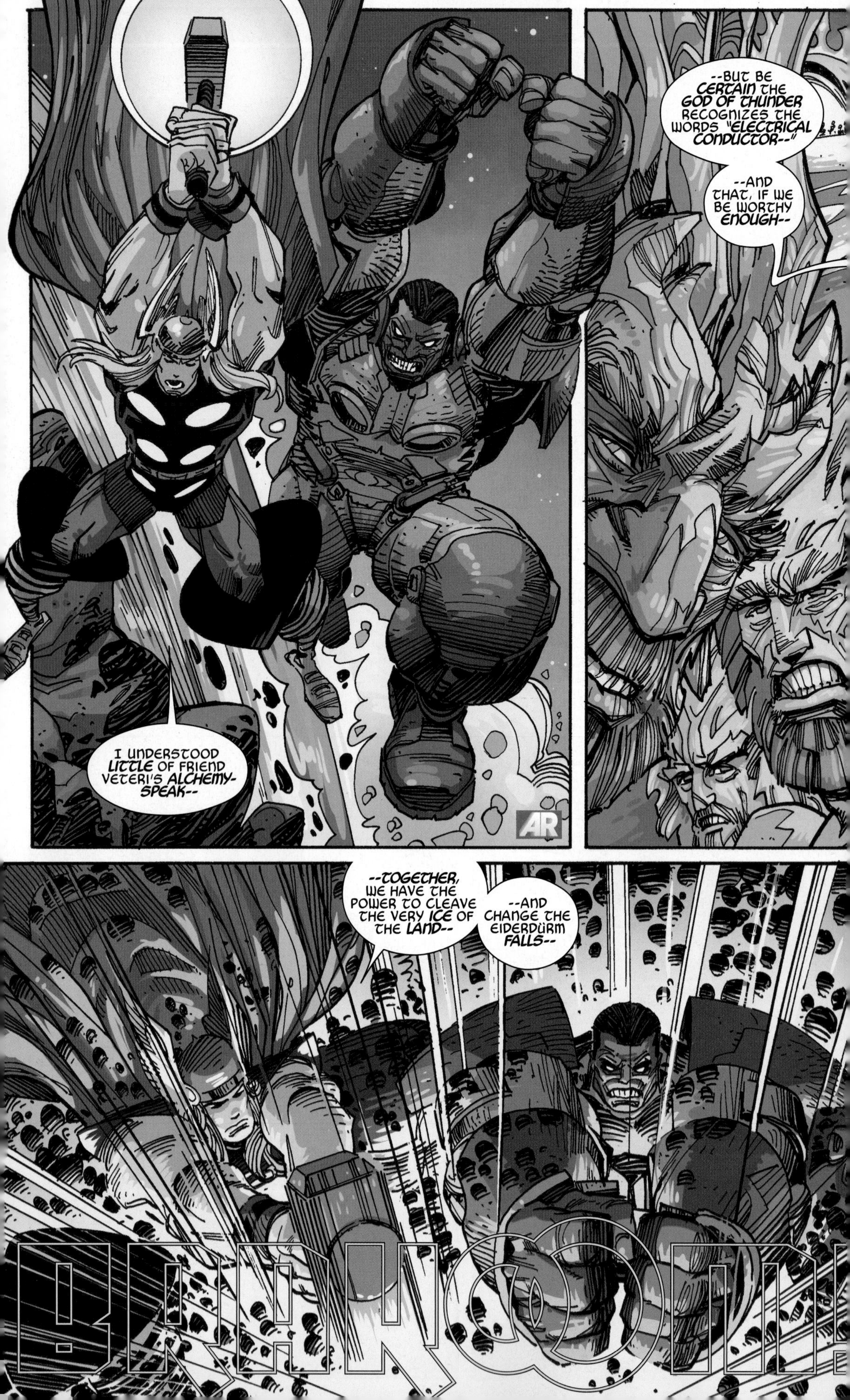
I UNDERSTOOD LITTLE OF FRIEND VETERI'S ALCHEMY-SPEAK--
--BUT BE CERTAIN THE GOD OF THUNDER RECOGNIZES THE WORDS "ELECTRICAL CONDUCTOR--"
--AND THAT, IF WE BE WORTHY ENOUGH--
--TOGETHER, WE HAVE THE POWER TO CLEAVE THE VERY ICE OF THE LAND--
--AND CHANGE THE EIDERDÜRM FALLS--
BRAKOOM!

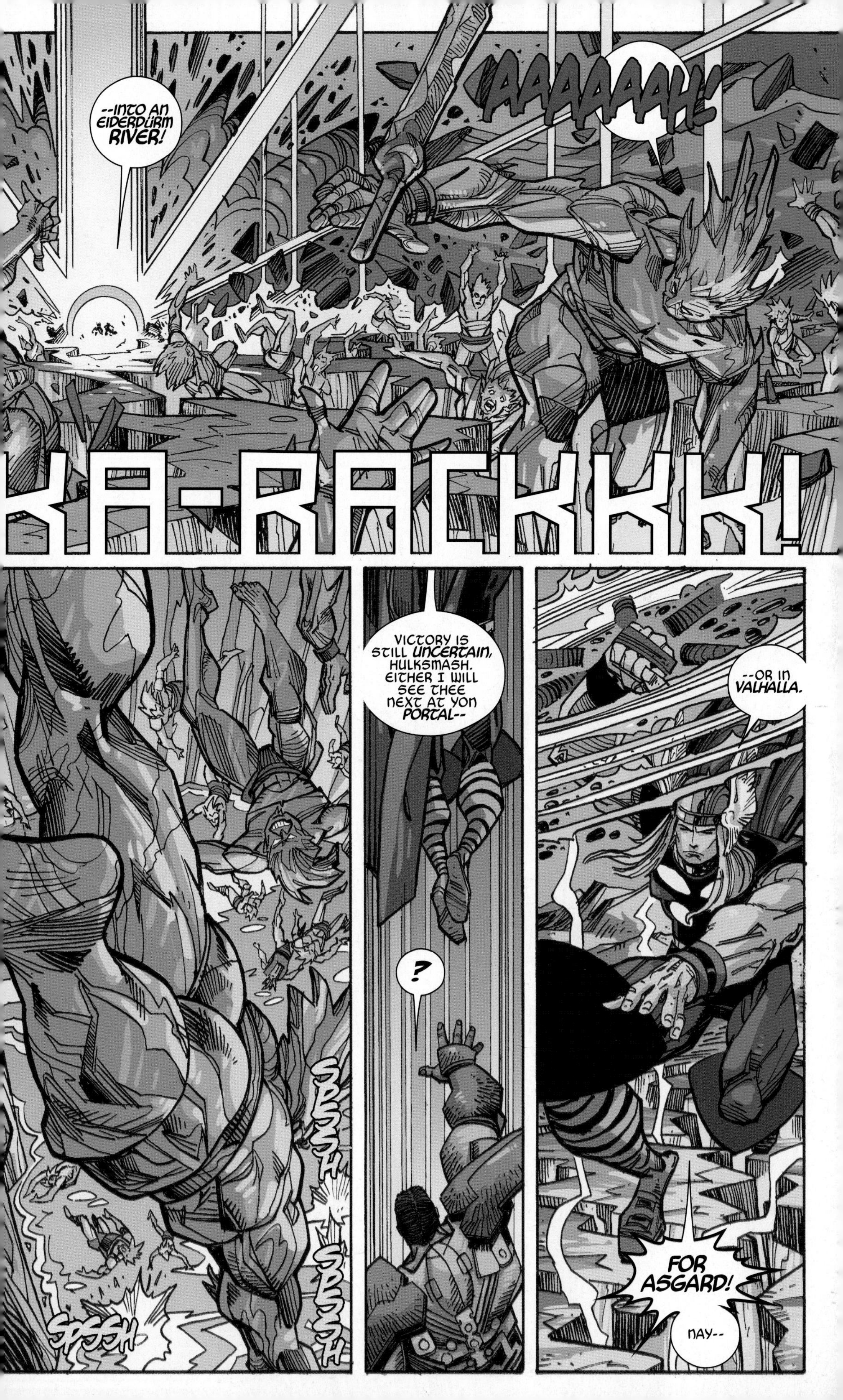
--INTO AN EIDERDÜRM RIVER!
AAAAAAH!
KA-RACKKKK!
SPSSH
SPSSH
SPSSH
VICTORY IS STILL UNCERTAIN, HULKSMASH. EITHER I WILL SEE THEE NEXT AT YON PORTAL--
?
--OR IN VALHALLA.
FOR ASGARD!
NAY--

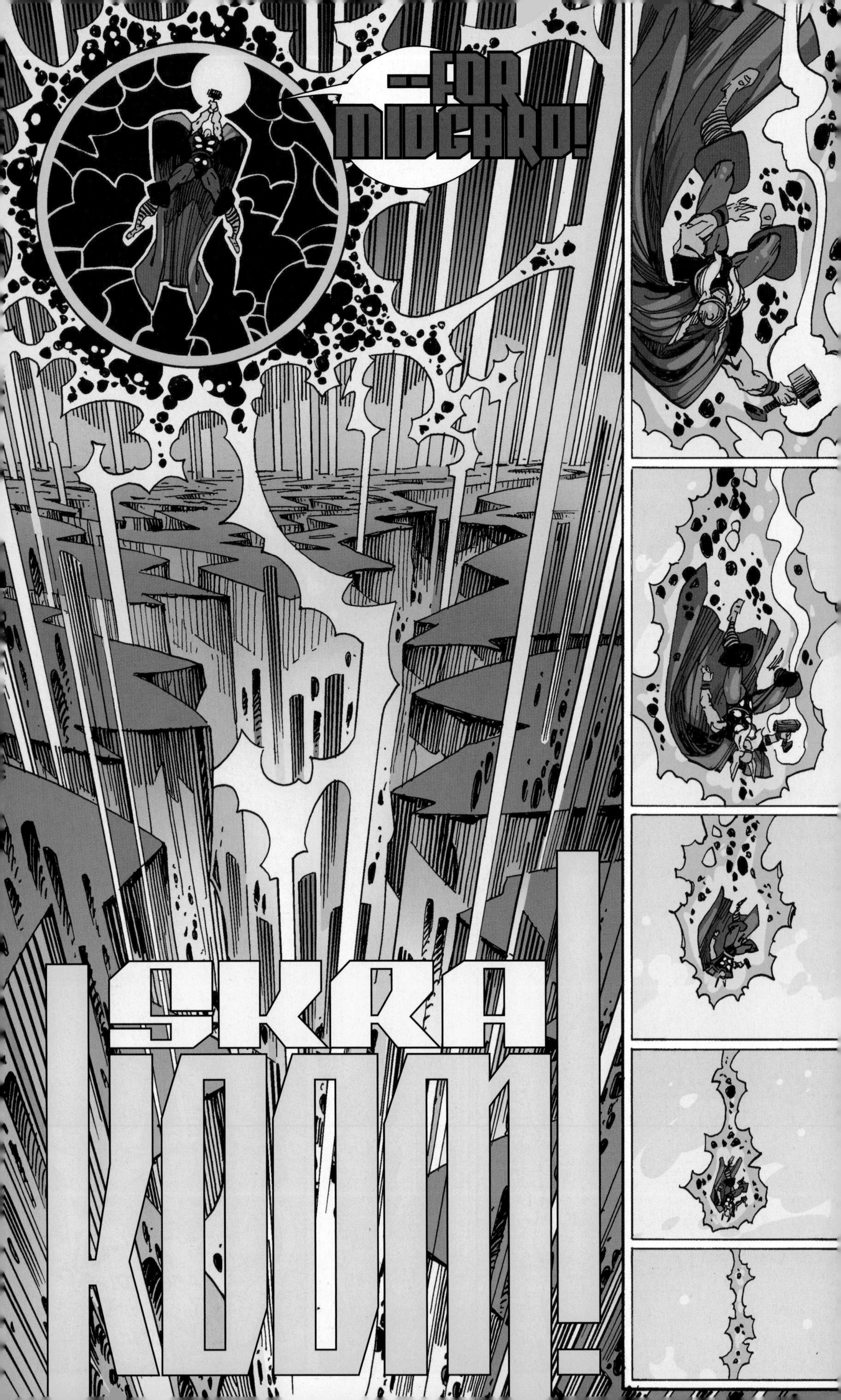
--FOR MIDGARD!
SKRA KOOM!

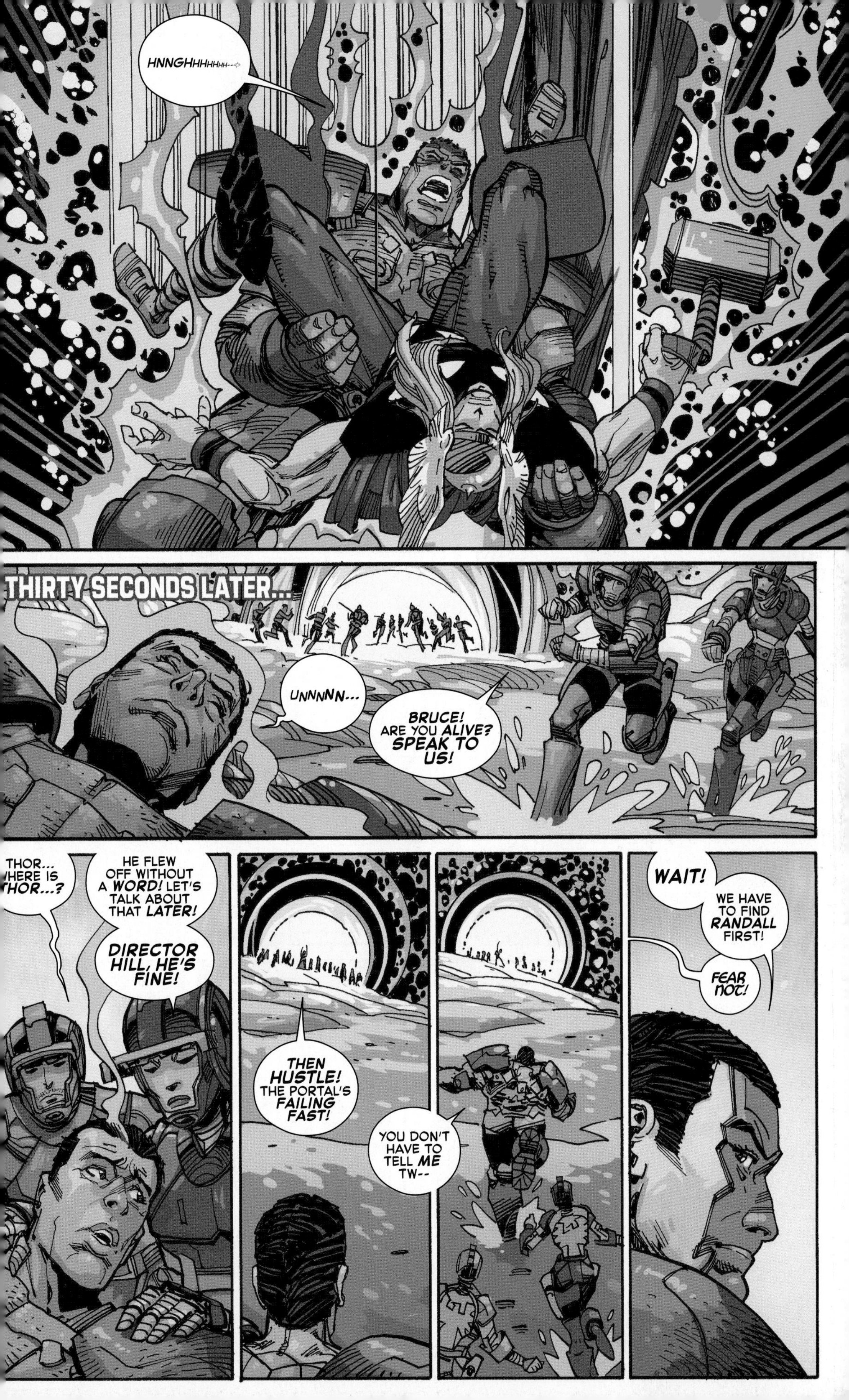
HNNGHHHHHH--
THIRTY SECONDS LATER...
UNNNNN...
BRUCE! ARE YOU ALIVE? SPEAK TO US!
THOR... WHERE IS THOR...?
HE FLEW OFF WITHOUT A WORD! LET'S TALK ABOUT THAT LATER!
DIRECTOR HILL, HE'S FINE!
THEN HUSTLE! THE PORTAL'S FAILING FAST!
YOU DON'T HAVE TO TELL ME TW--
WAIT!
WE HAVE TO FIND RANDALL FIRST!
FEAR NOT!

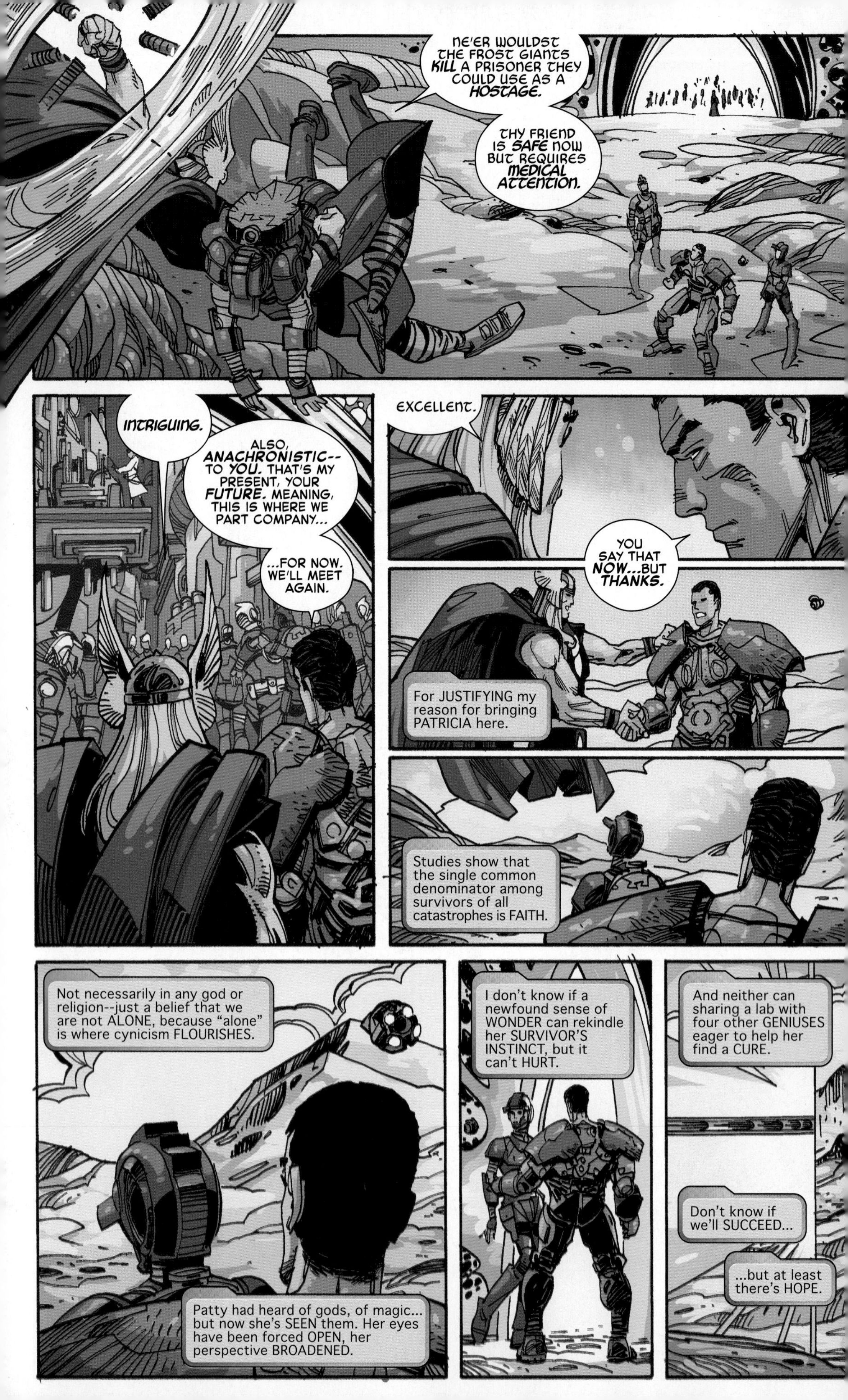
NE'ER WOULDST THE FROST GIANTS KILL A PRISONER THEY COULD USE AS A HOSTAGE.
THY FRIEND IS SAFE NOW BUT REQUIRES MEDICAL ATTENTION.
INTRIGUING.
ALSO, ANACHRONISTIC--TO YOU. THAT'S MY PRESENT, YOUR FUTURE. MEANING, THIS IS WHERE WE PART COMPANY...
...FOR NOW. WE'LL MEET AGAIN.
EXCELLENT.
YOU SAY THAT NOW...BUT THANKS.
For JUSTIFYING my reason for bringing PATRICIA here.
Studies show that the single common denominator among survivors of all catastrophes is FAITH.
Not necessarily in any god or religion--just a belief that we are not ALONE, because "alone" is where cynicism FLOURISHES.
Patty had heard of gods, of magic... but now she's SEEN them. Her eyes have been forced OPEN, her perspective BROADENED.
I don't know if a newfound sense of WONDER can rekindle her SURVIVOR'S INSTINCT, but it can't HURT.
And neither can sharing a lab with four other GENIUSES eager to help her find a CURE.
Don't know if we'll SUCCEED...
...but at least there's HOPE.

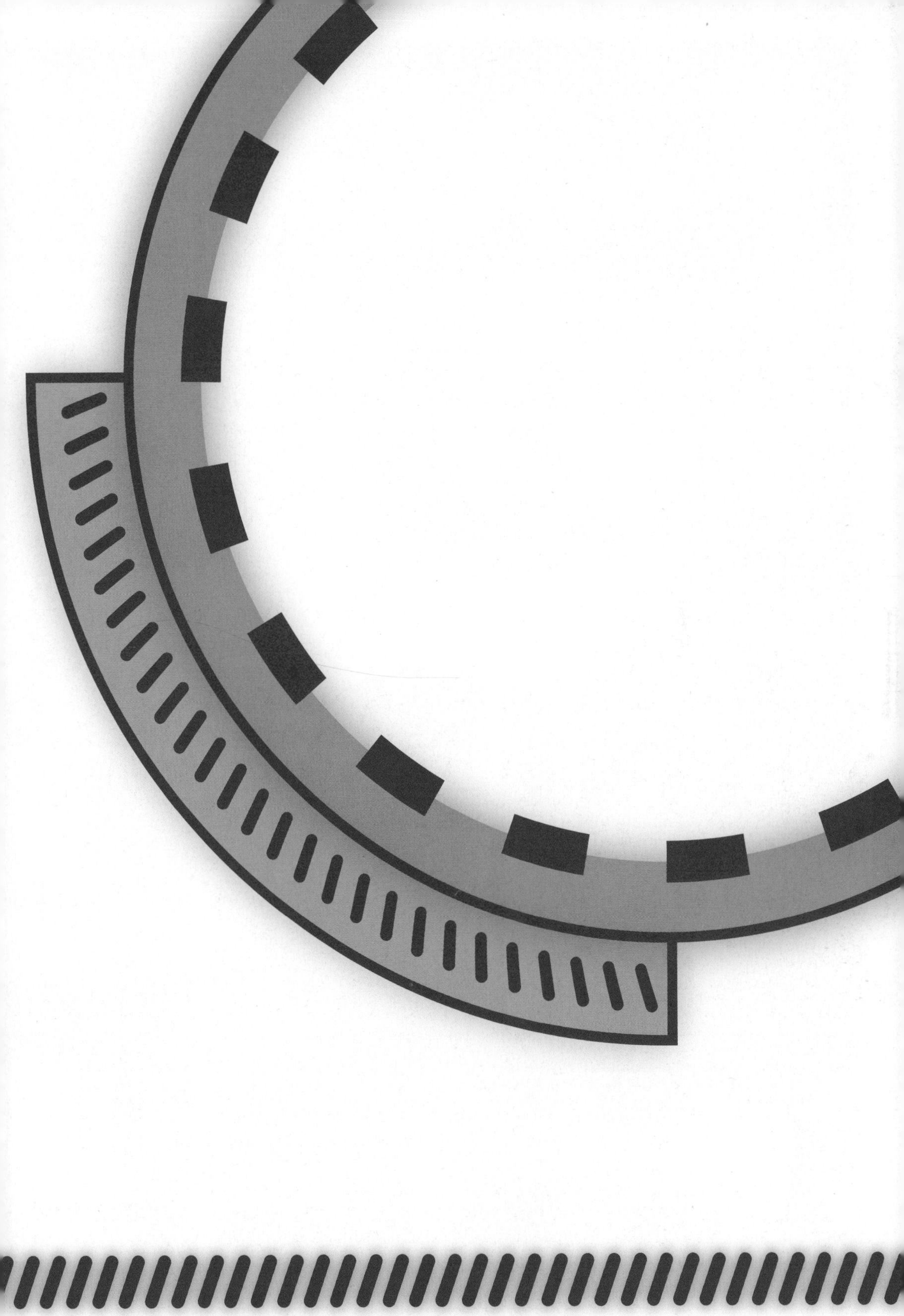

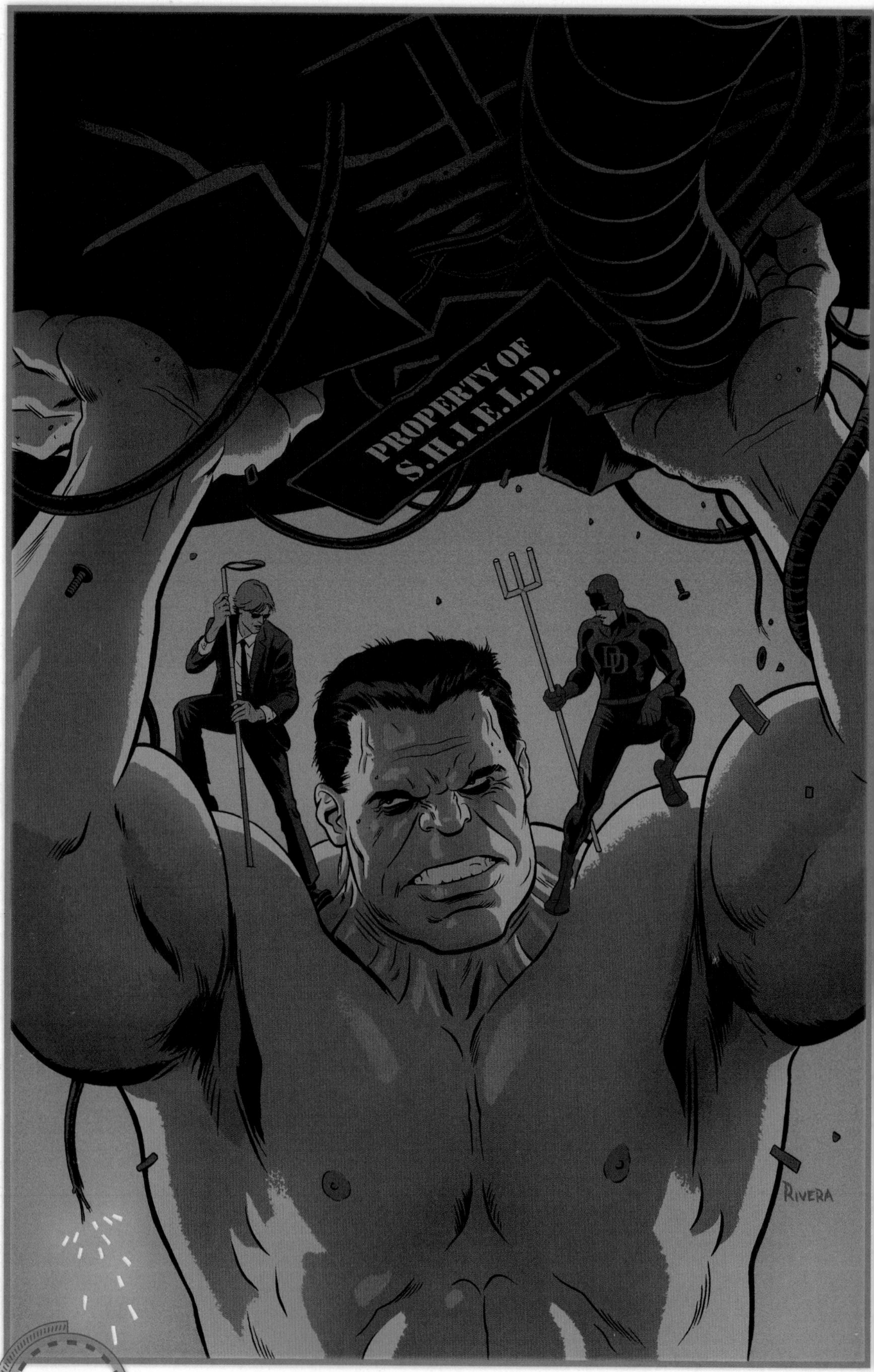
PROPERTY OF
S.H.I.E.L.D.
RIVERA

RELAX. YOU KNOW WHO THAT WAS. HE'S COOL.

HE'S JUST DOING HIS DUE DILIGENCE, THAT'S ALL.

...I WANT... TO KILL YOU... SO MUCH...

YOU'LL GET ME BACK. YOU ALWAYS DO. BUT YOU AND I MADE A DEAL, REMEMBER?

And it was THIS:

"Hulk smashes, Banner BUILDS." I get a lab and resources. In exchange, HULK works for S.H.I.E.L.D. as a one-man W.M.D.

My insurance against S.H.I.E.L.D. just dropping Hulk into the SUN and being DONE with him is this:

Once a week, my OUTSIDE MAN has to hear FROM ME that I'm alive, healthy, and not being MISTREATED in ANY WAY.

HOLD MY CALLS, ALYSSA.

His name is MATT MURDOCK.

That man is my LAWYER.

His OTHER name is...

DAREDEVIL

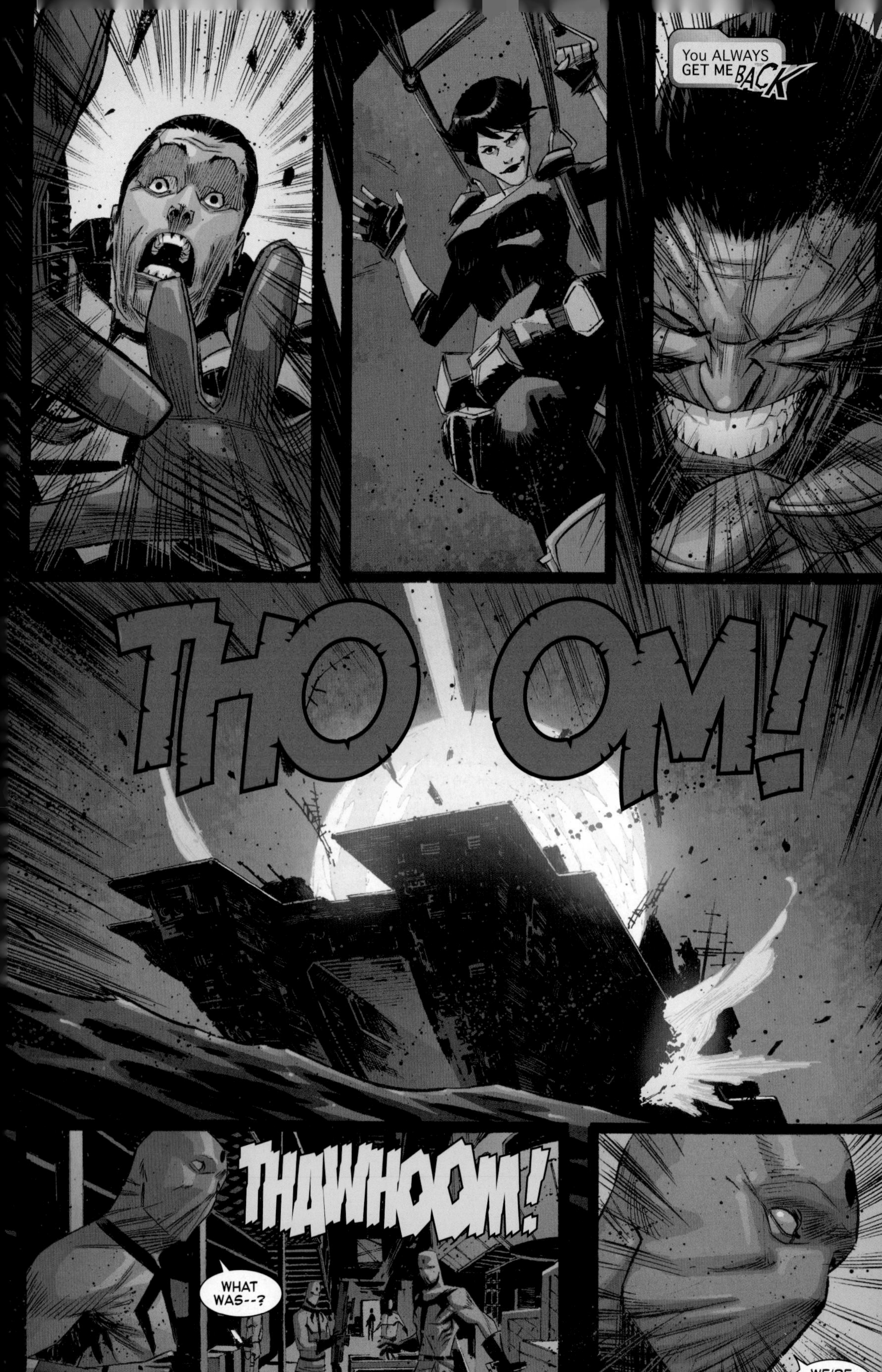
You ALWAYS GET ME BACK
THO OM!
THAWHOOM!
WHAT WAS--?
WE'RE UNDER SIEGE!

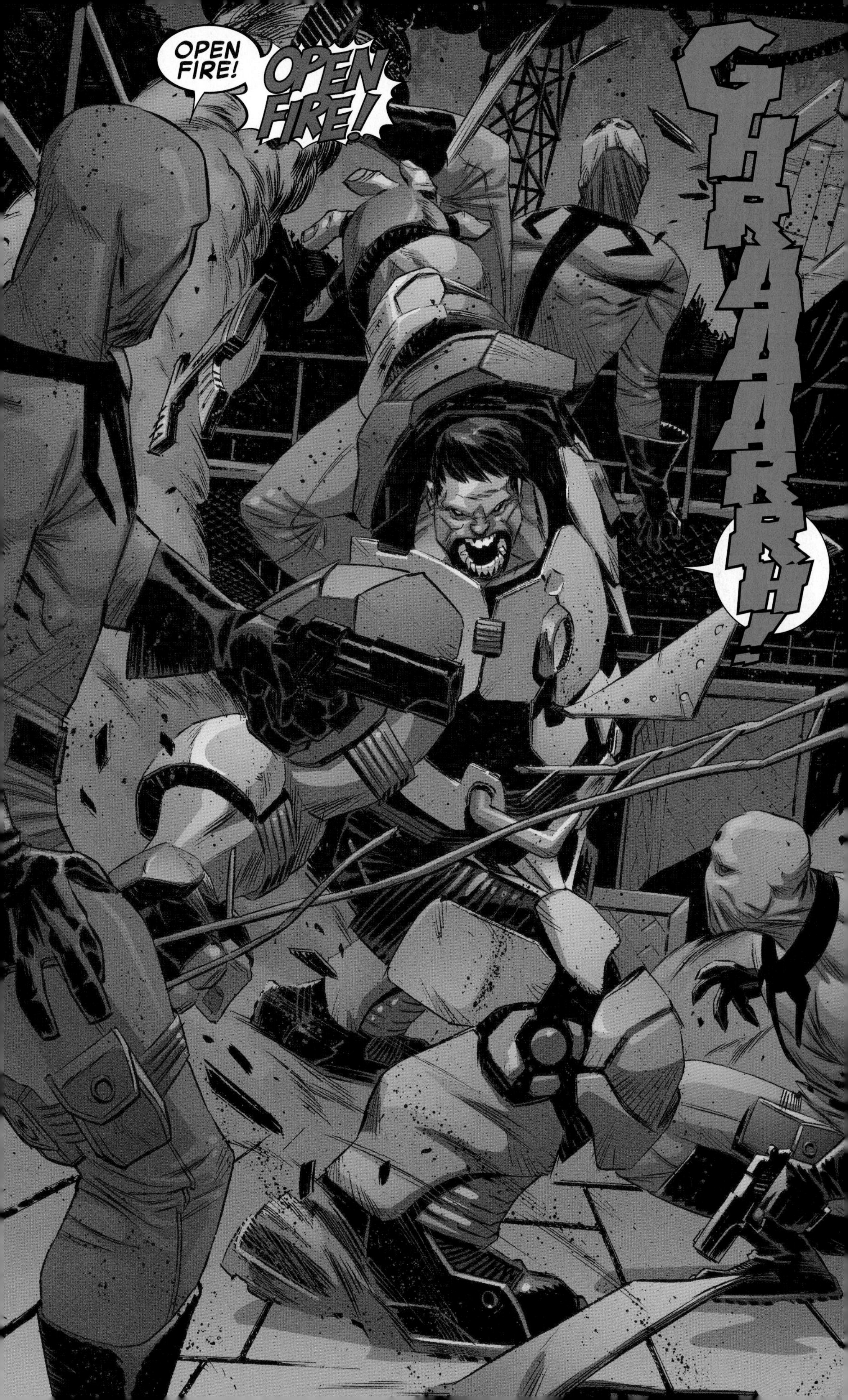
OPEN FIRE!
OPEN FIRE!
GHRAAARRH!

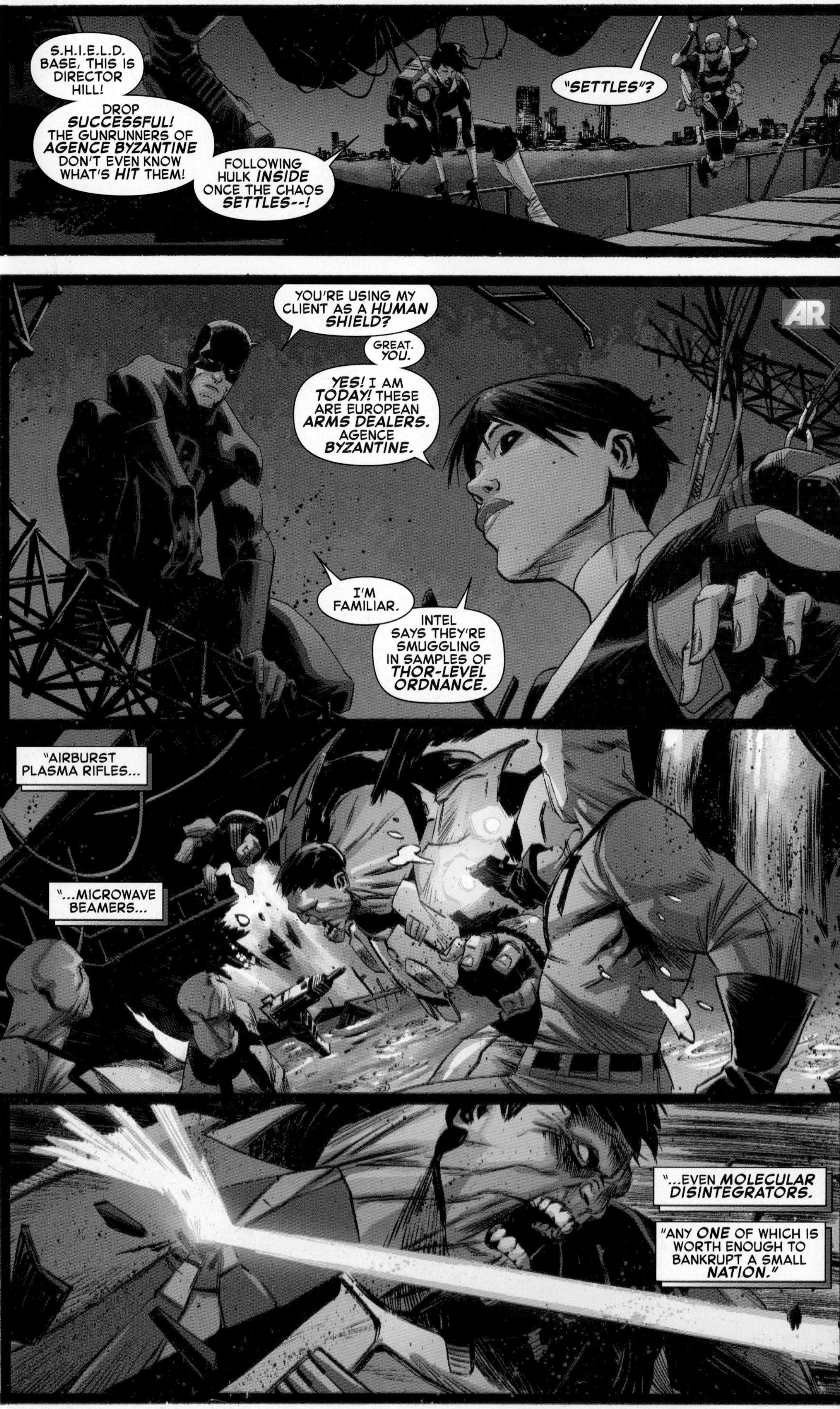
S.H.I.E.L.D. BASE, THIS IS DIRECTOR HILL!
DROP SUCCESSFUL! THE GUNRUNNERS OF AGENCE BYZANTINE DON'T EVEN KNOW WHAT'S HIT THEM!
FOLLOWING HULK INSIDE ONCE THE CHAOS SETTLES--!
"SETTLES"?
YOU'RE USING MY CLIENT AS A HUMAN SHIELD?
GREAT. YOU.
YES! I AM TODAY! THESE ARE EUROPEAN ARMS DEALERS. AGENCE BYZANTINE.
I'M FAMILIAR.
INTEL SAYS THEY'RE SMUGGLING IN SAMPLES OF THOR-LEVEL ORDNANCE.
"AIRBURST PLASMA RIFLES...
"...MICROWAVE BEAMERS...
"...EVEN MOLECULAR DISINTEGRATORS.
"ANY ONE OF WHICH IS WORTH ENOUGH TO BANKRUPT A SMALL NATION."

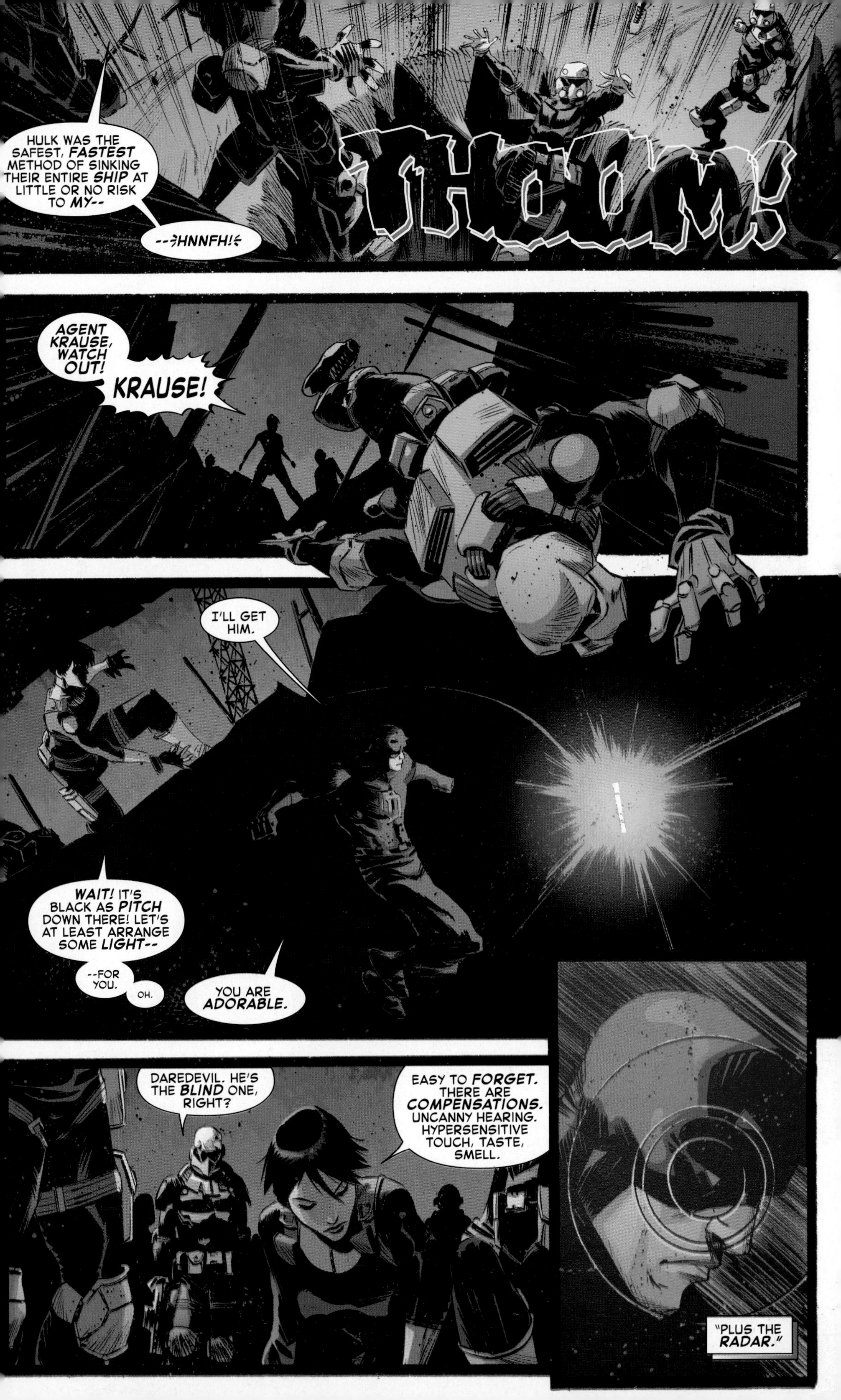
HULK WAS THE SAFEST, FASTEST METHOD OF SINKING THEIR ENTIRE SHIP AT LITTLE OR NO RISK TO MY--
--HNNFH!
THOOM!
AGENT KRAUSE, WATCH OUT!
KRAUSE!
I'LL GET HIM.
WAIT! IT'S BLACK AS PITCH DOWN THERE! LET'S AT LEAST ARRANGE SOME LIGHT--
--FOR YOU.
OH.
YOU ARE ADORABLE.
DAREDEVIL. HE'S THE BLIND ONE, RIGHT?
EASY TO FORGET. THERE ARE COMPENSATIONS. UNCANNY HEARING. HYPERSENSITIVE TOUCH, TASTE, SMELL.
"PLUS THE RADAR."

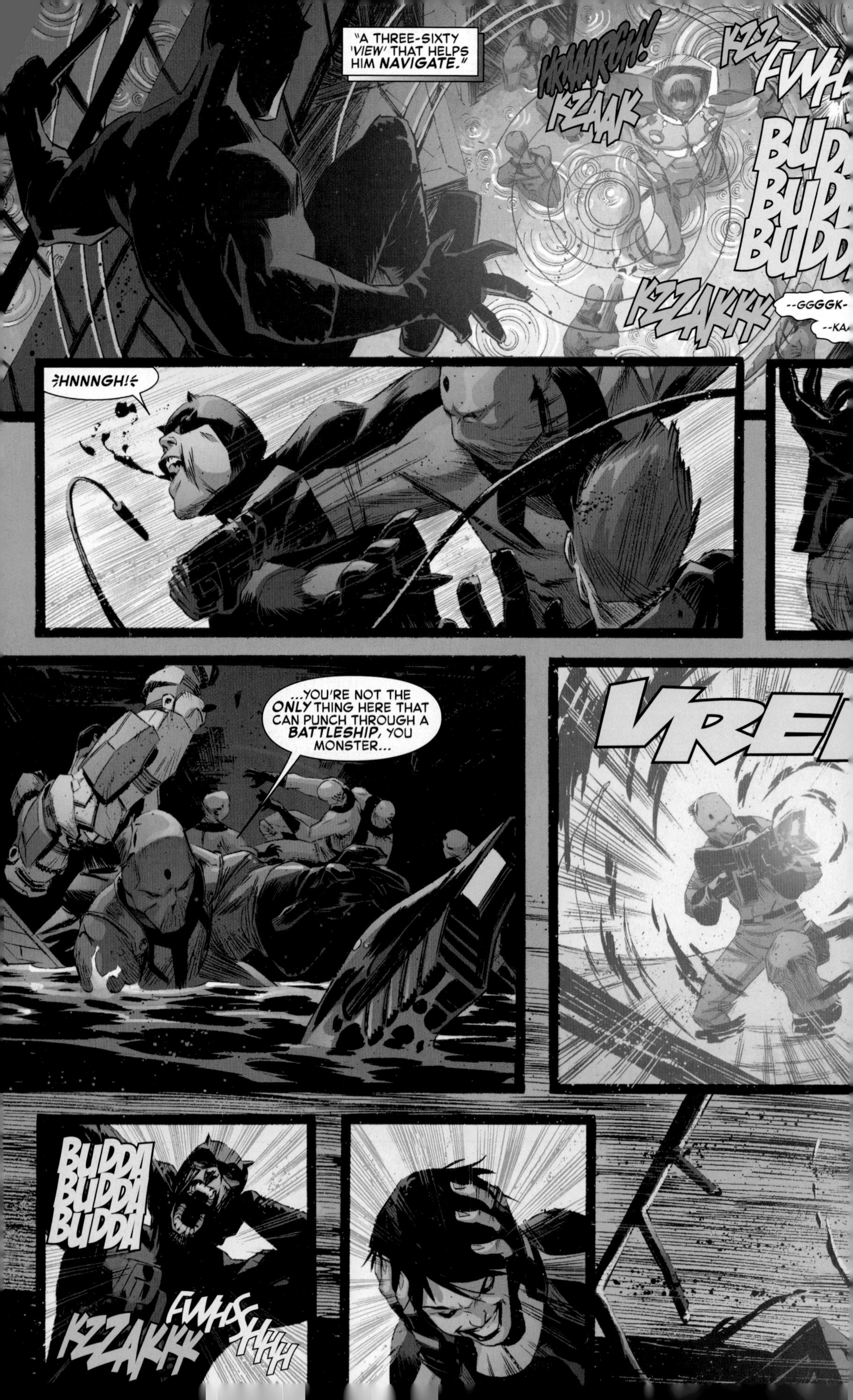
"A THREE-SIXTY 'VIEW' THAT HELPS HIM NAVIGATE."
HRAAARGH!
KZAAK
KZZ
FWH
BUD
BUD
BUDD
KZZAKKK
--GGGGK-
--KA
HNNNGH!
...YOU'RE NOT THE ONLY THING HERE THAT CAN PUNCH THROUGH A BATTLESHIP, YOU MONSTER...
VRE
BUDDA
BUDDA
BUDDA
KZZAKKK
FWHSHHH

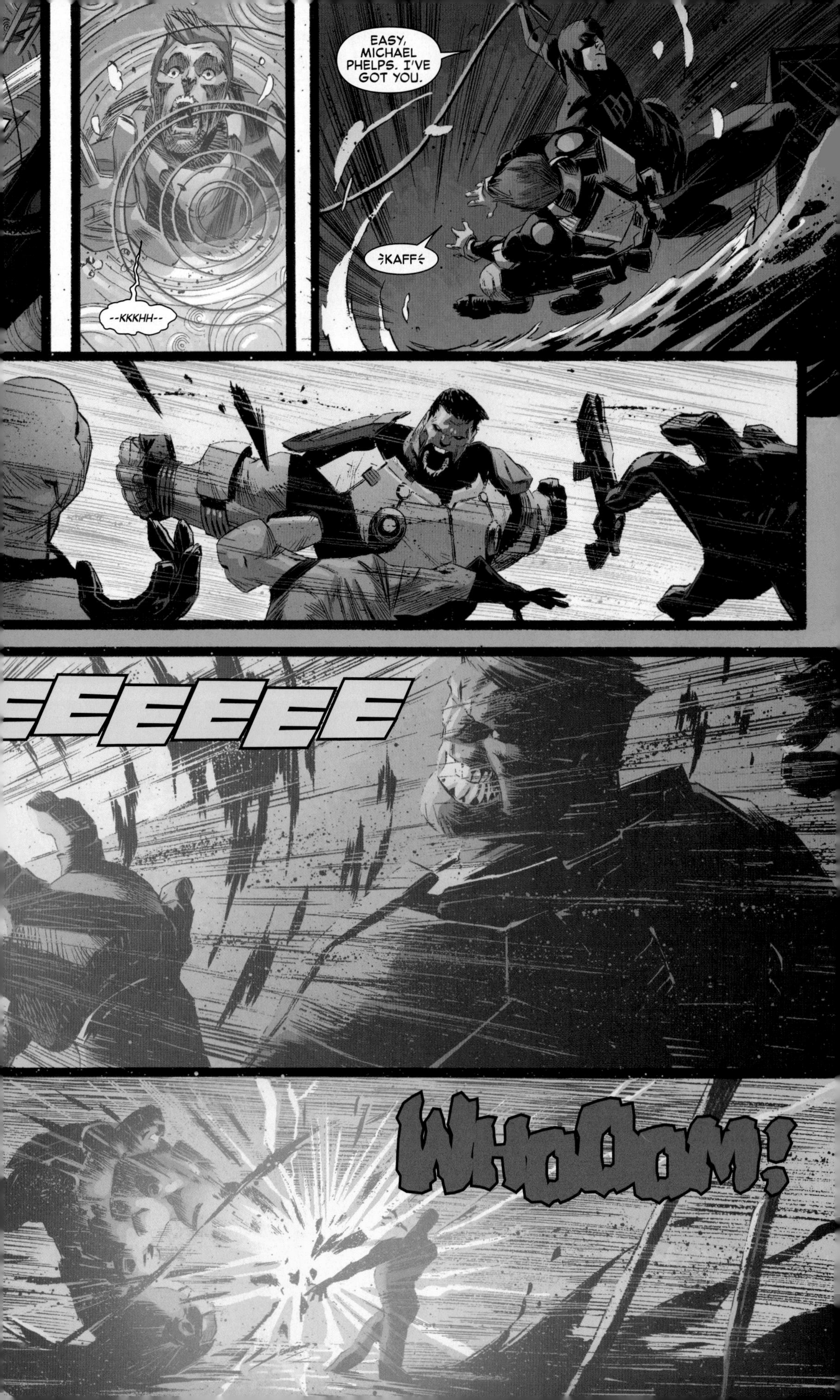
--KKKHH--
EASY, MICHAEL PHELPS. I'VE GOT YOU.
KAFF
EEEEEE
WHOOOM!

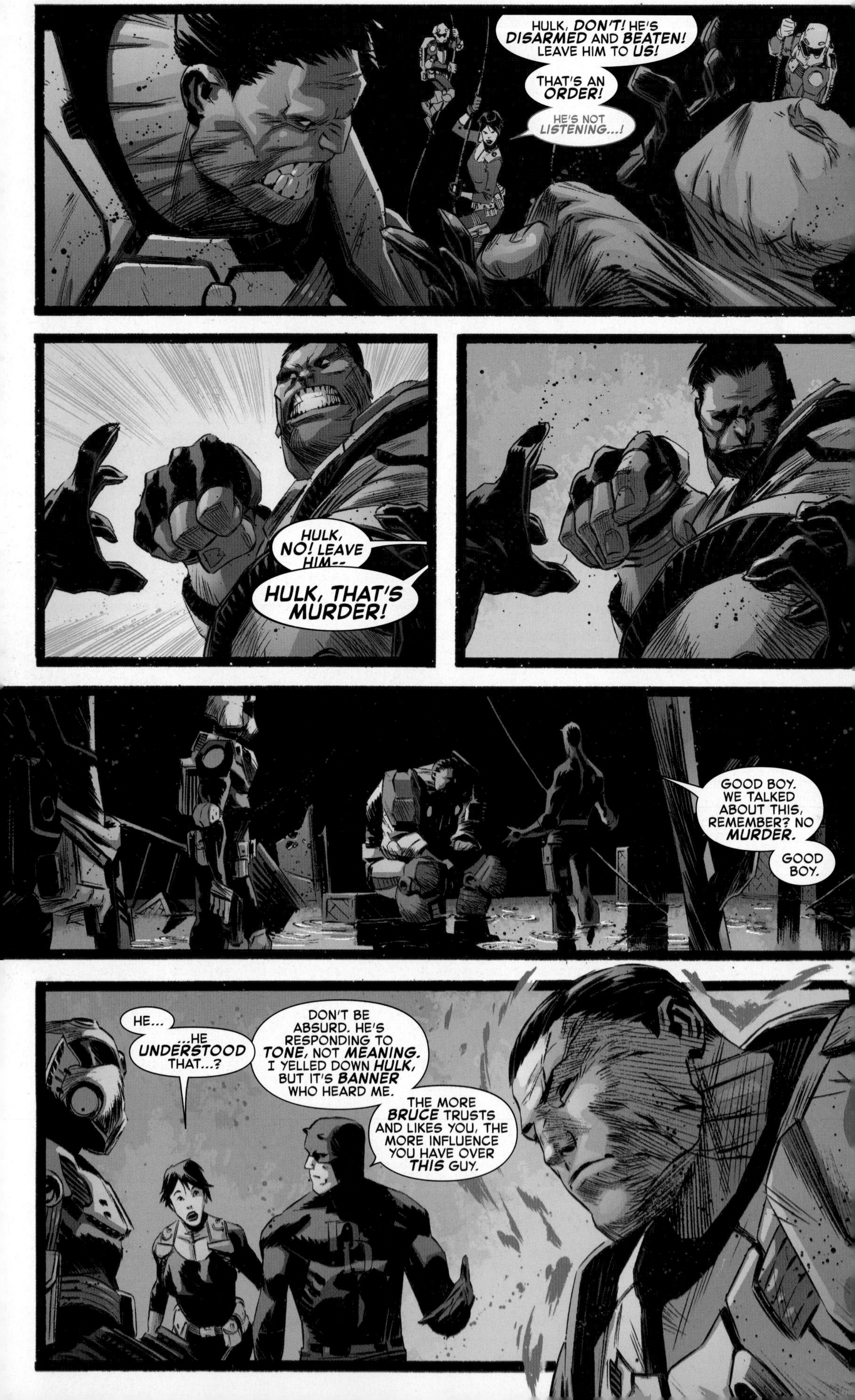
HULK, DON'T! HE'S DISARMED AND BEATEN! LEAVE HIM TO US!
THAT'S AN ORDER!
HE'S NOT LISTENING...!
HULK, NO! LEAVE HIM--
HULK, THAT'S MURDER!
GOOD BOY. WE TALKED ABOUT THIS, REMEMBER? NO MURDER.
GOOD BOY.
HE...
...HE UNDERSTOOD THAT...?
DON'T BE ABSURD. HE'S RESPONDING TO TONE, NOT MEANING. I YELLED DOWN HULK, BUT IT'S BANNER WHO HEARD ME.
THE MORE BRUCE TRUSTS AND LIKES YOU, THE MORE INFLUENCE YOU HAVE OVER THIS GUY.

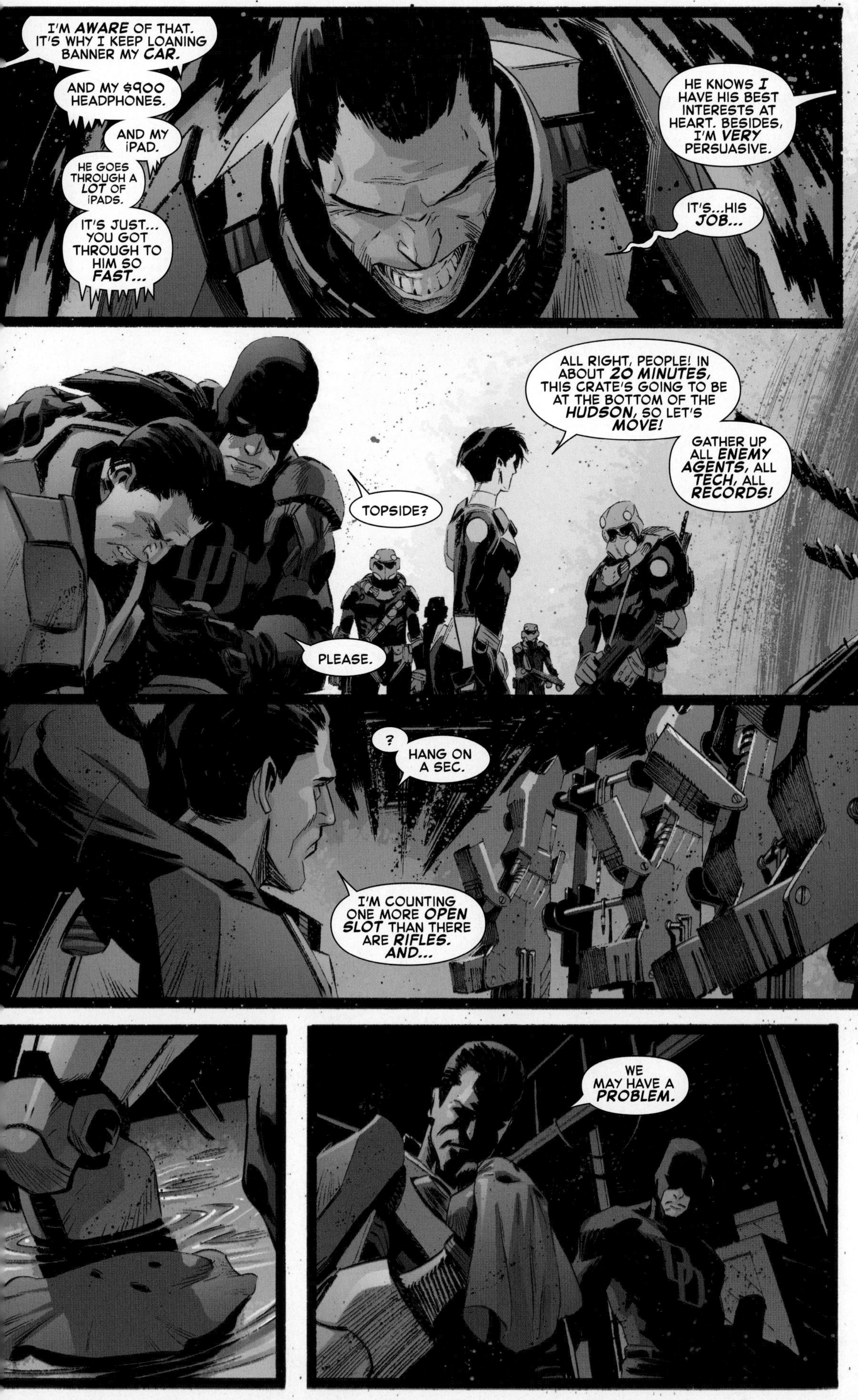
I'M AWARE OF THAT. IT'S WHY I KEEP LOANING BANNER MY CAR.
AND MY $900 HEADPHONES.
AND MY iPAD.
HE GOES THROUGH A LOT OF iPADS.
IT'S JUST... YOU GOT THROUGH TO HIM SO FAST...
HE KNOWS I HAVE HIS BEST INTERESTS AT HEART. BESIDES, I'M VERY PERSUASIVE.
IT'S...HIS JOB...
ALL RIGHT, PEOPLE! IN ABOUT 20 MINUTES, THIS CRATE'S GOING TO BE AT THE BOTTOM OF THE HUDSON, SO LET'S MOVE!
GATHER UP ALL ENEMY AGENTS, ALL TECH, ALL RECORDS!
TOPSIDE?
PLEASE.
?
HANG ON A SEC.
I'M COUNTING ONE MORE OPEN SLOT THAN THERE ARE RIFLES. AND...
WE MAY HAVE A PROBLEM.

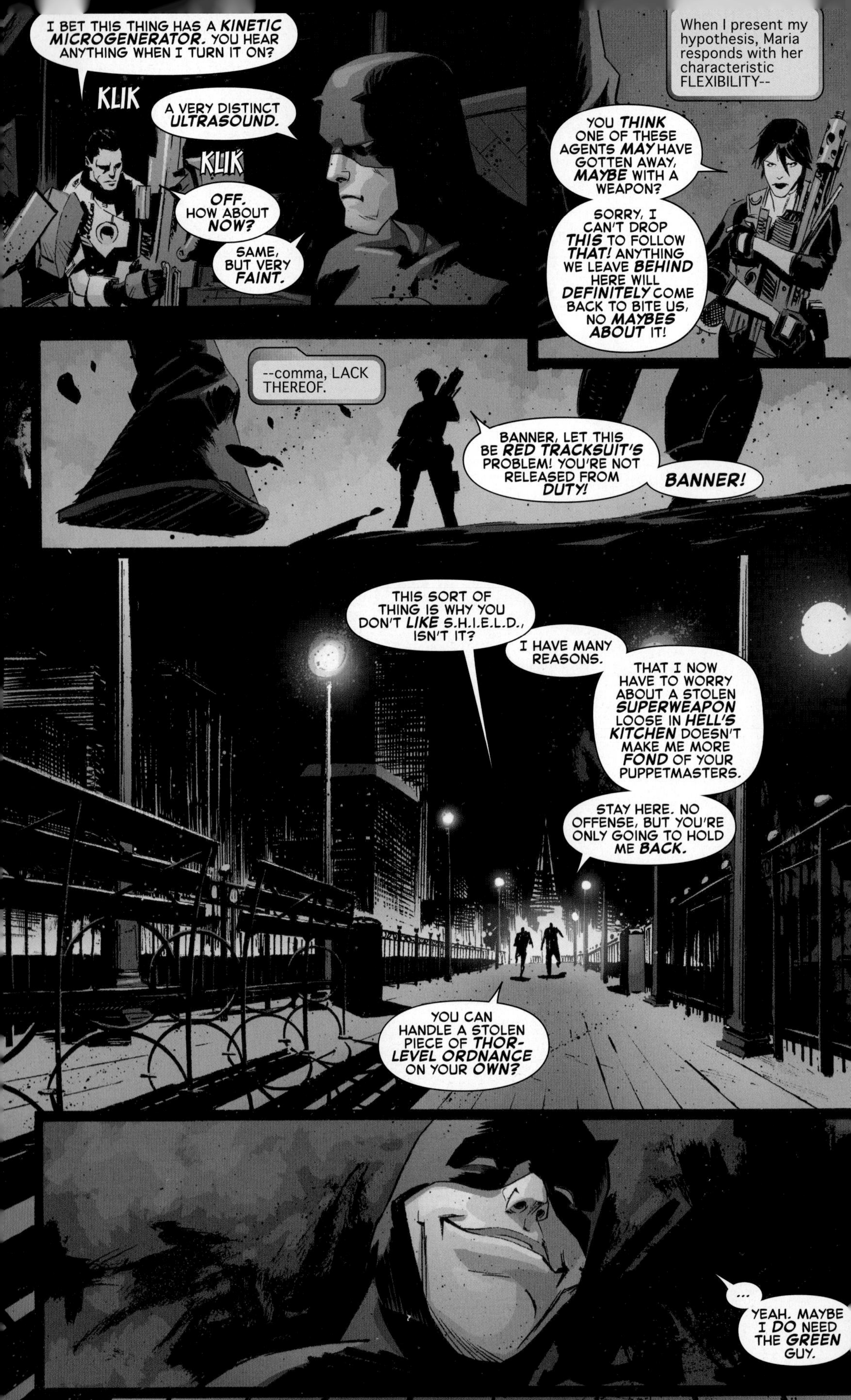
I BET THIS THING HAS A KINETIC MICROGENERATOR. YOU HEAR ANYTHING WHEN I TURN IT ON?
KLIK
A VERY DISTINCT ULTRASOUND.
KLIK
OFF. HOW ABOUT NOW?
SAME, BUT VERY FAINT.
When I present my hypothesis, Maria responds with her characteristic FLEXIBILITY--
YOU THINK ONE OF THESE AGENTS MAY HAVE GOTTEN AWAY, MAYBE WITH A WEAPON?
SORRY, I CAN'T DROP THIS TO FOLLOW THAT! ANYTHING WE LEAVE BEHIND HERE WILL DEFINITELY COME BACK TO BITE US, NO MAYBES ABOUT IT!
--comma, LACK THEREOF.
BANNER, LET THIS BE RED TRACKSUIT'S PROBLEM! YOU'RE NOT RELEASED FROM DUTY!
BANNER!
THIS SORT OF THING IS WHY YOU DON'T LIKE S.H.I.E.L.D., ISN'T IT?
I HAVE MANY REASONS.
THAT I NOW HAVE TO WORRY ABOUT A STOLEN SUPERWEAPON LOOSE IN HELL'S KITCHEN DOESN'T MAKE ME MORE FOND OF YOUR PUPPETMASTERS.
STAY HERE. NO OFFENSE, BUT YOU'RE ONLY GOING TO HOLD ME BACK.
YOU CAN HANDLE A STOLEN PIECE OF THOR-LEVEL ORDNANCE ON YOUR OWN?
...
YEAH. MAYBE I DO NEED THE GREEN GUY.

YOU HEAR THE *GUN*?

RIGHT DOWN TO MY *FILLINGS*. OUR RUNNER'S DUCKED IN *THERE*.

YOU *KNOW* THIS PLACE?

HALF-BAR, HALF-UNDERWORLD *ARMAMENT EXCHANGE*. LOWLIFE CENTRAL. THE *ANTI-CHEERS*.

THEY DON'T EVEN LET YOU *IN* IF YOU'RE NOT PACKING.

SO THEY'LL SHOOT *YOU* THE MOMENT YOU SET FOOT INSIDE.

THEY'LL *TRY.*

CABBIE, POP THE TRUNK AND THE HOOD.

LOOK, NOT TO TELL YOU YOUR BUSINESS, BEING THAT I'M THE OUT-OF-TOWNER AND ALL...

...BUT, TO REPEAT: AN *ULTRASOUND GUN.* BUILT TO, AMONG *OTHER* THINGS...

...RADIATE *EXCRUCIATING SOUNDWAVES* FROM A *DISTANCE*, BYPASSING THE *EARS* AND ENTERING DIRECTLY THROUGH THE *SKULL.*

AND FORGIVE ME, BUT YOU *ESPECIALLY* ARE VULNERABLE TO *SONIC ATTACKS.*

SO...

...LET'S TRY THIS *MY* WAY.

LOVE TO.

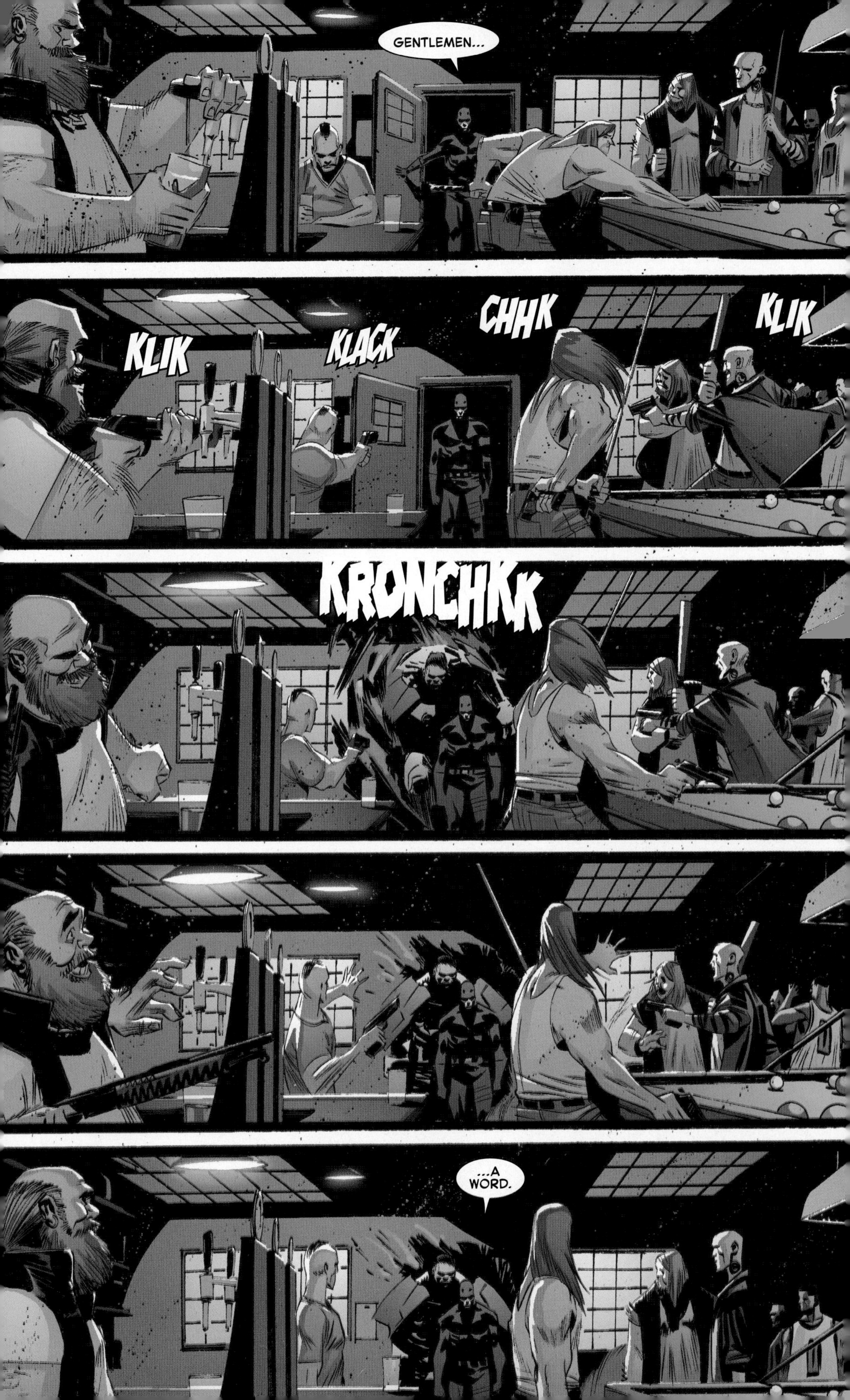
GENTLEMEN...
KLIK
KLACK
CHHK
KLIK
KRONCHKK
...A WORD.

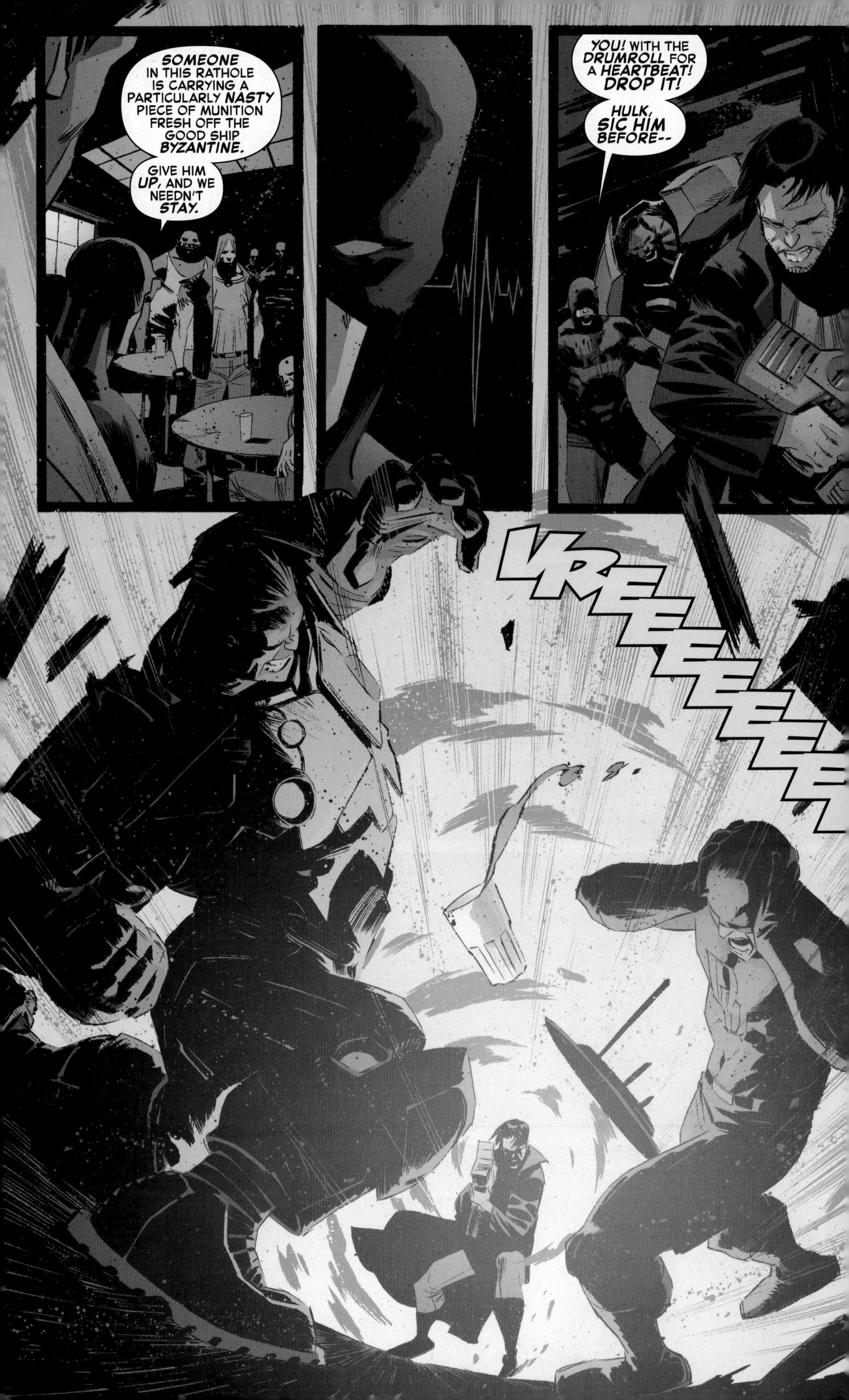
SOMEONE IN THIS RATHOLE IS CARRYING A PARTICULARLY NASTY PIECE OF MUNITION FRESH OFF THE GOOD SHIP BYZANTINE.
GIVE HIM UP, AND WE NEEDN'T STAY.
YOU! WITH THE DRUMROLL FOR A HEARTBEAT! DROP IT!
HULK, SIC HIM BEFORE--
VREEEEEEEEE

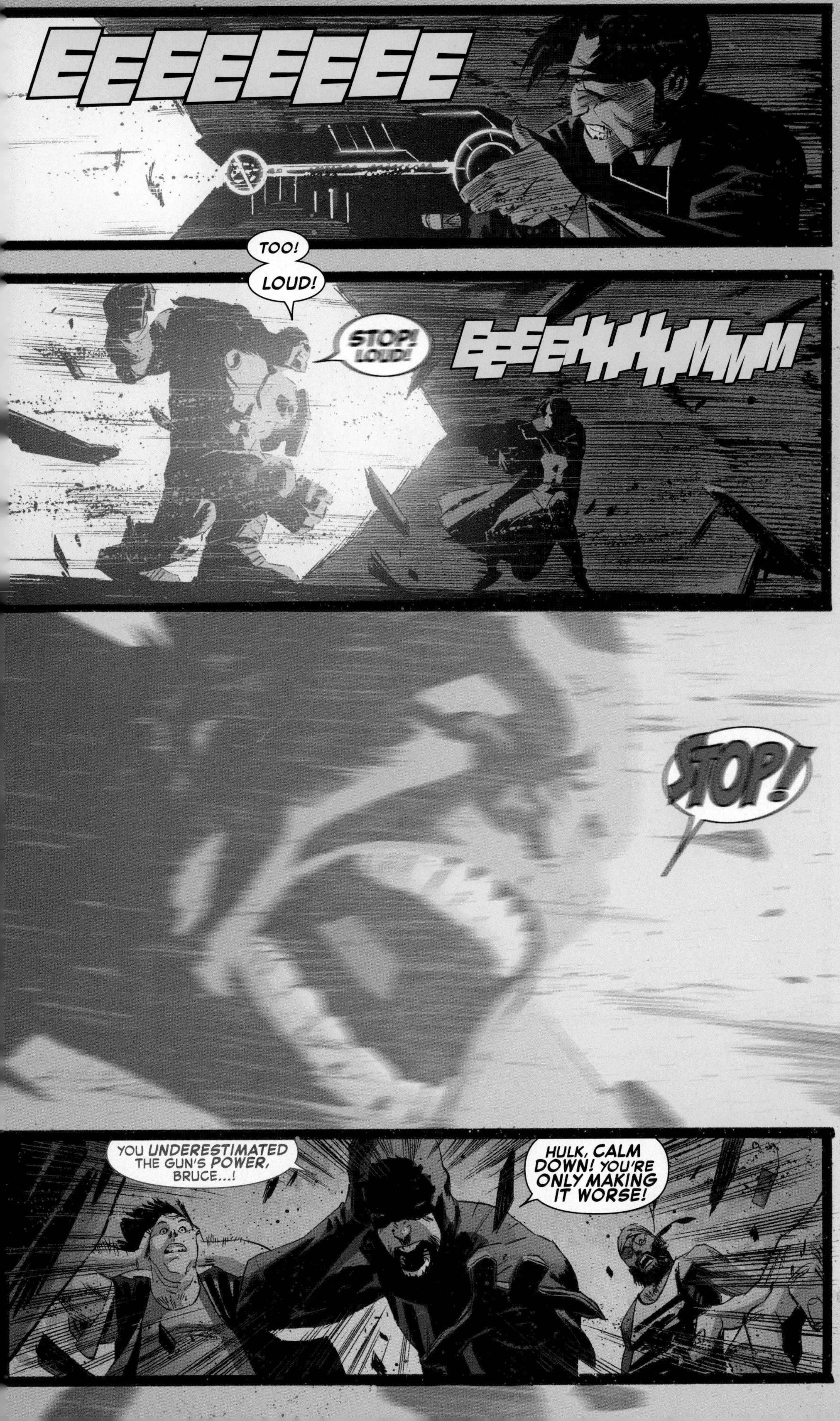

EEEEEEEEE
TOO!
LOUD!
STOP! LOUD!
EEEEHHHHMMMM
STOP!
YOU UNDERESTIMATED THE GUN'S POWER, BRUCE...!
HULK, CALM DOWN! YOU'RE ONLY MAKING IT WORSE!

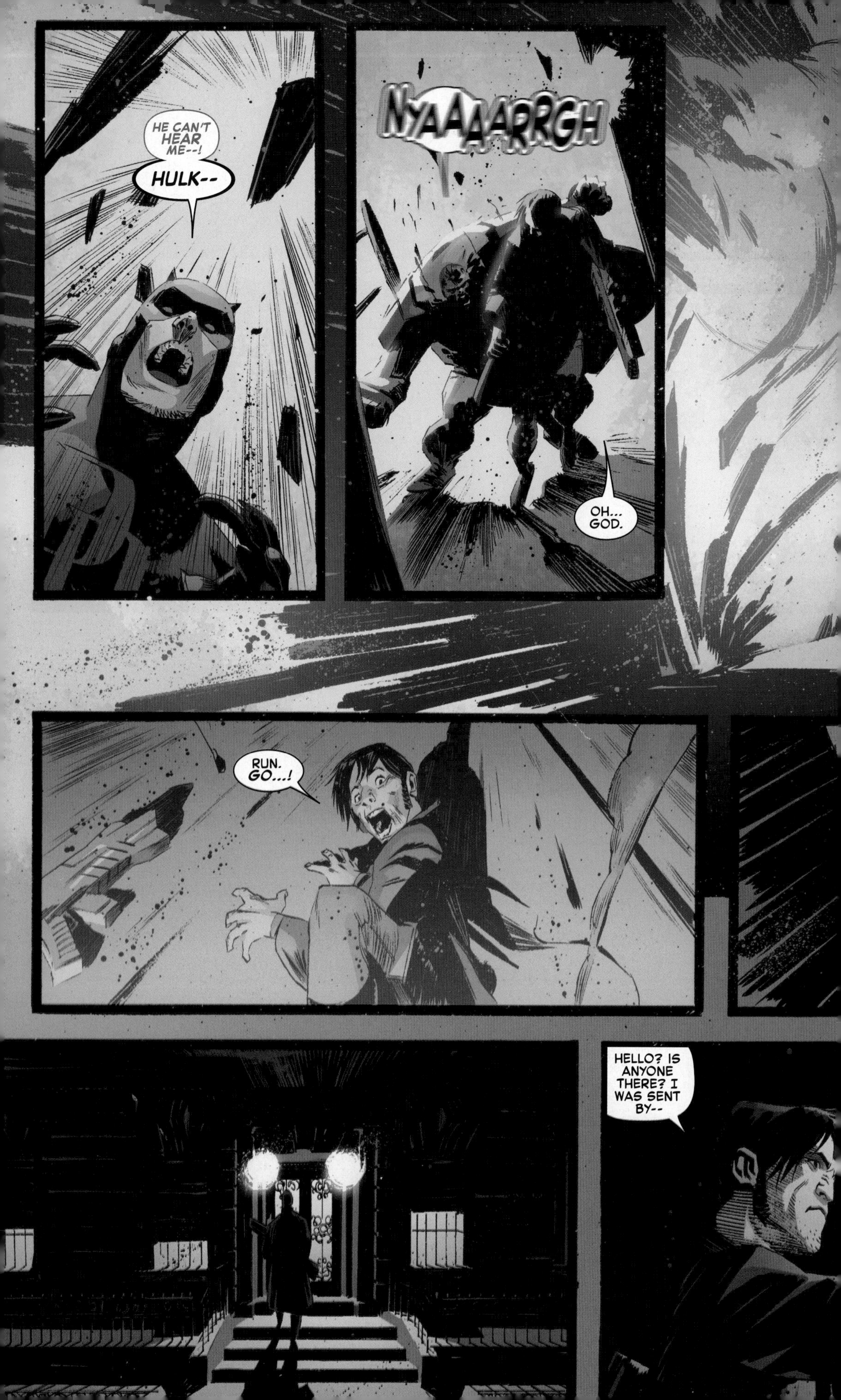
HE CAN'T HEAR ME--!
HULK--
NYAAAARRGH
OH... GOD.
RUN. GO...!
HELLO? IS ANYONE THERE? I WAS SENT BY--

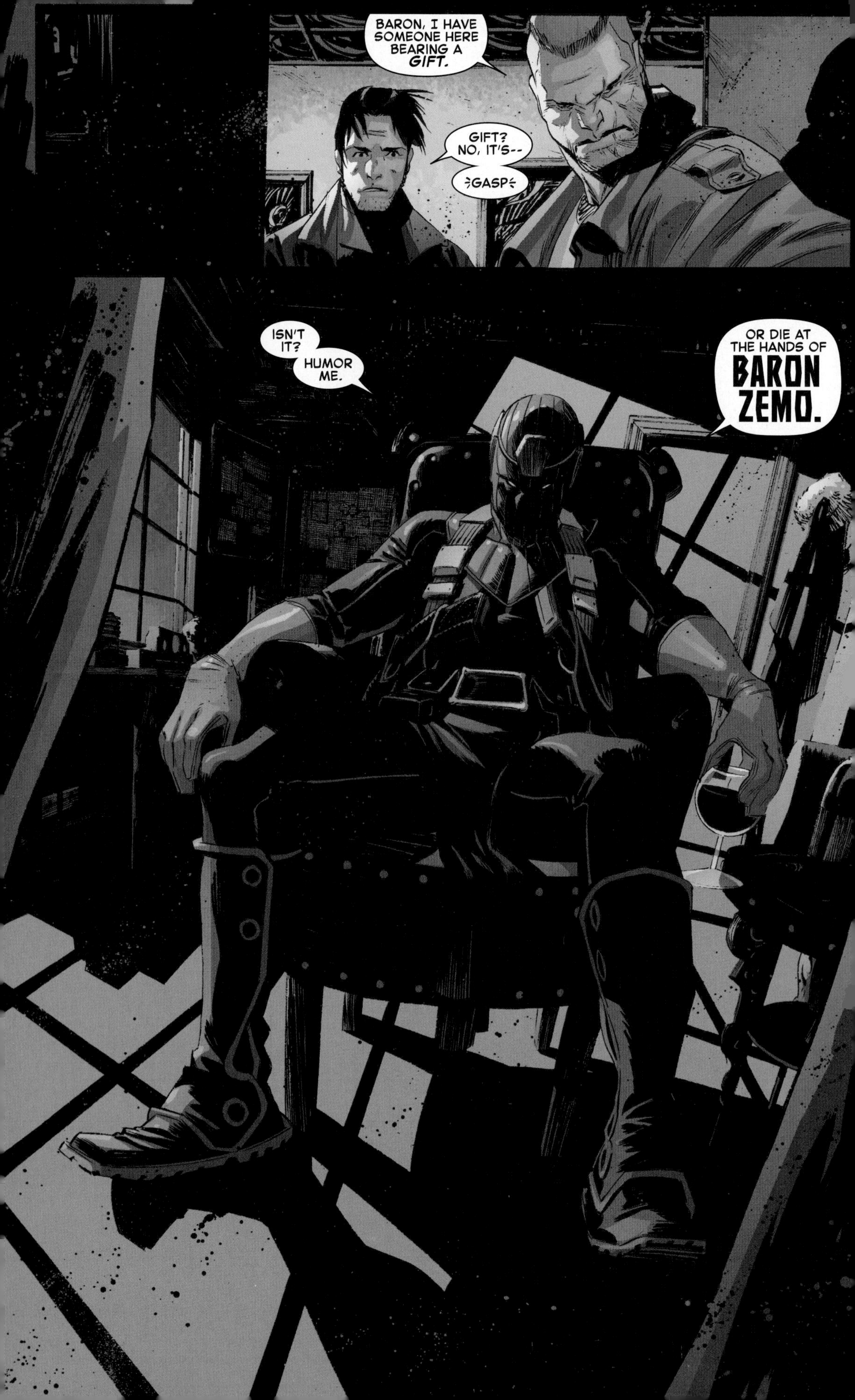
BARON, I HAVE SOMEONE HERE BEARING A GIFT.
GIFT? NO, IT'S--
GASP
ISN'T IT?
HUMOR ME.
OR DIE AT THE HANDS OF BARON ZEMO.

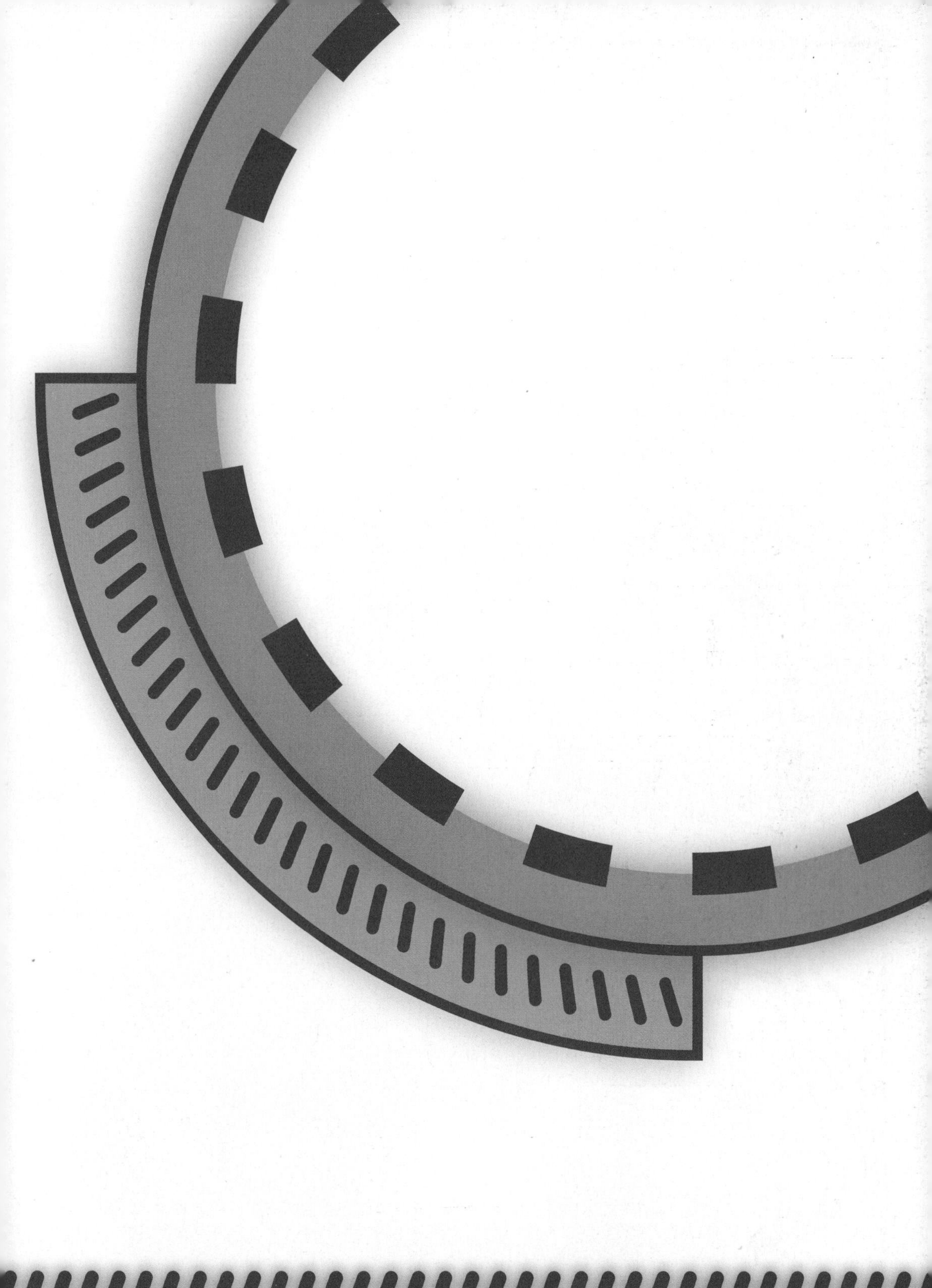

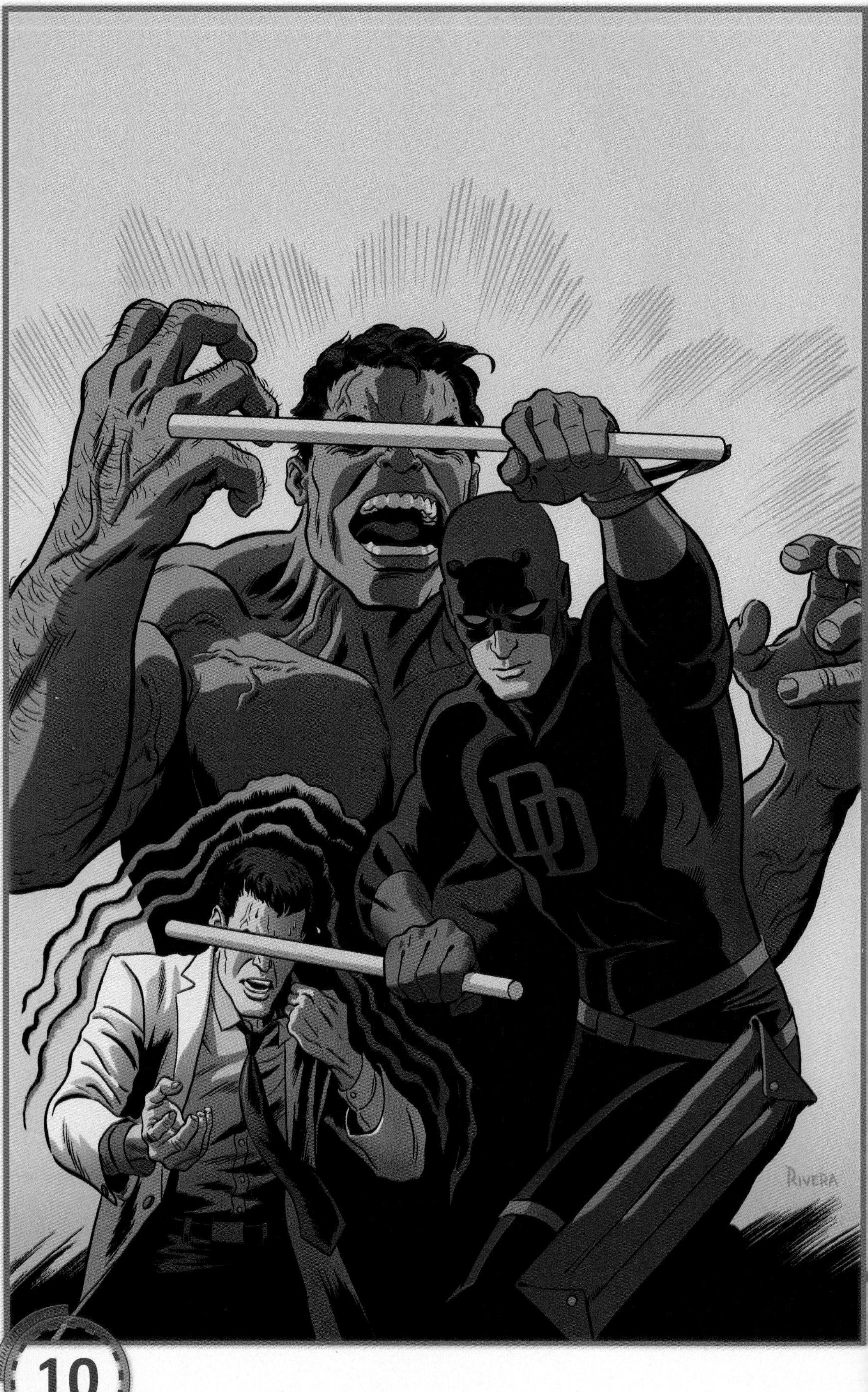
RIVERA

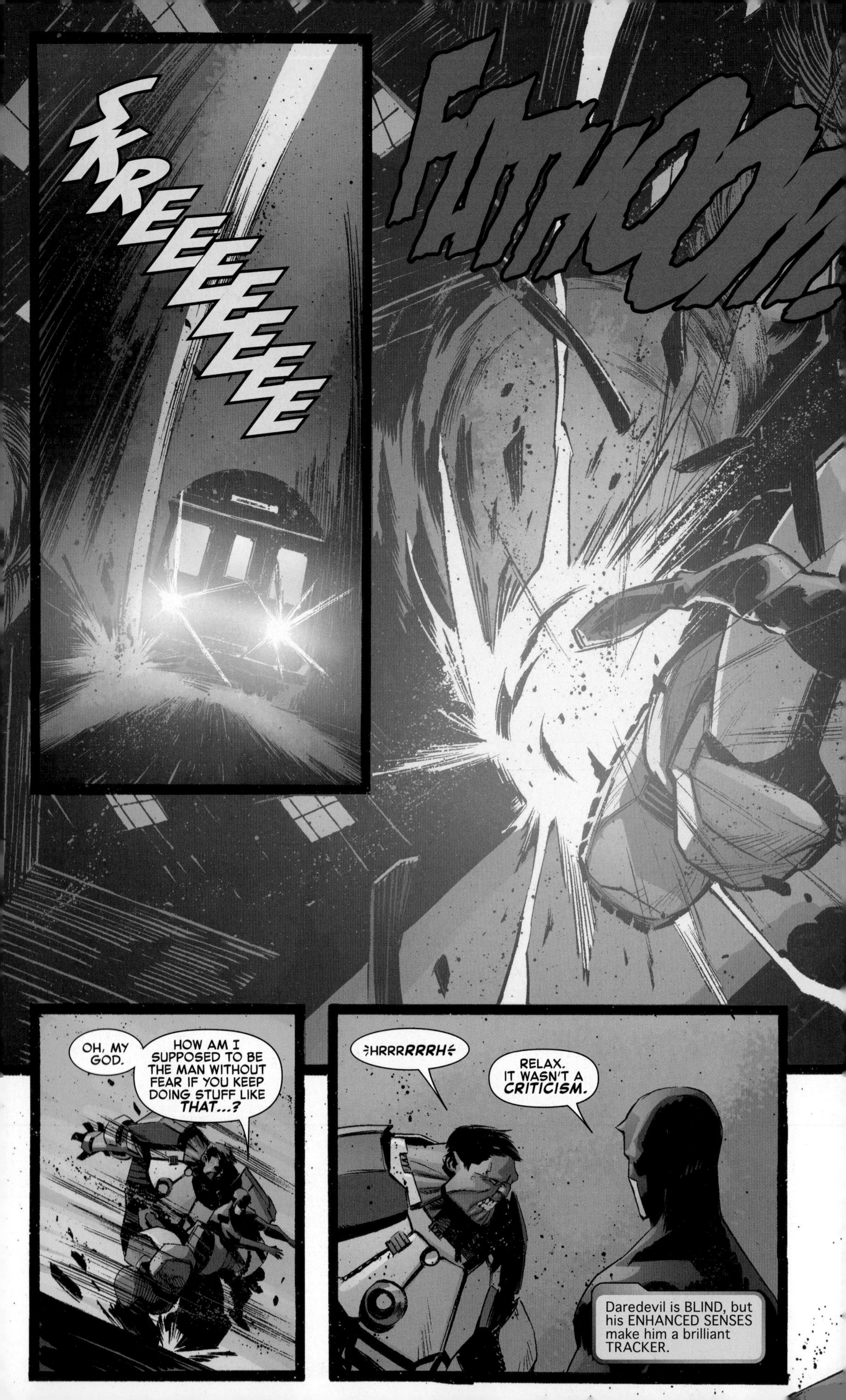

SKREEEEEEEEE
FATHOOM!
OH, MY GOD.
HOW AM I SUPPOSED TO BE THE MAN WITHOUT FEAR IF YOU KEEP DOING STUFF LIKE THAT...?
HRRRRRRH
RELAX. IT WASN'T A CRITICISM.
Daredevil is BLIND, but his ENHANCED SENSES make him a brilliant TRACKER.

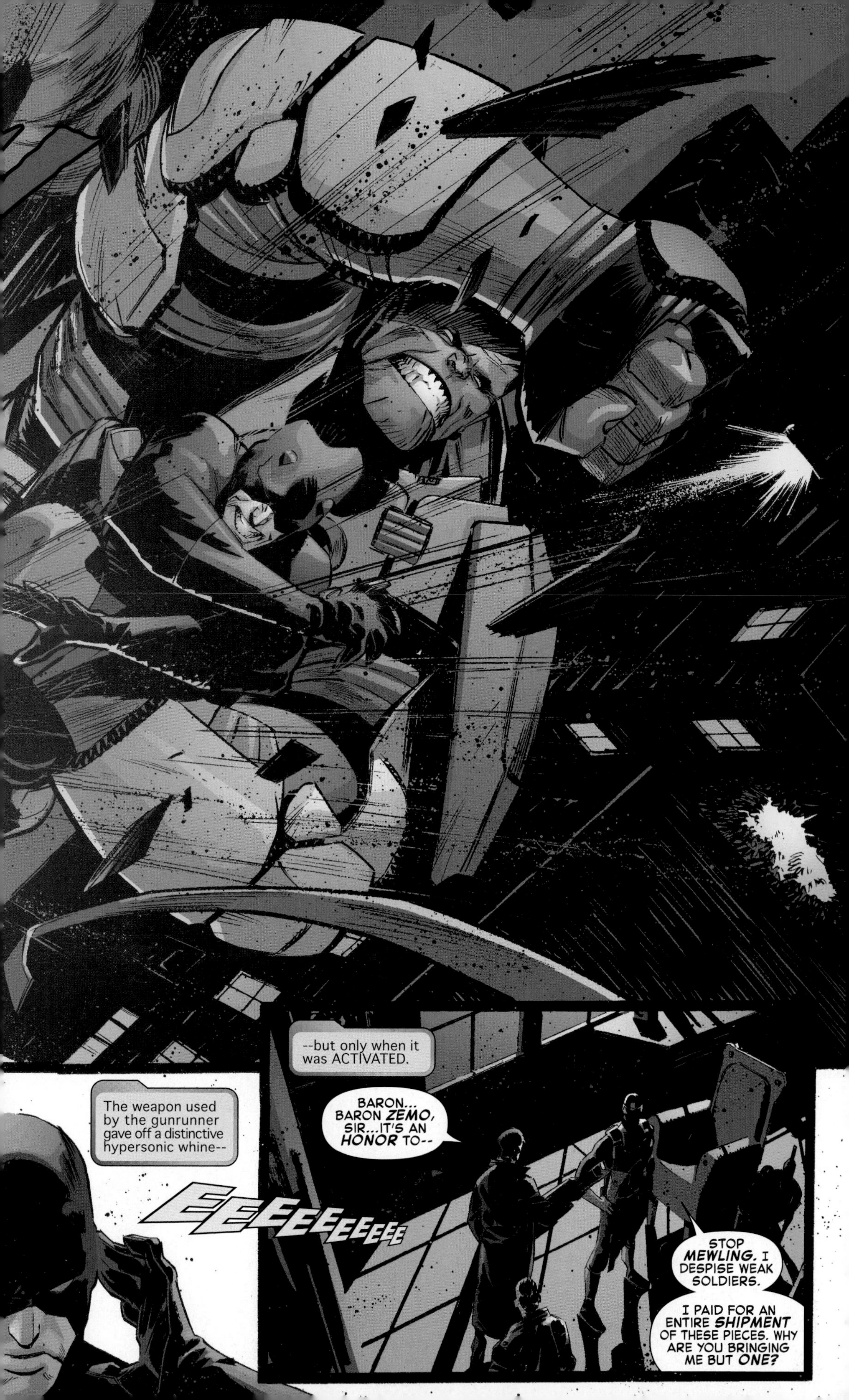

The weapon used by the gunrunner gave off a distinctive hypersonic whine--
EEEEEEEEEEE
--but only when it was ACTIVATED.
BARON... BARON ZEMO, SIR...IT'S AN HONOR TO--
STOP MEWLING. I DESPISE WEAK SOLDIERS.
I PAID FOR AN ENTIRE SHIPMENT OF THESE PIECES. WHY ARE YOU BRINGING ME BUT ONE?

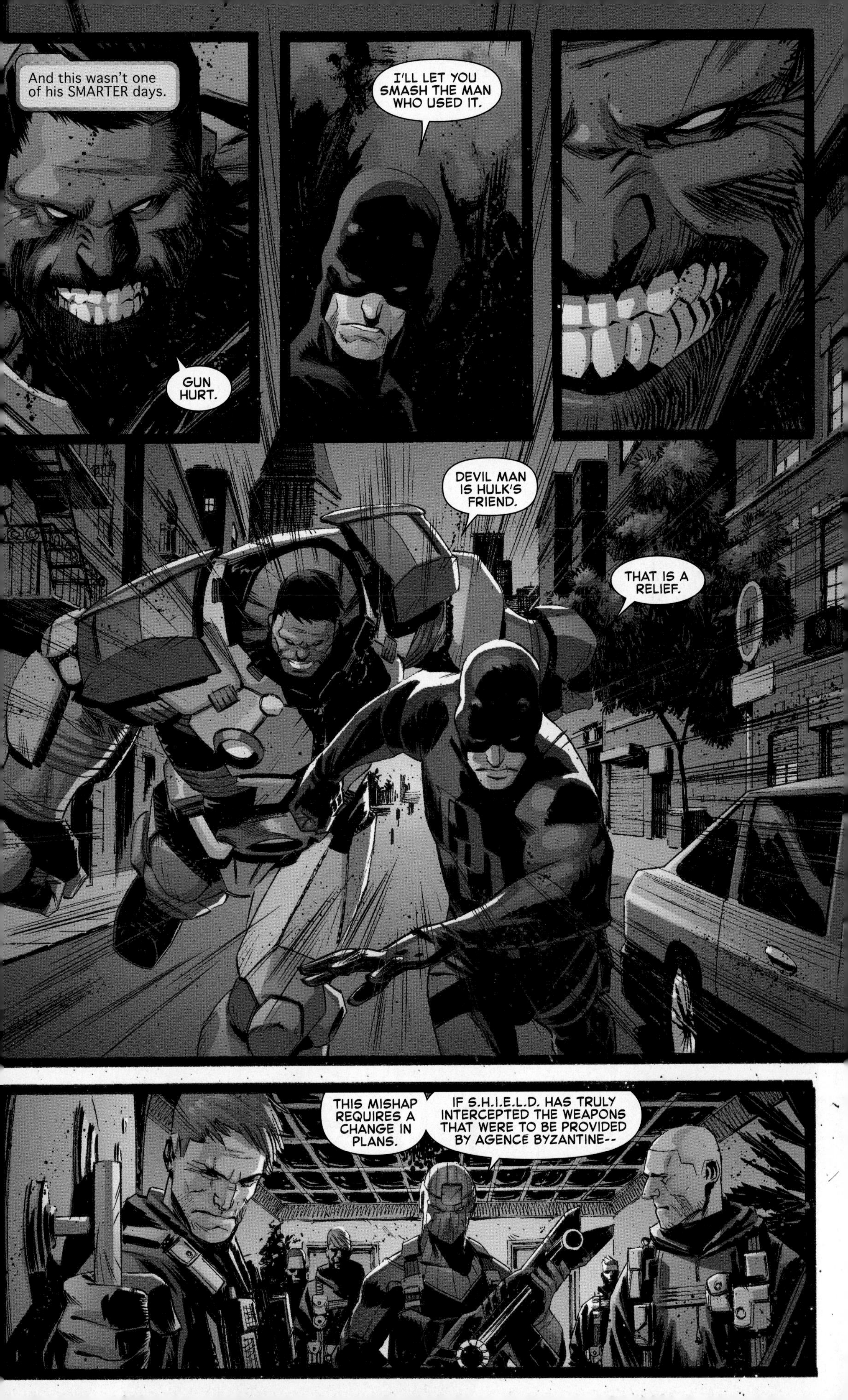
And this wasn't one of his SMARTER days.
GUN HURT.
I'LL LET YOU SMASH THE MAN WHO USED IT.
DEVIL MAN IS HULK'S FRIEND.
THAT IS A RELIEF.
THIS MISHAP REQUIRES A CHANGE IN PLANS.
IF S.H.I.E.L.D. HAS TRULY INTERCEPTED THE WEAPONS THAT WERE TO BE PROVIDED BY AGENCE BYZANTINE--

THOOM

WHHA'AARRHH!

EXACTLY.

Apparently, Zemo's ARMS DEPOT was filled with everything from plasma-ammo rail guns to EMPs to dark-matter BAZOOKAS.

And, of course...

...the SONIC ASSAULT RIFLE.

SOUNDWAVES can't hurt Hulk--but the gun's actual NOISES, as it turned out, were just a BUG.

NYAAAARRGH

THAT'S the STING.

GNNGH

THWOK

Its REAL purpose was to rewrite MOLECULES on a SUBATOMIC LEVEL using a SONIC VORTEX.
[Drinkwater, Prof. Bruce, 2011, unpublished data, Faculty of Engineering, Univ. of Bristol]

TELEPORTAL *ENGAGED!* BARON, THIS WAY-- BEFORE HULK *RECOVERS!*

HULK'S NOT YOUR *PROBLEM.*

NEITHER IS A GLORIFIED *ACROBAT.*

KZMMMMM

Had I been present as BANNER, I would have recognized the particle beam Zemo deployed.

It transmits a binding radiation that blocks PHOTONS.
[Englur, Prof. Craig, 2012 Univ. of Latveria]

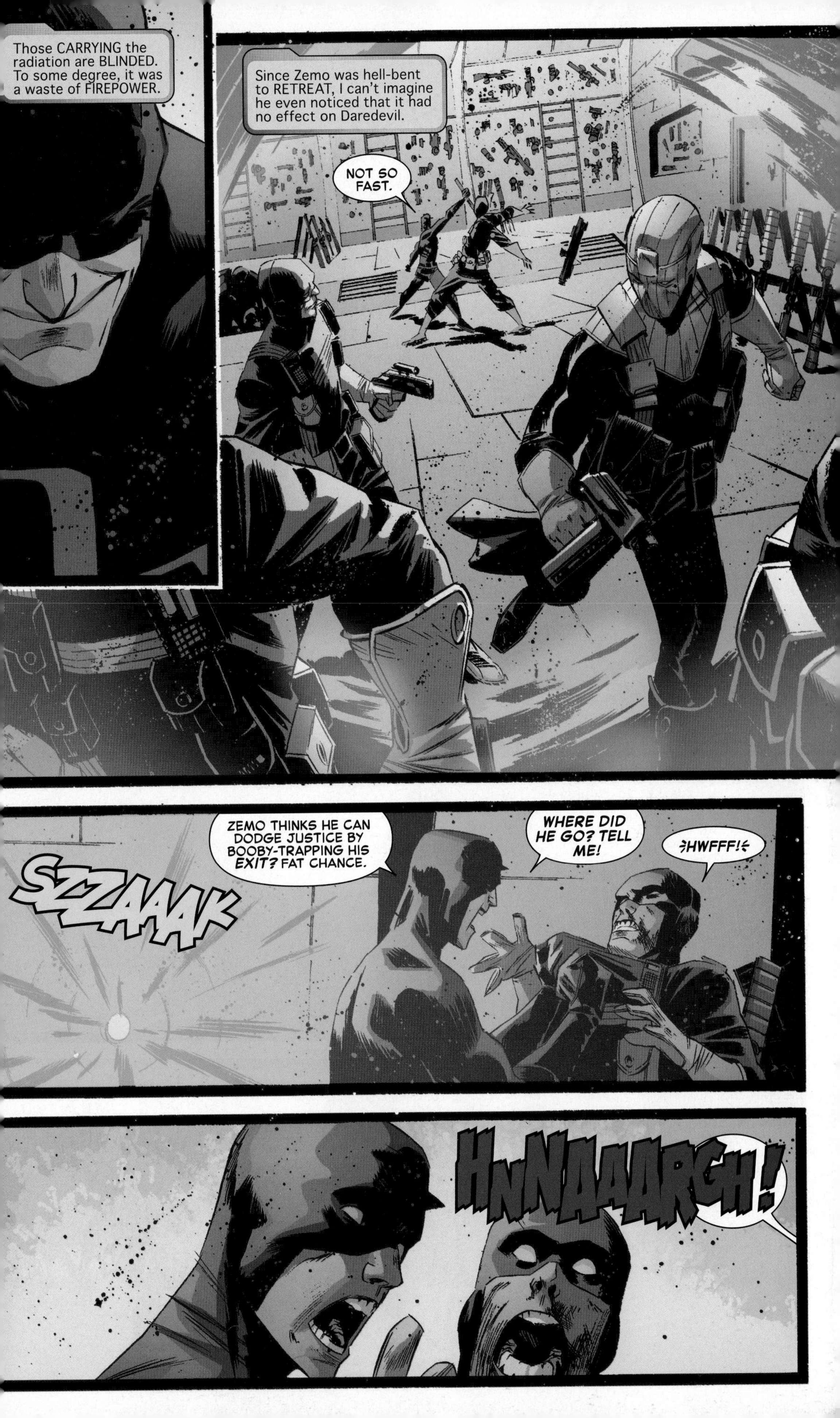

Those CARRYING the radiation are BLINDED. To some degree, it was a waste of FIREPOWER.
Since Zemo was hell-bent to RETREAT, I can't imagine he even noticed that it had no effect on Daredevil.
NOT SO FAST.
SZZAAAK
ZEMO THINKS HE CAN DODGE JUSTICE BY BOOBY-TRAPPING HIS EXIT? FAT CHANCE.
WHERE DID HE GO? TELL ME!
HWFFF!
HNNAAARGH!

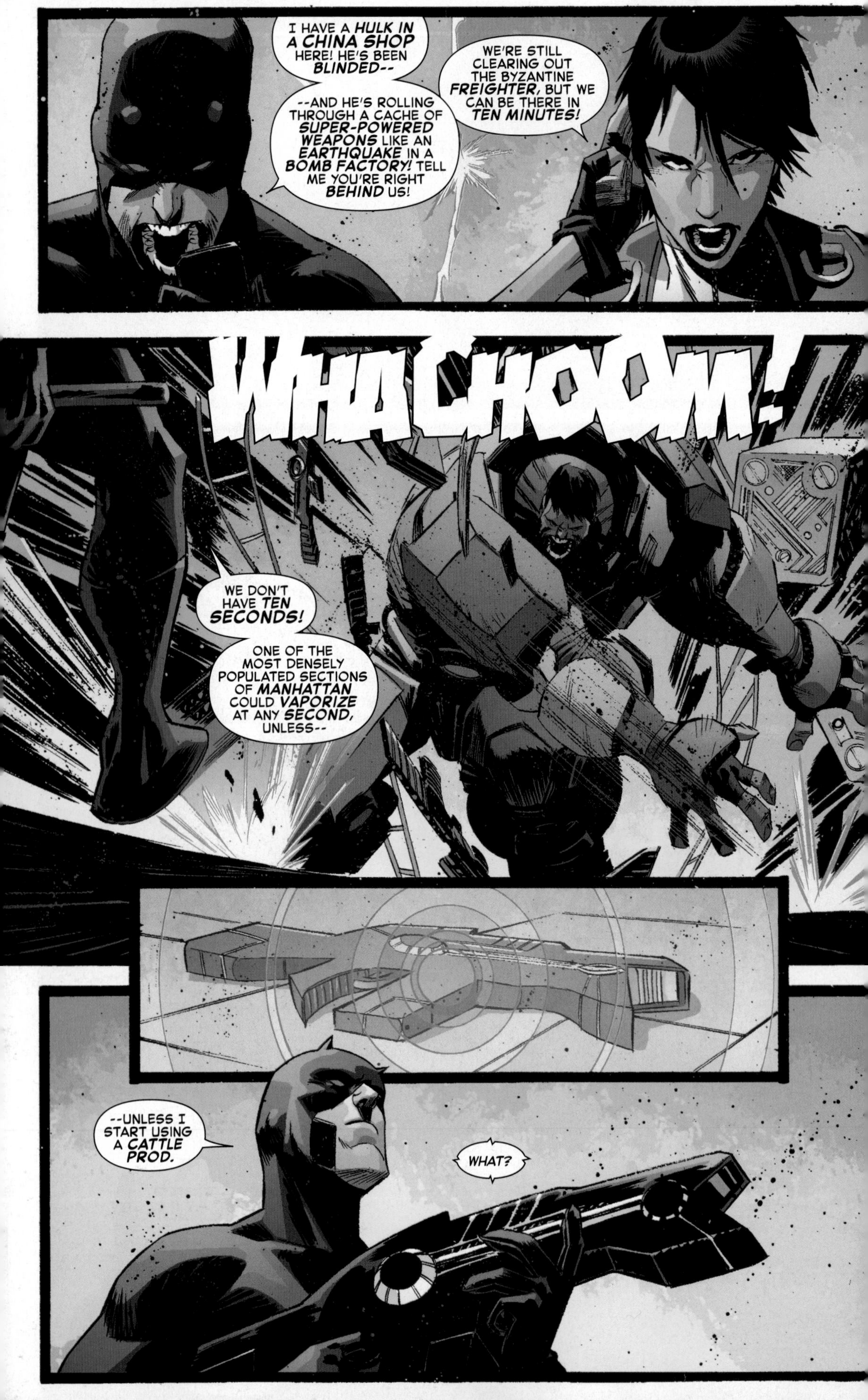
I HAVE A HULK IN A CHINA SHOP HERE! HE'S BEEN BLINDED--
--AND HE'S ROLLING THROUGH A CACHE OF SUPER-POWERED WEAPONS LIKE AN EARTHQUAKE IN A BOMB FACTORY! TELL ME YOU'RE RIGHT BEHIND US!
WE'RE STILL CLEARING OUT THE BYZANTINE FREIGHTER, BUT WE CAN BE THERE IN TEN MINUTES!
WHACHOOM!
WE DON'T HAVE TEN SECONDS!
ONE OF THE MOST DENSELY POPULATED SECTIONS OF MANHATTAN COULD VAPORIZE AT ANY SECOND, UNLESS--
--UNLESS I START USING A CATTLE PROD.
WHAT?

GREEN ALERT! I REPEAT, GREEN ALERT! PATCH BANNER'S LAB RATS INTO THIS LINE NOW!

VETERI, ARE YOU THERE?

He was. All the assistants were. And they are QUICK STUDIES.

OPTIONS!

THERE'S RESEARCH ON USING ULTRASOUND AS A MOOD STABILIZER IN THE 60 KILOHERTZ RANGE! THAT MIGHT CALM HULK! DAREDEVIL, CAN YOU SEE SETTINGS ON THIS WEAPON?

THERE'S WHAT SEEMS TO BE AN ADJUSTMENT DIAL, BUT I...

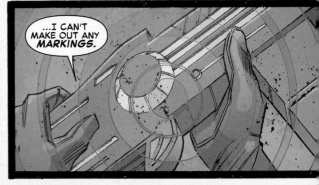

...I CAN'T MAKE OUT ANY MARKINGS.

I'LL HAVE TO DO THIS BY EAR.

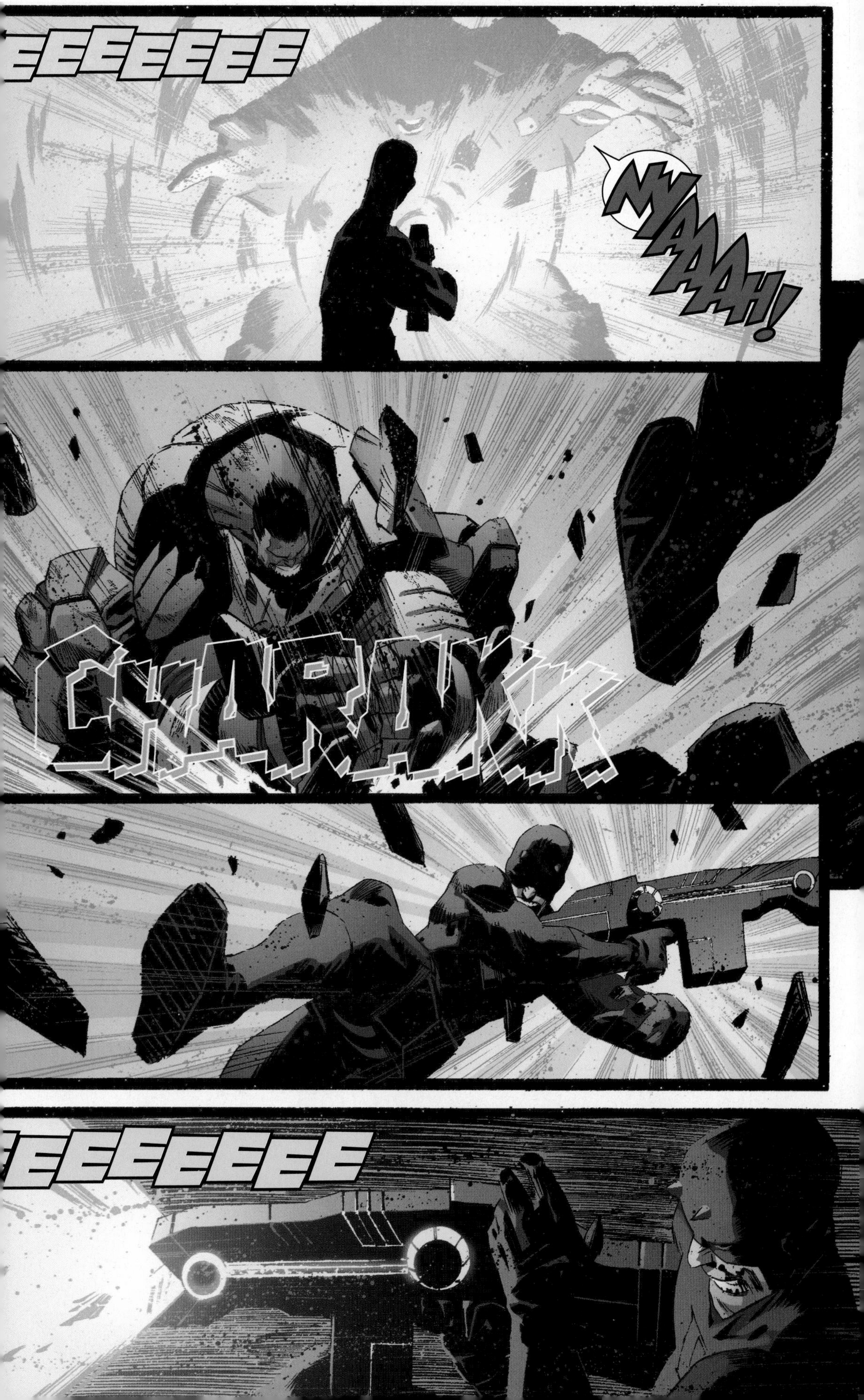
EEEEEEE
NYAAAAH!
CHRAKK
EEEEEEEE

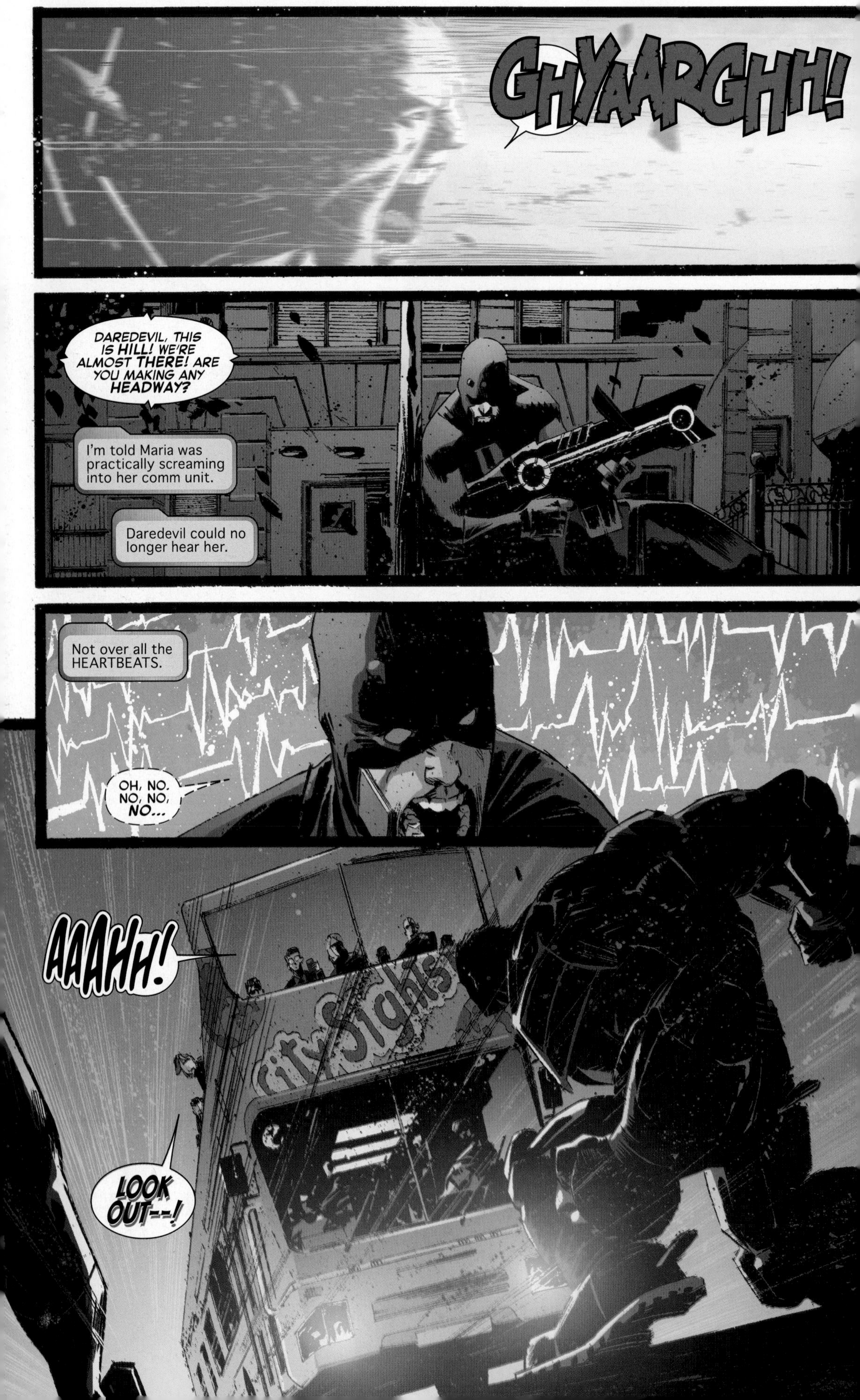
GHYAARGHH!
DAREDEVIL, THIS IS HILL! WE'RE ALMOST THERE! ARE YOU MAKING ANY HEADWAY?
I'm told Maria was practically screaming into her comm unit.
Daredevil could no longer hear her.
Not over all the HEARTBEATS.
OH, NO. NO, NO, NO...
AAAHH!
LOOK OUT--!

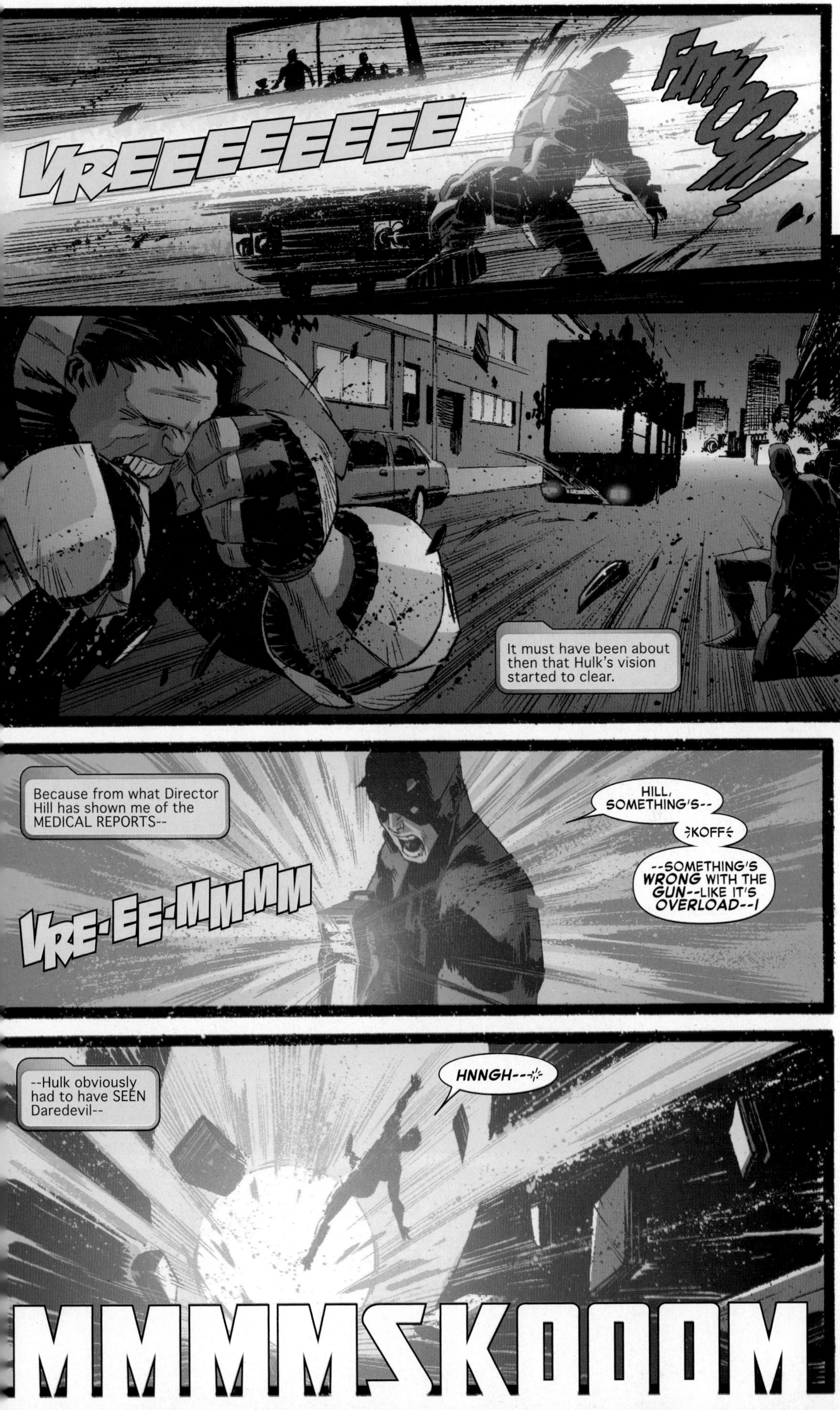
VREEEEEEEEE
FATHOOM!!
It must have been about then that Hulk's vision started to clear.
Because from what Director Hill has shown me of the MEDICAL REPORTS--
HILL, SOMETHING'S--
KOFF
--SOMETHING'S WRONG WITH THE GUN--LIKE IT'S OVERLOAD--!
VRE-EE-MMMM
--Hulk obviously had to have SEEN Daredevil--
HNNGH--
MMMMSKOOOM

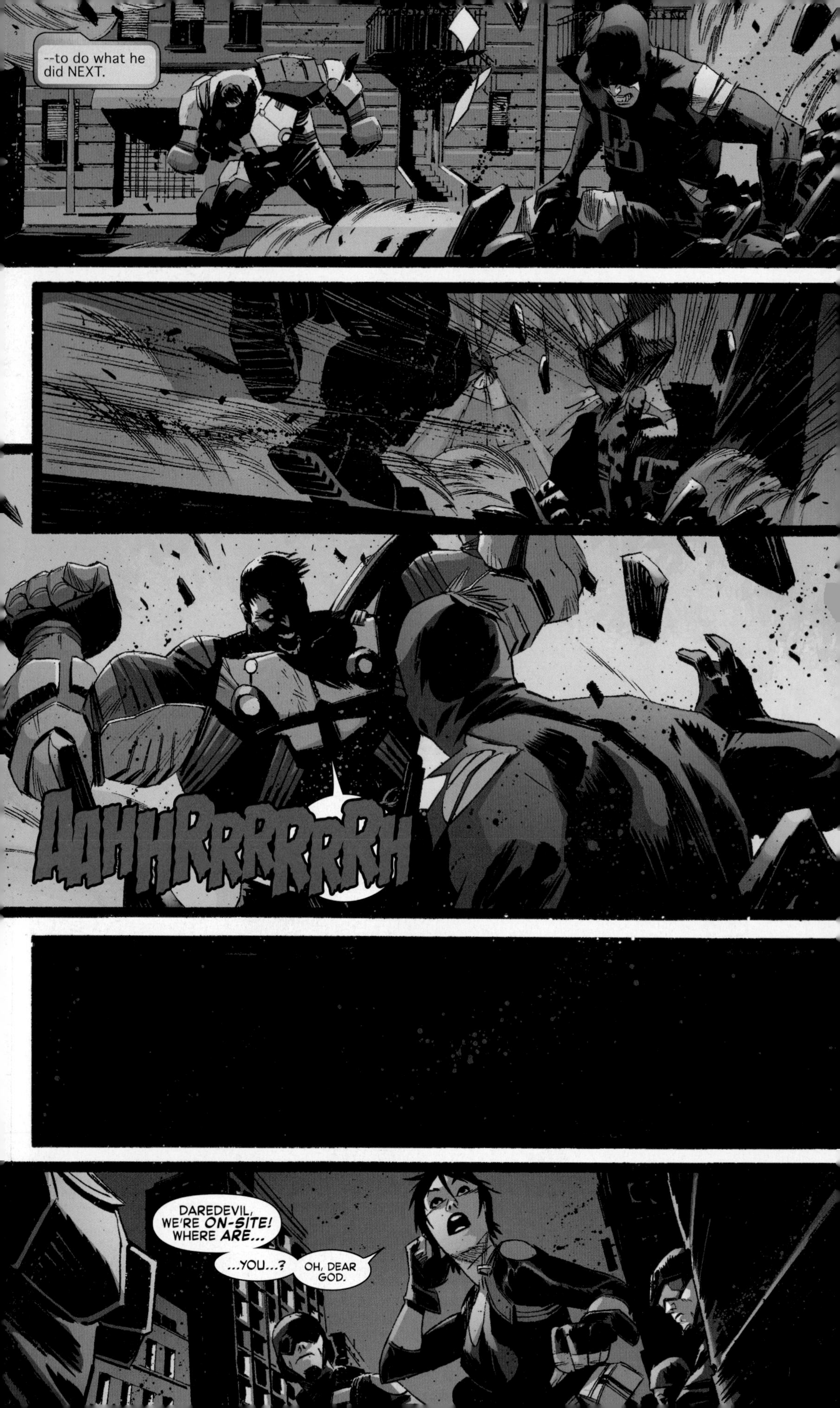
--to do what he did NEXT.
AAHHRRRRRRRH
DAREDEVIL, WE'RE ON-SITE! WHERE ARE...
...YOU...?
OH, DEAR GOD.

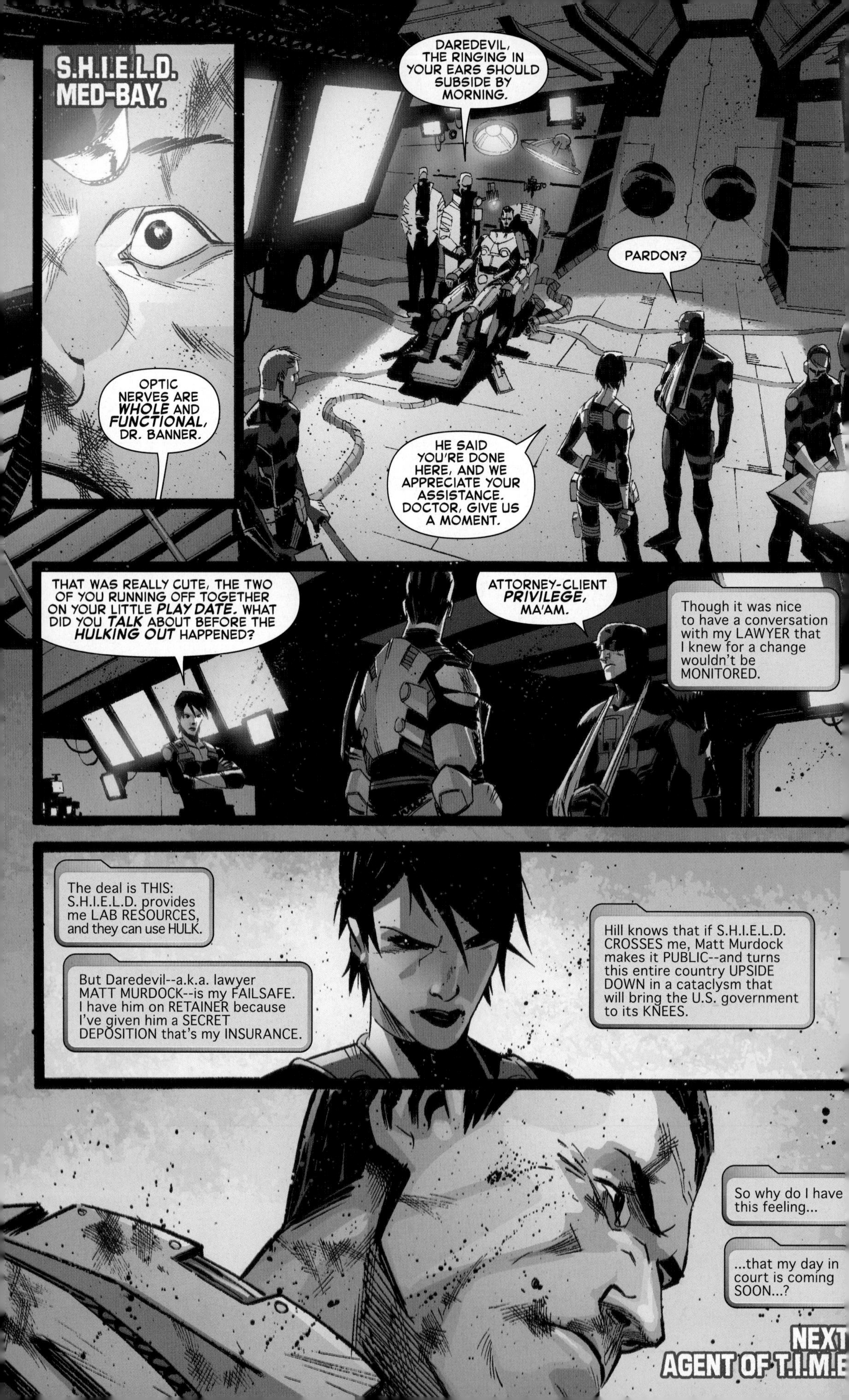

S.H.I.E.L.D. MED-BAY.
DAREDEVIL, THE RINGING IN YOUR EARS SHOULD SUBSIDE BY MORNING.
PARDON?
OPTIC NERVES ARE WHOLE AND FUNCTIONAL, DR. BANNER.
HE SAID YOU'RE DONE HERE, AND WE APPRECIATE YOUR ASSISTANCE. DOCTOR, GIVE US A MOMENT.
THAT WAS REALLY CUTE, THE TWO OF YOU RUNNING OFF TOGETHER ON YOUR LITTLE PLAY DATE. WHAT DID YOU TALK ABOUT BEFORE THE HULKING OUT HAPPENED?
ATTORNEY-CLIENT PRIVILEGE, MA'AM.
Though it was nice to have a conversation with my LAWYER that I knew for a change wouldn't be MONITORED.
The deal is THIS: S.H.I.E.L.D. provides me LAB RESOURCES, and they can use HULK.
But Daredevil--a.k.a. lawyer MATT MURDOCK--is my FAILSAFE. I have him on RETAINER because I've given him a SECRET DEPOSITION that's my INSURANCE.
Hill knows that if S.H.I.E.L.D. CROSSES me, Matt Murdock makes it PUBLIC--and turns this entire country UPSIDE DOWN in a cataclysm that will bring the U.S. government to its KNEES.
So why do I have this feeling...
...that my day in court is coming SOON...?
NEXT
AGENT OF T.I.M.E

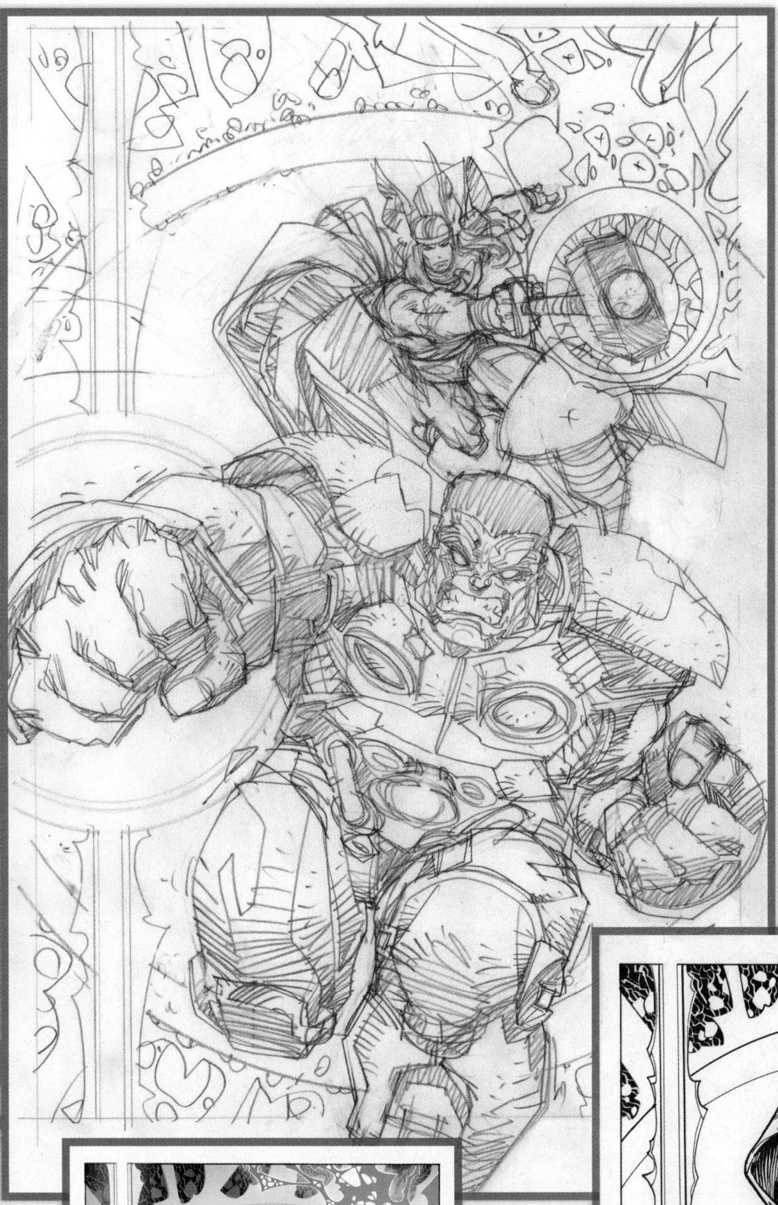

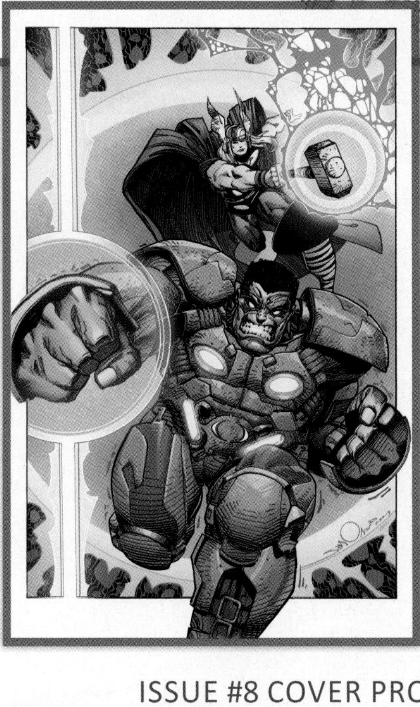

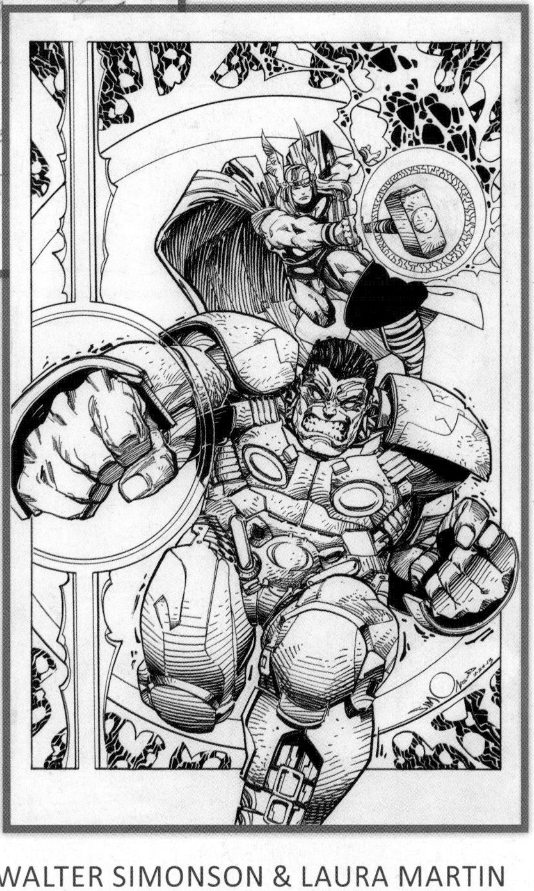

ISSUE #8 COVER PROCESS BY WALTER SIMONSON & LAURA MARTIN

ART PROCESS
BY WALTER SIMONSON

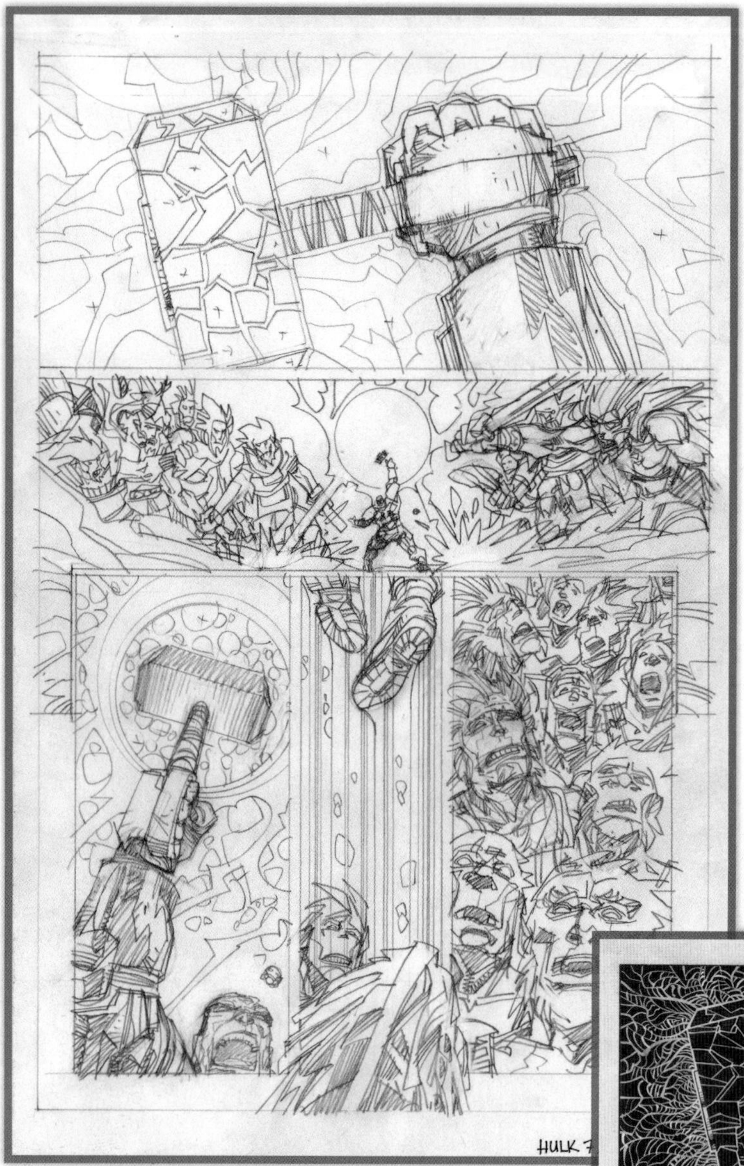

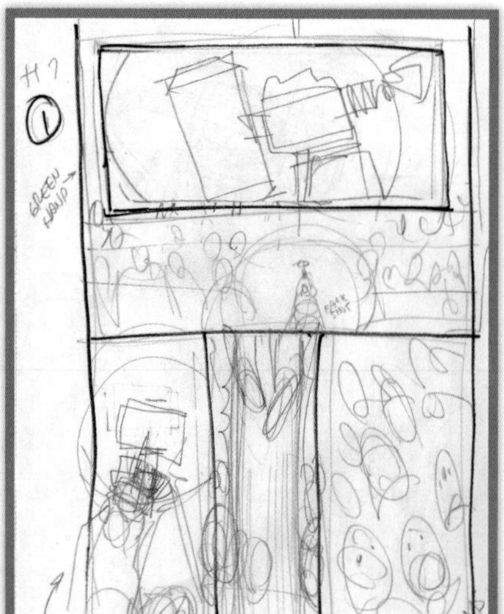

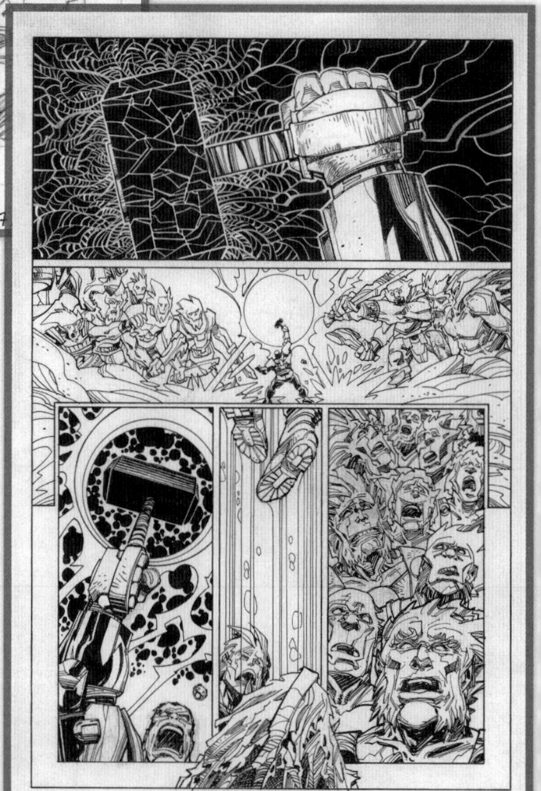
HULK 7/PG 1

#7, PAGE 1

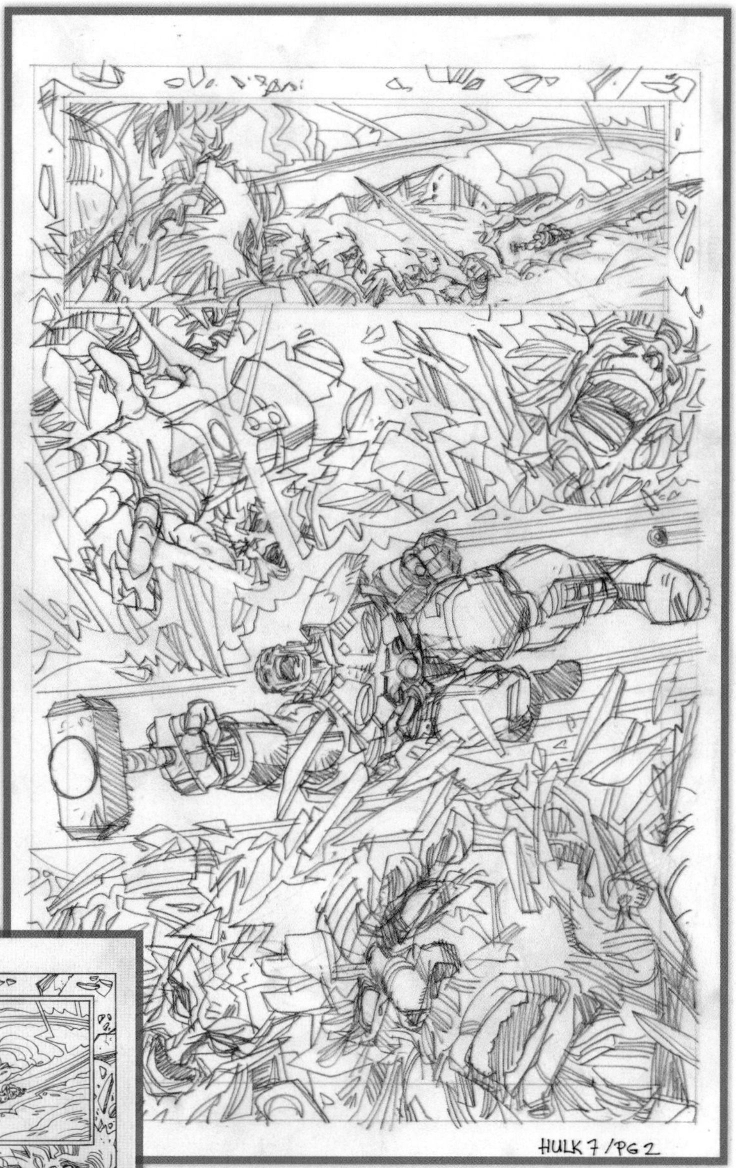
HULK 7 /PG 2

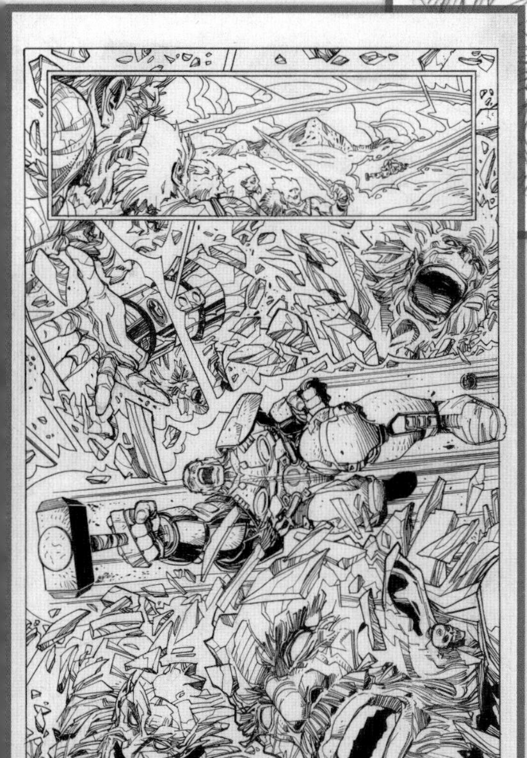
HULK 7 /PG 2

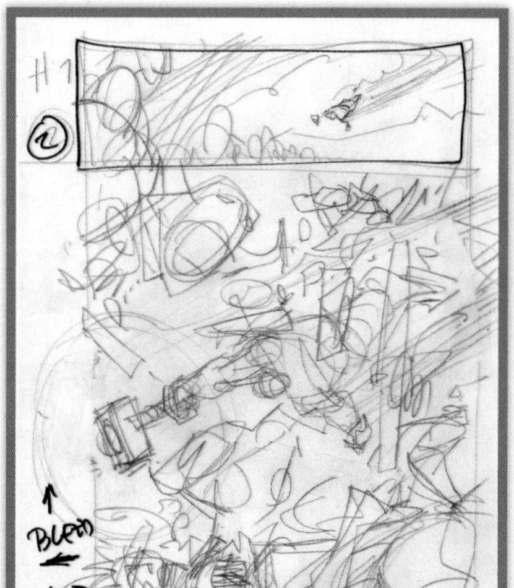

#7, PAGE 2

#7, PAGE 3

HULK 7 / PG 4

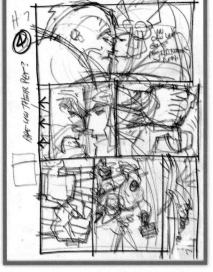

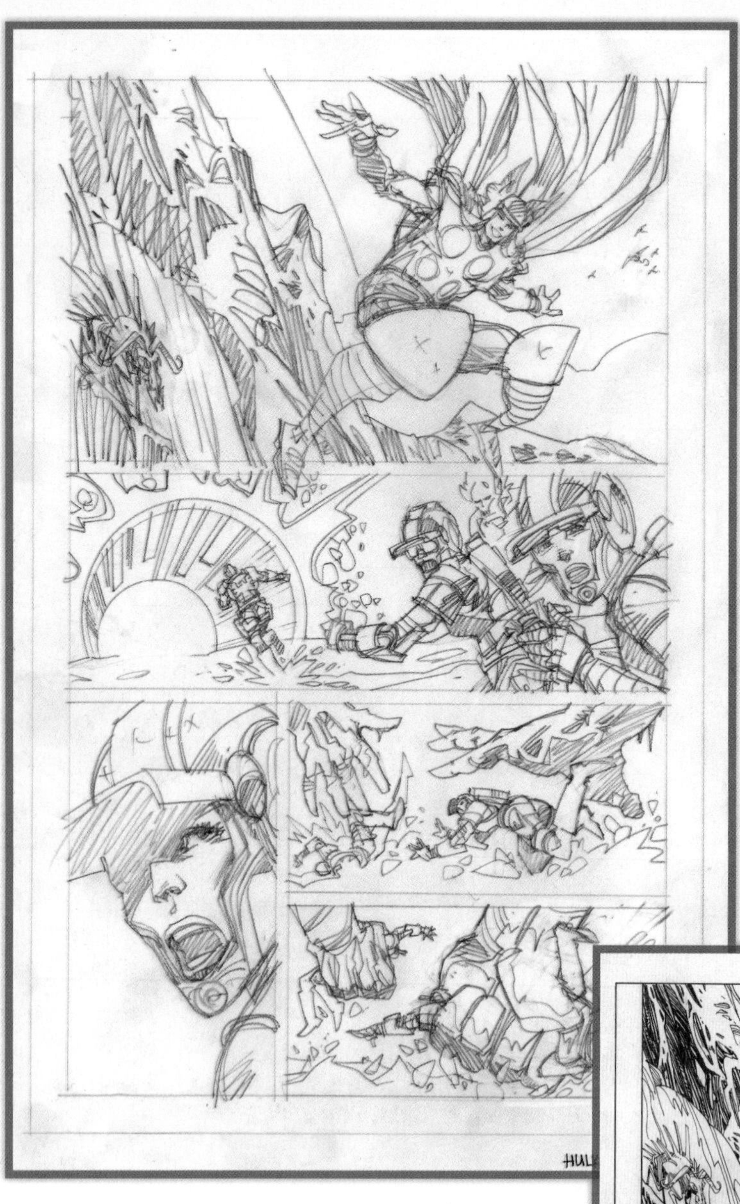

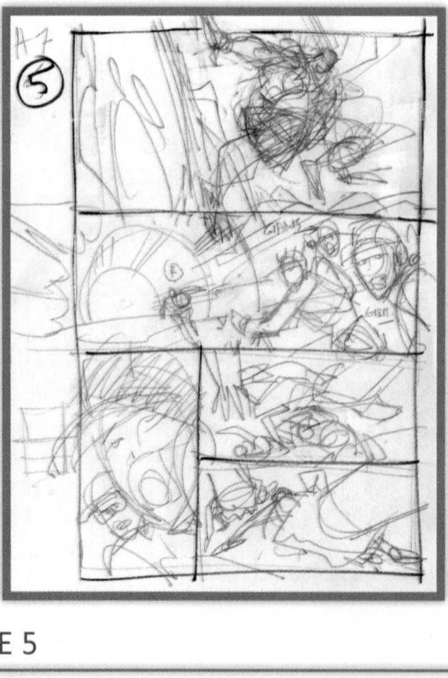

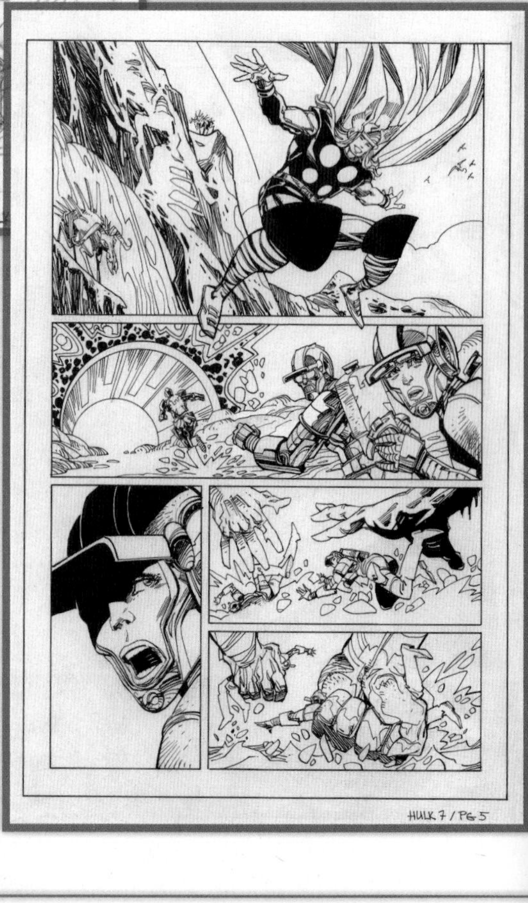
HULK 7 / PG 5

#7, PAGE 5

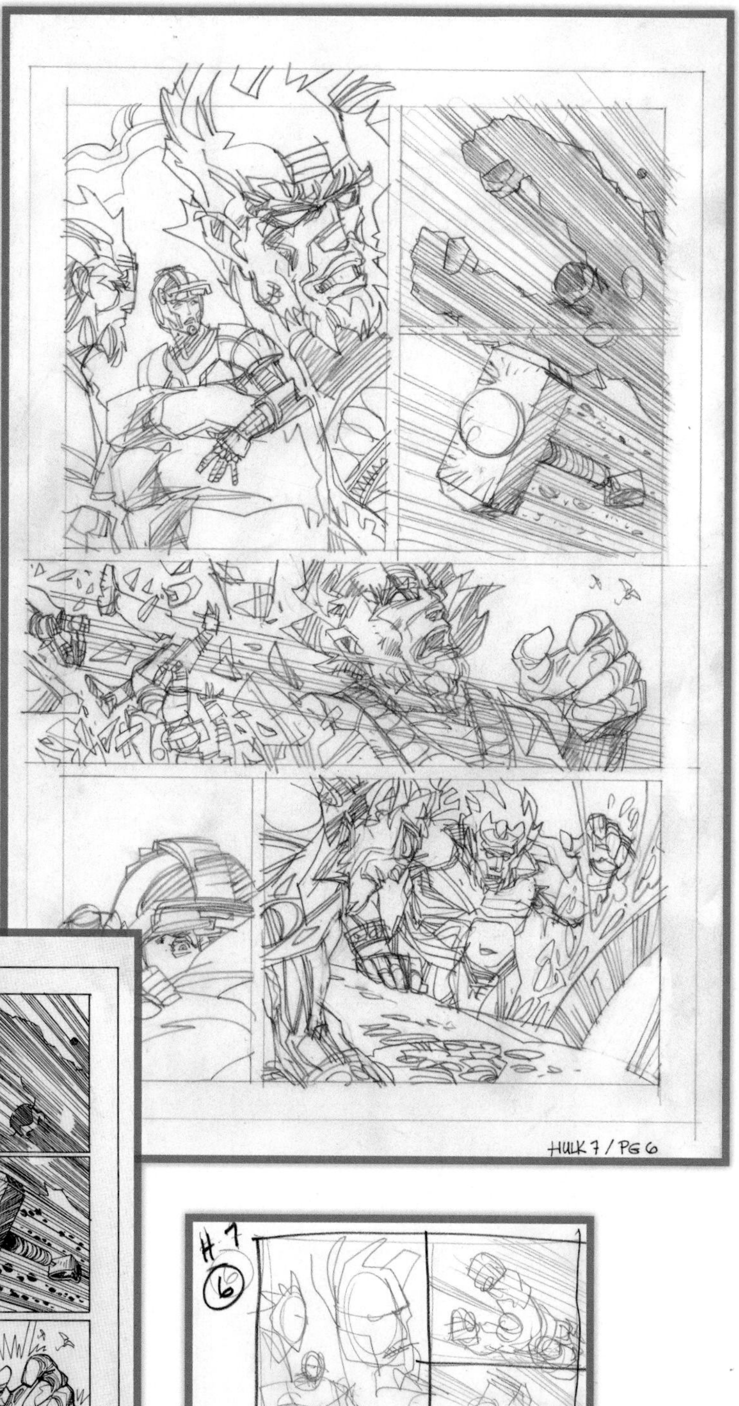
HULK 7 / PG 6

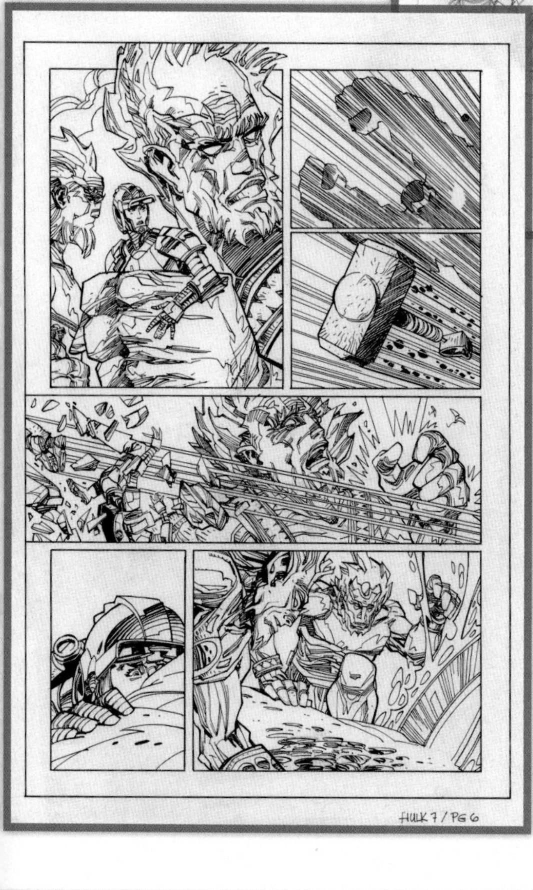
HULK 7 / PG 6

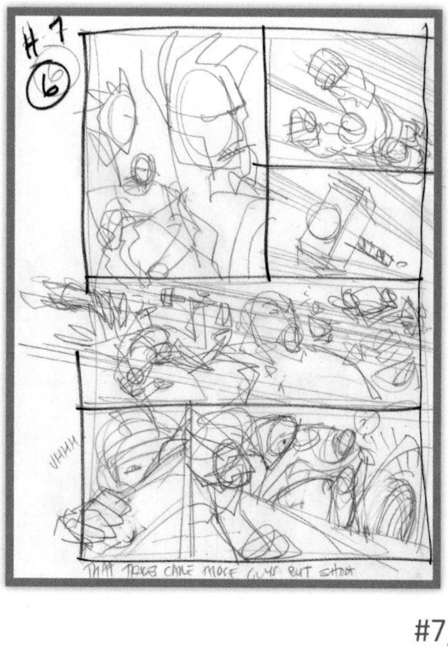
H 7
6

#7, PAGE 6

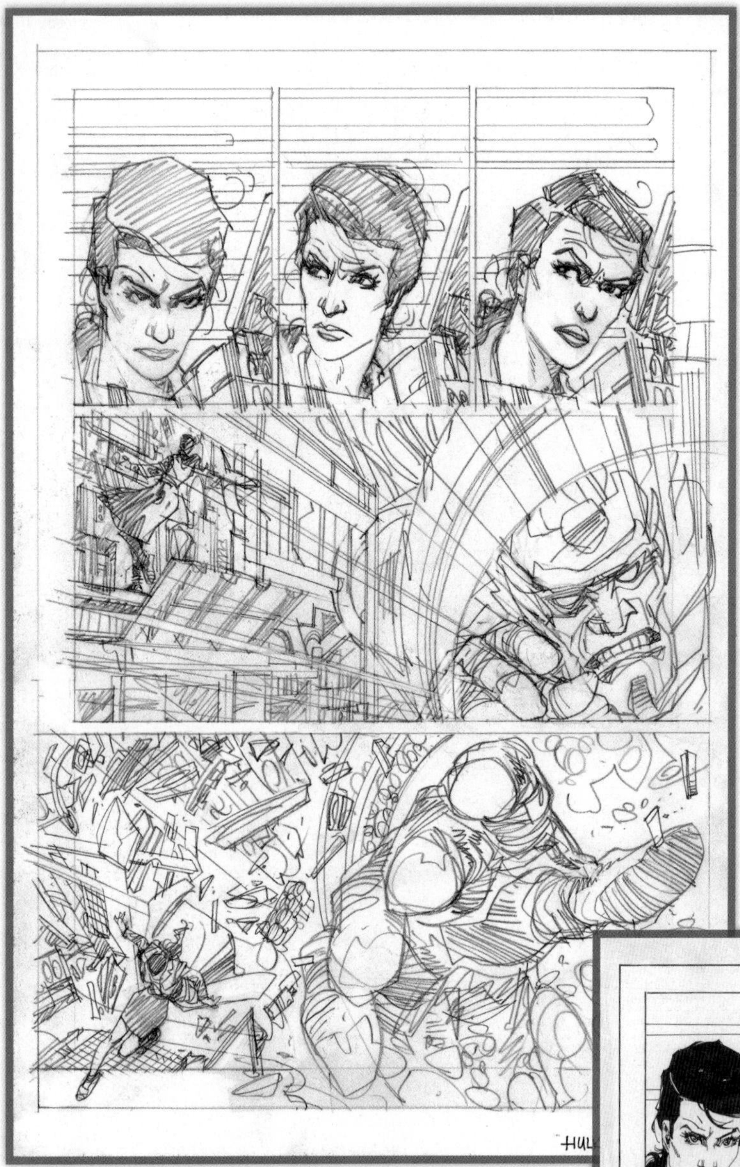

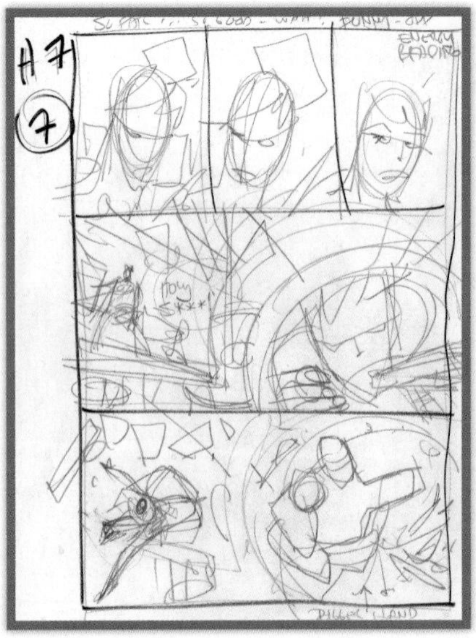

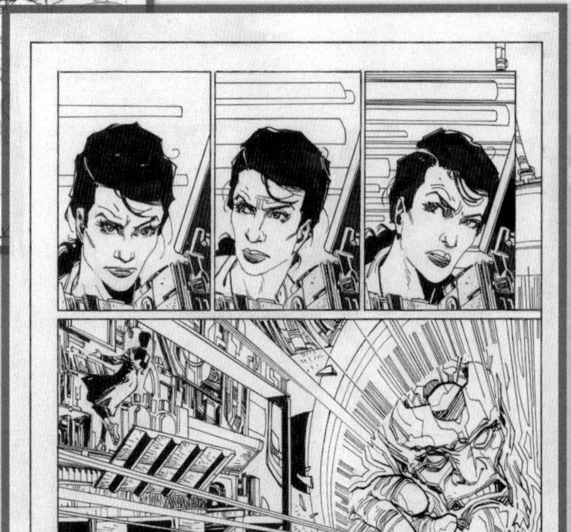
HULK 7 / PG 7

#7, PAGE 7

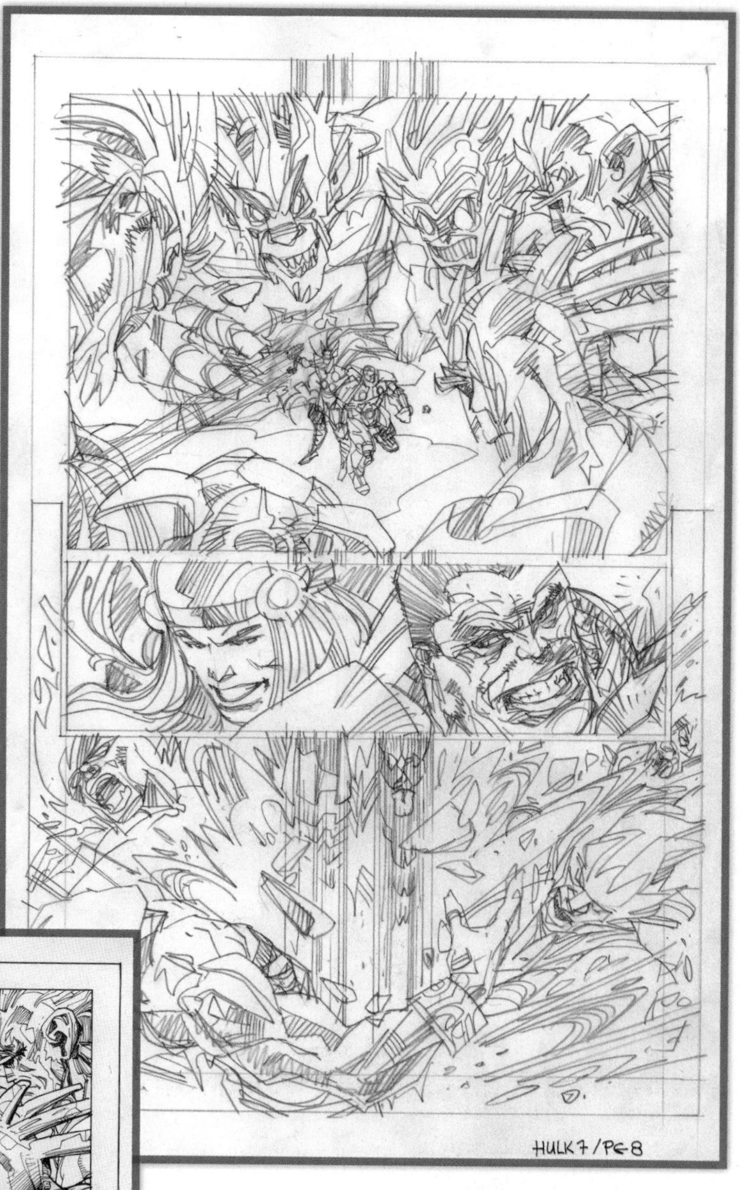
HULK7/PG8

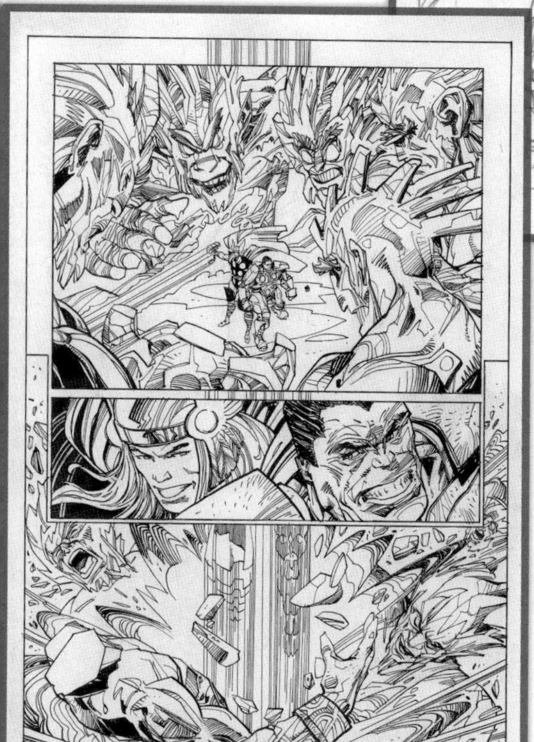
HULK7/PG8

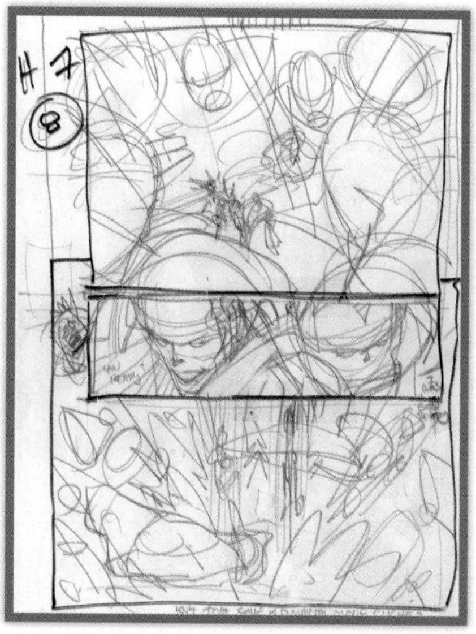
#7
8

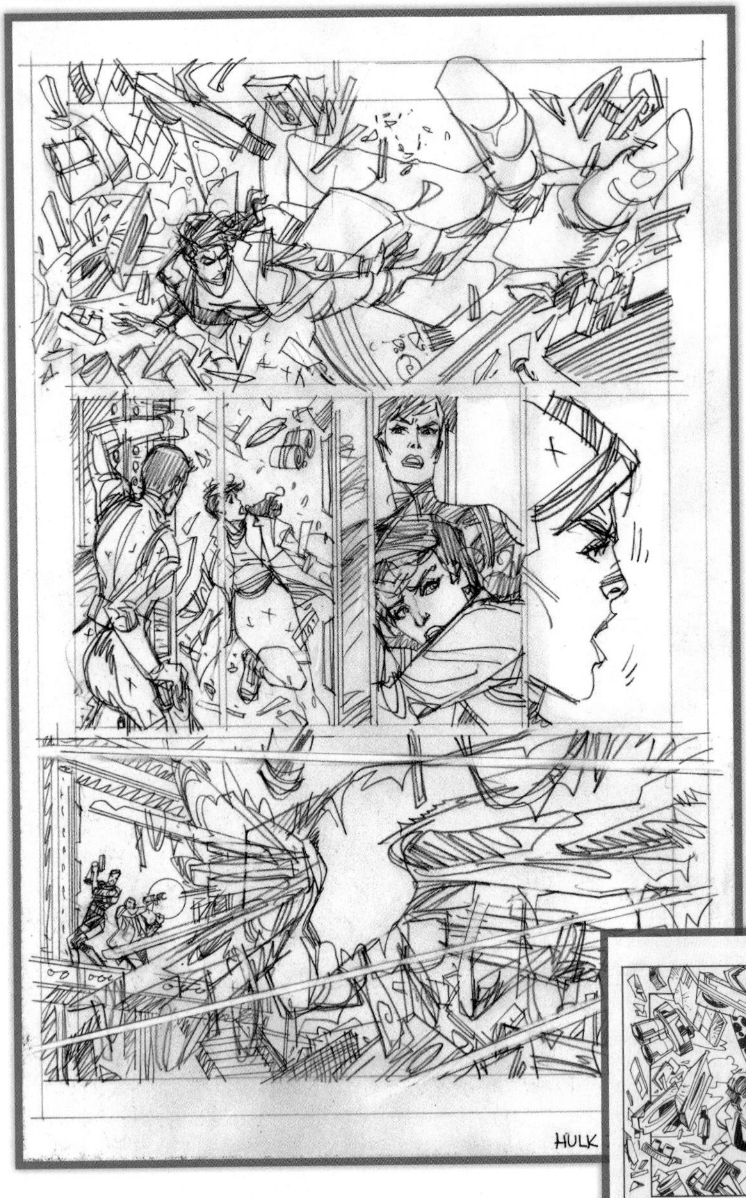
HULK

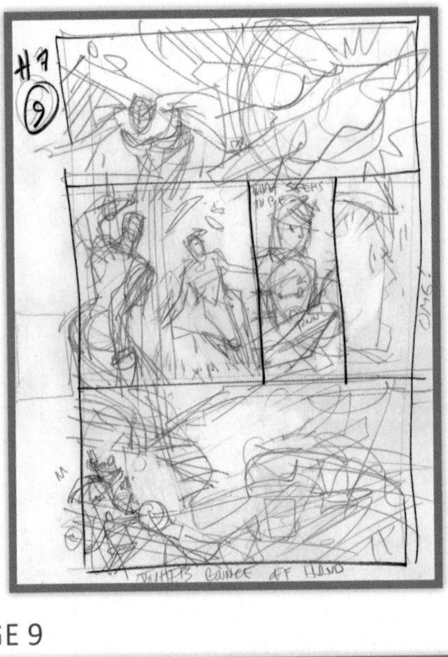
#7
9

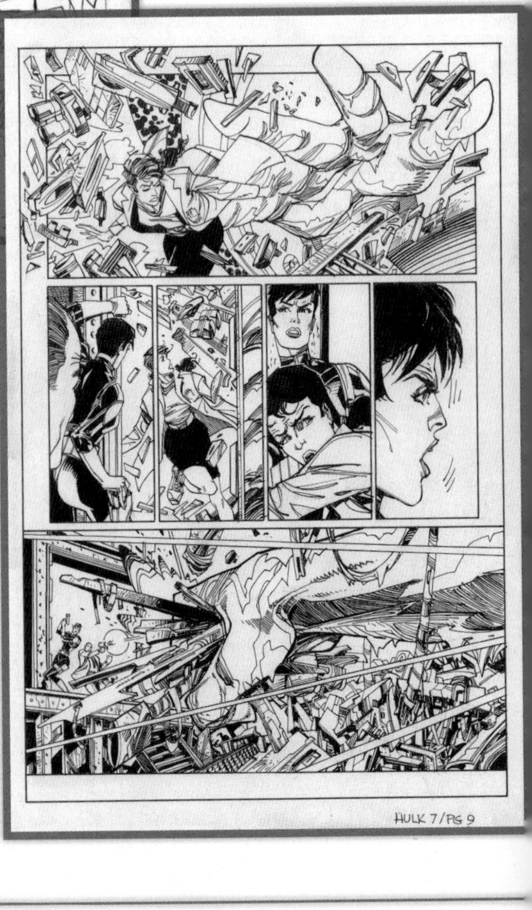
HULK 7/PG 9

#7, PAGE 9

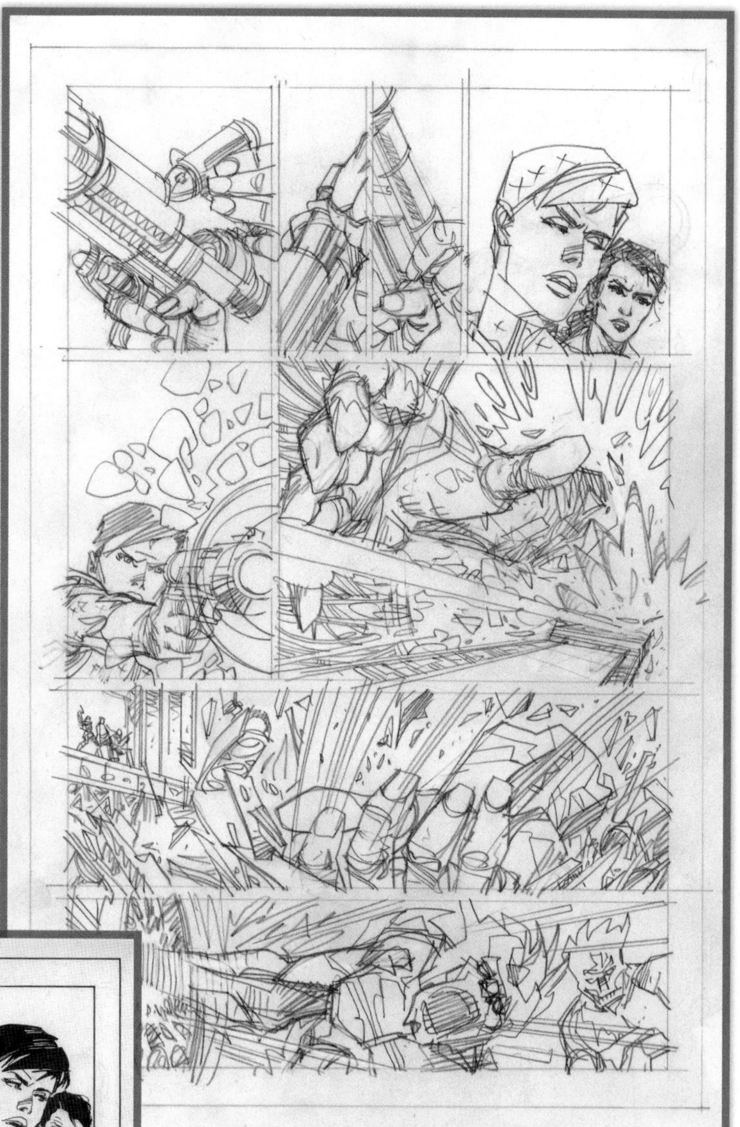
HULK 7/PG 10

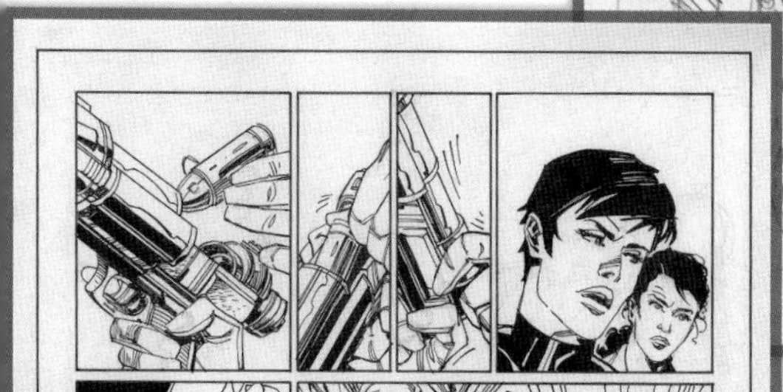
HULK 7/PG 10

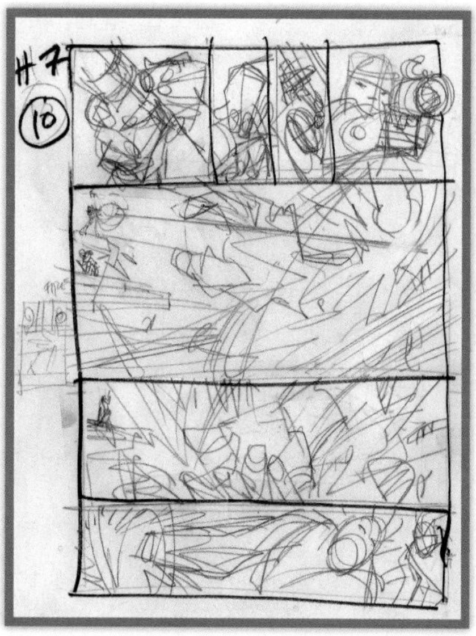
#7
10

#7, PAGE 10

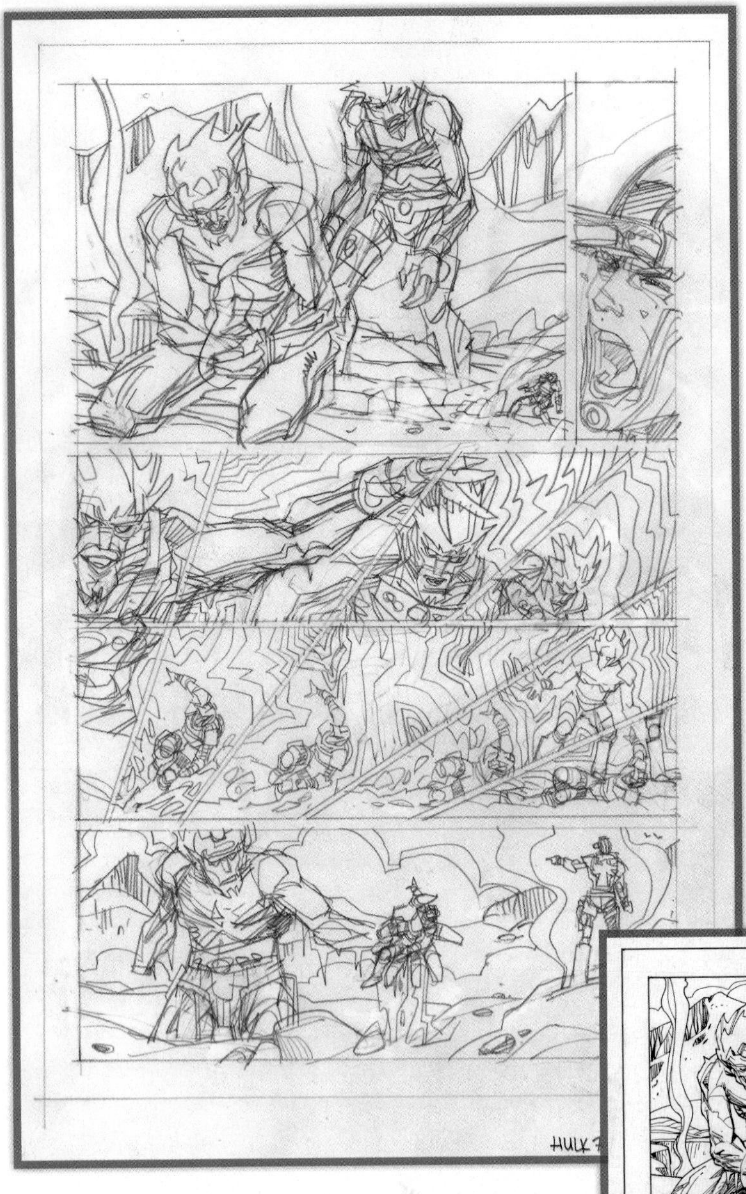

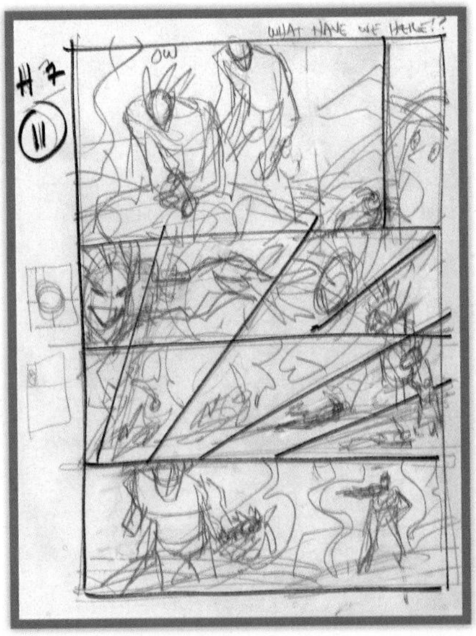
WHAT HAVE WE HERE!?
OW
#7
11

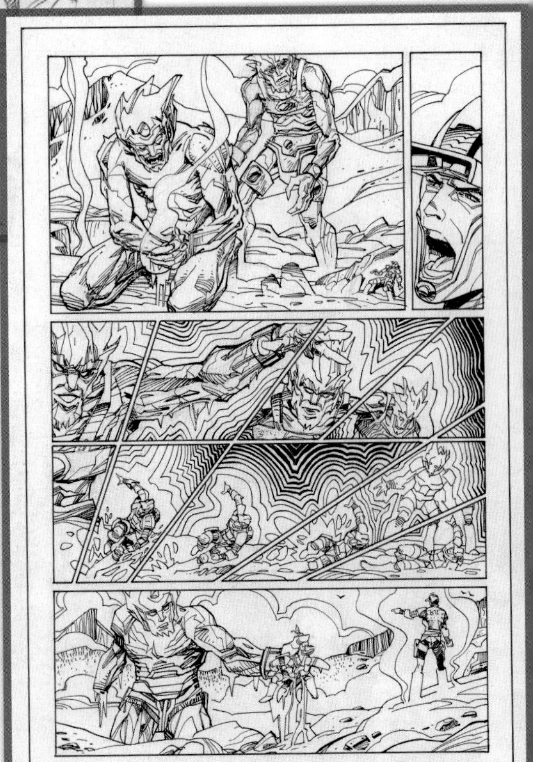
HULK 7/PG 11

#7, PAGE 11

ART PROCESS
BY MATTEO SCALERA

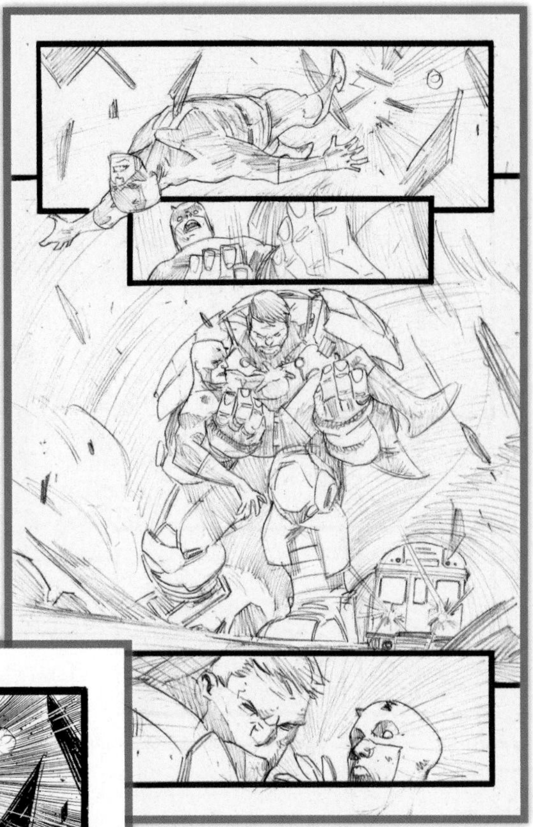

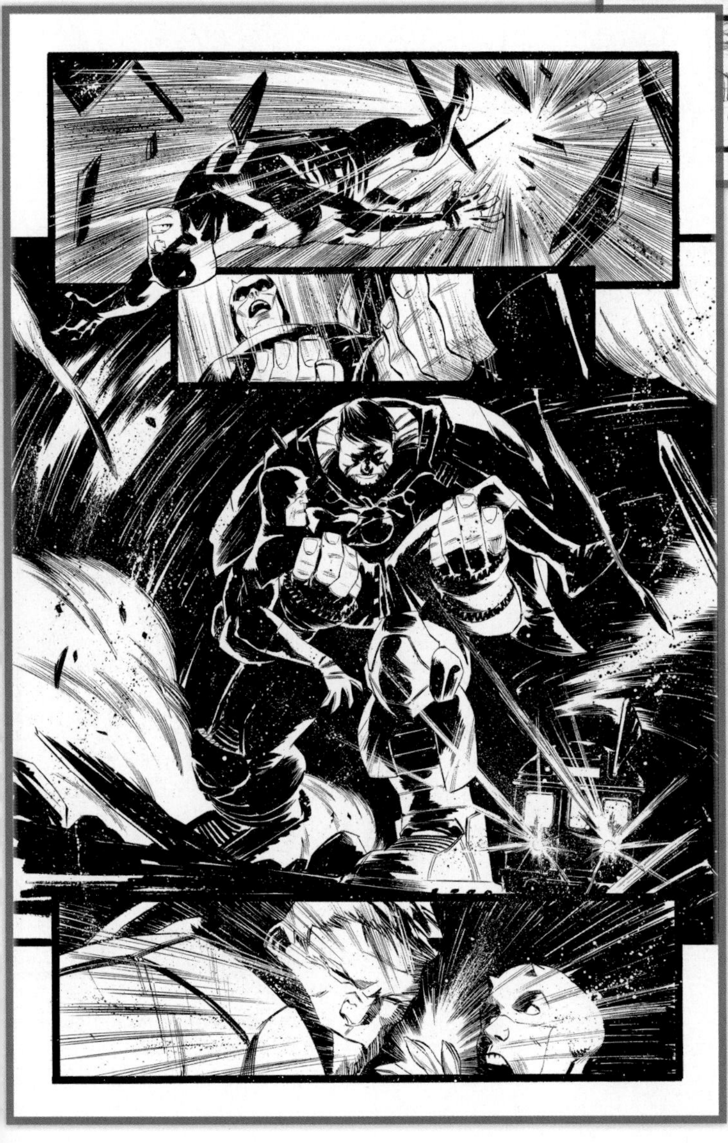

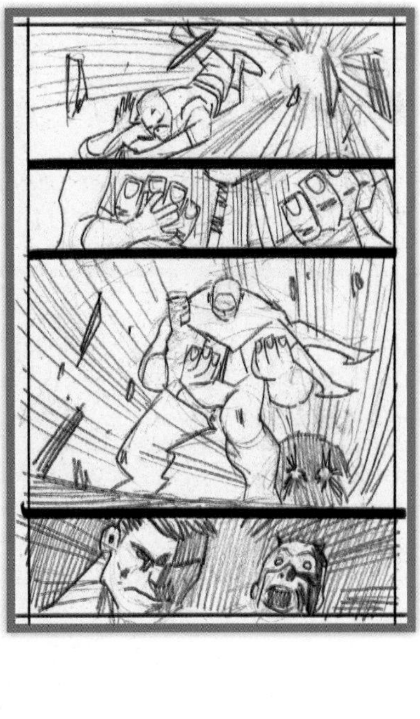

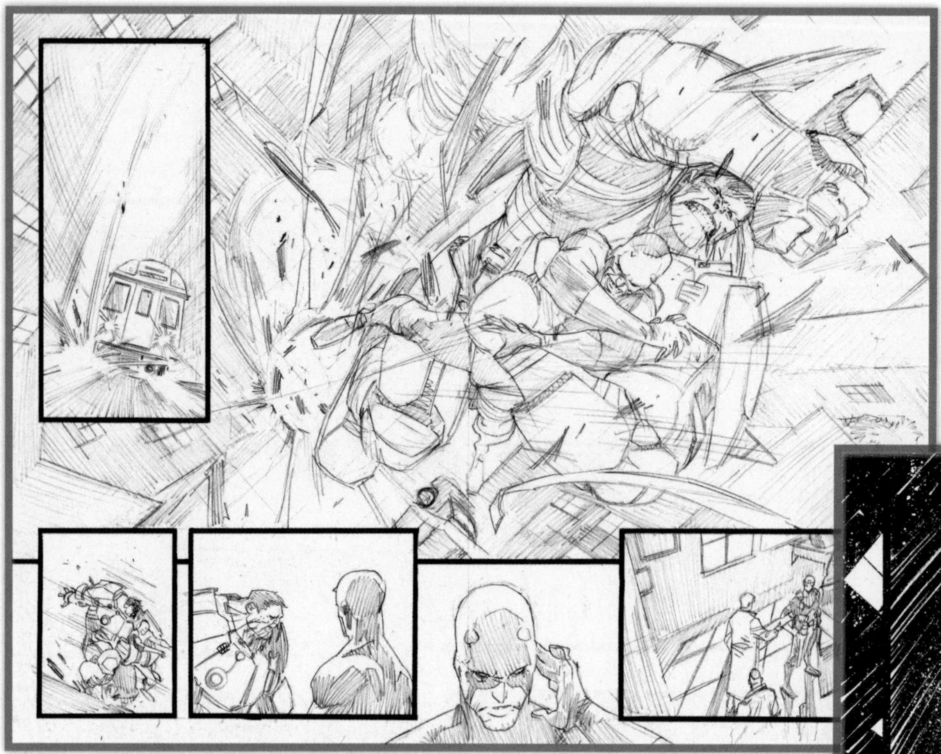

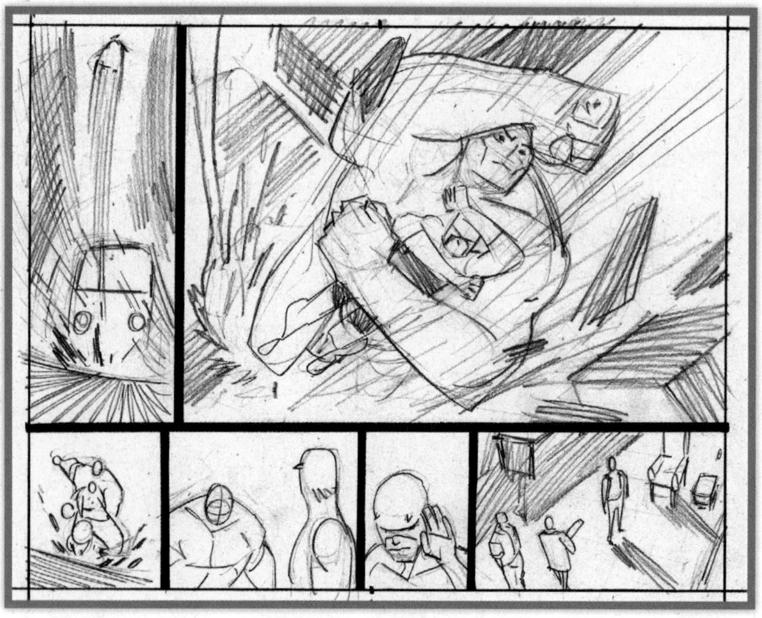

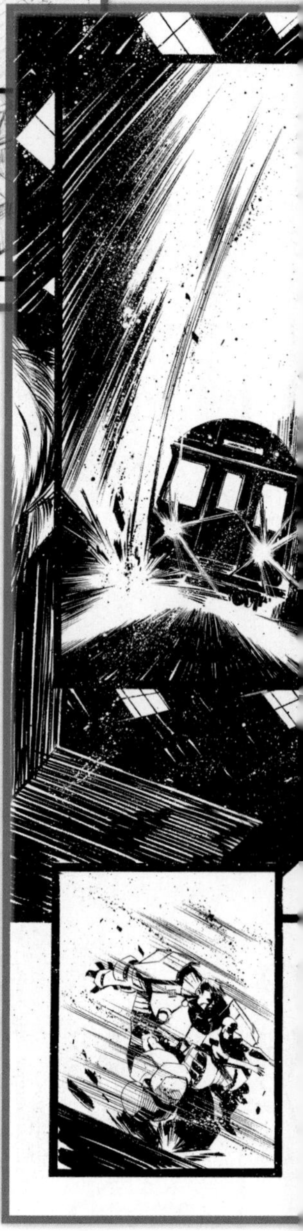

#10, PAGES 2-3

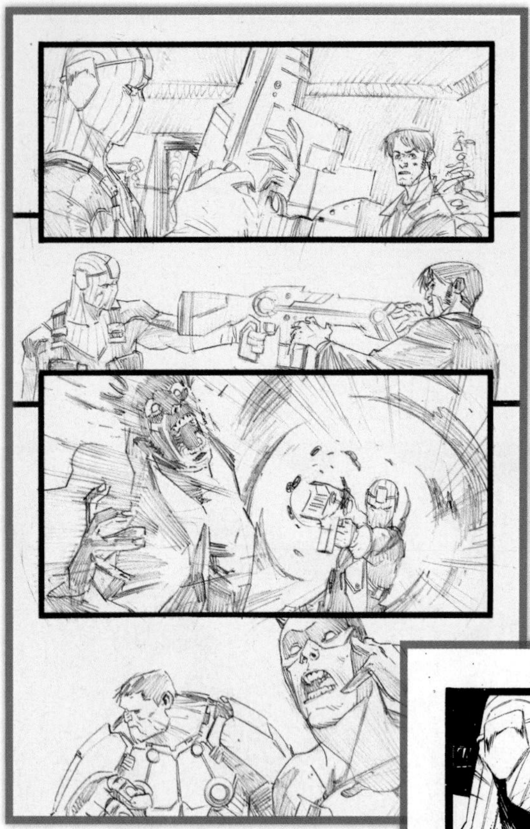

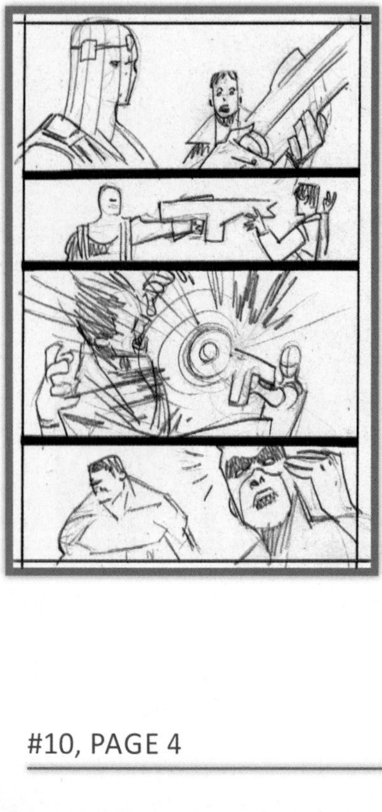

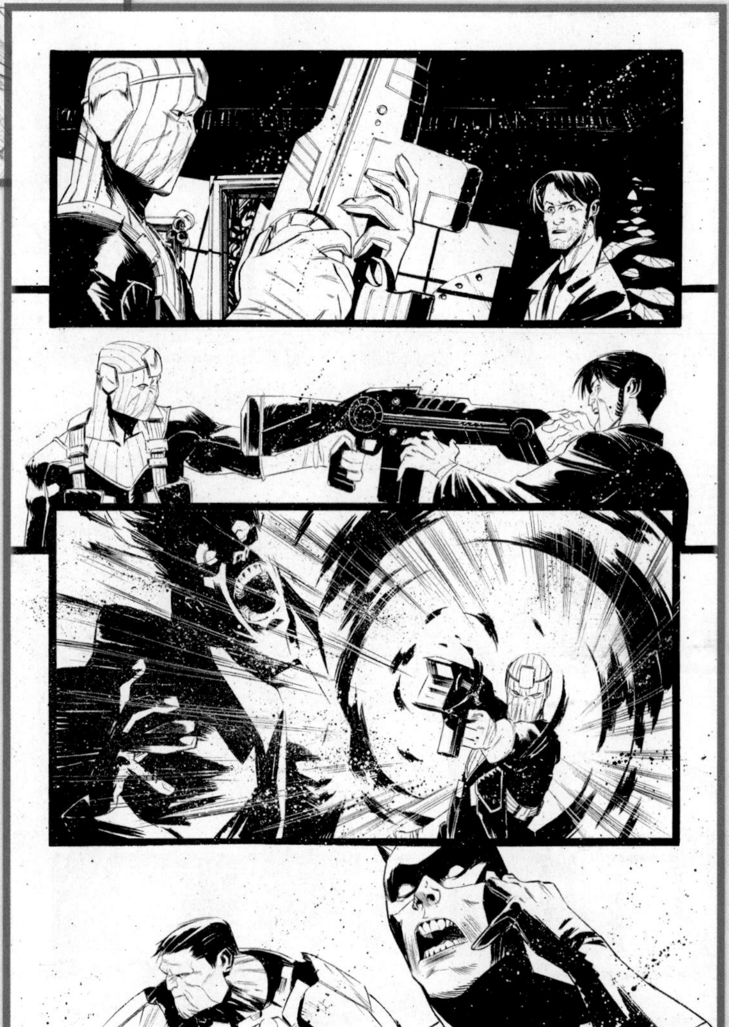

#10, PAGE 4

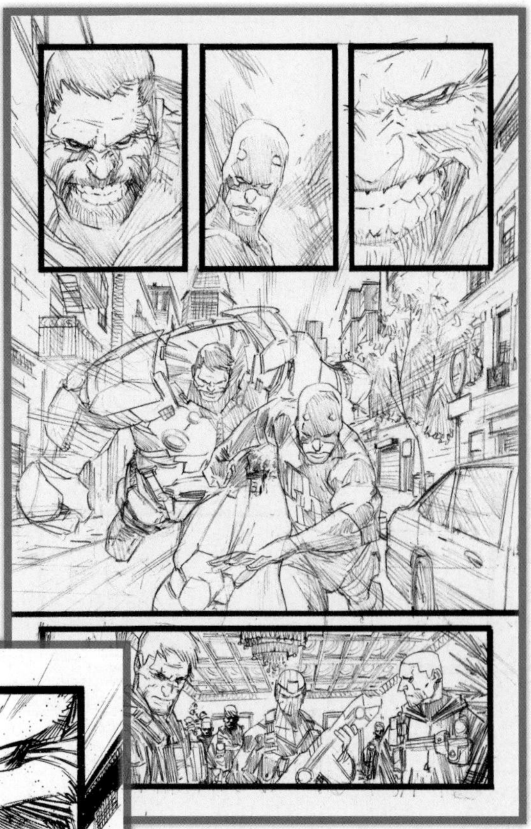

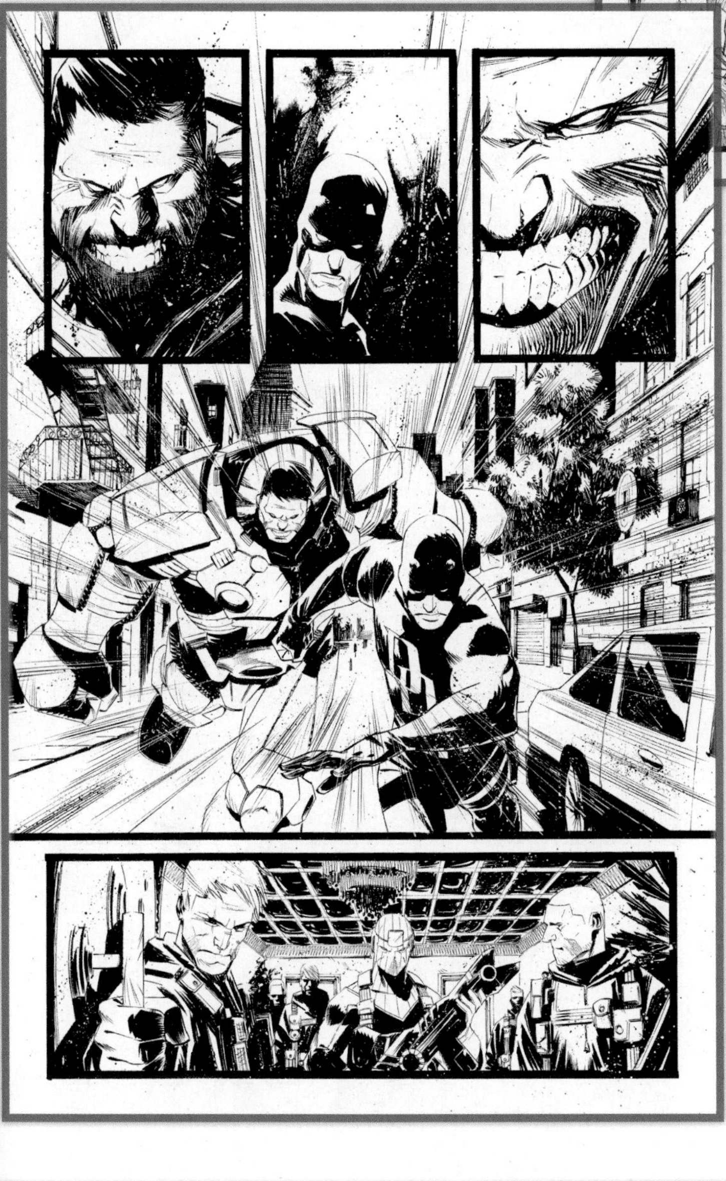

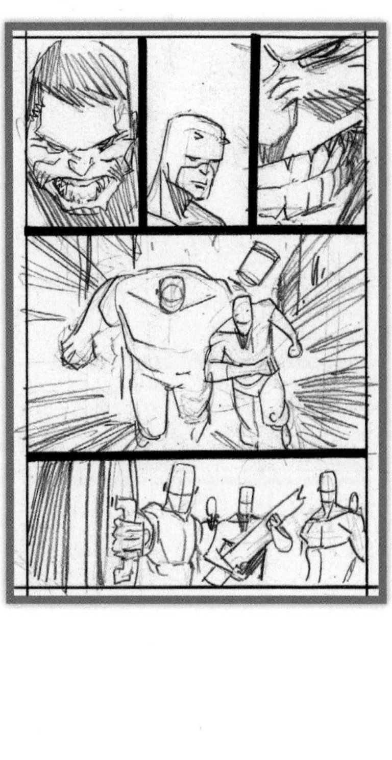

#10, PAGE 5

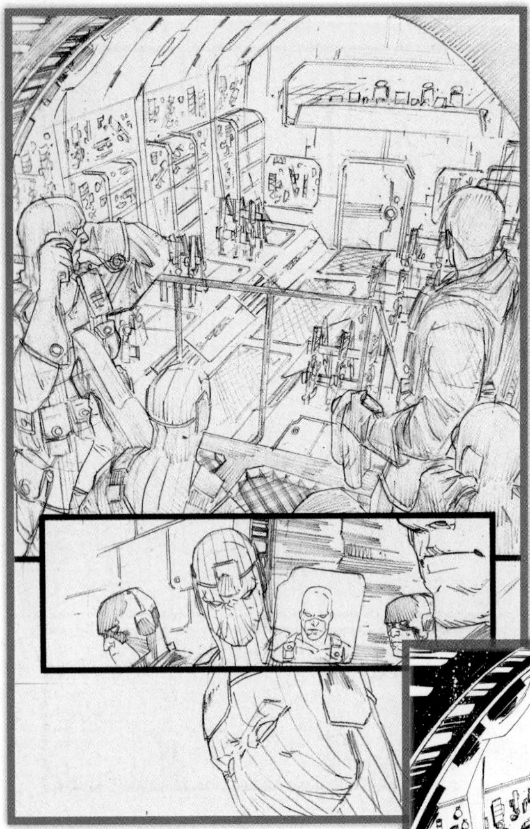

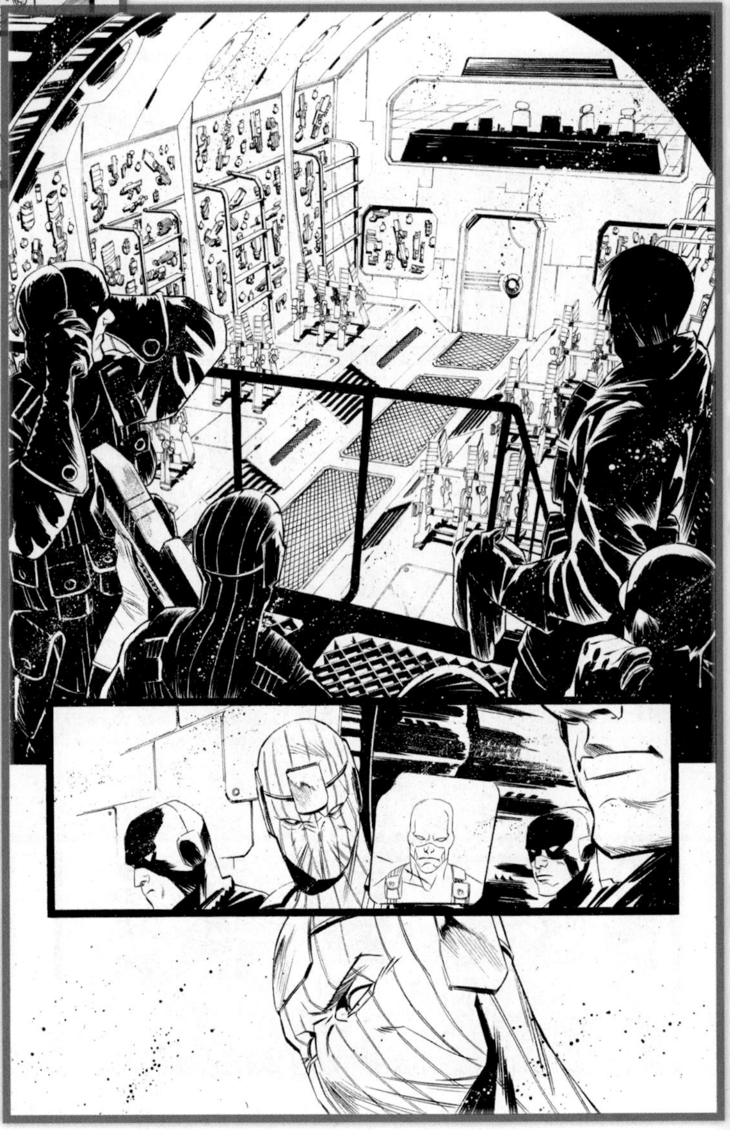

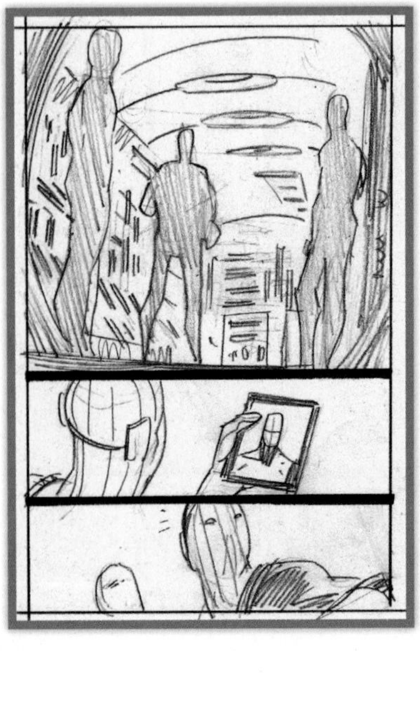

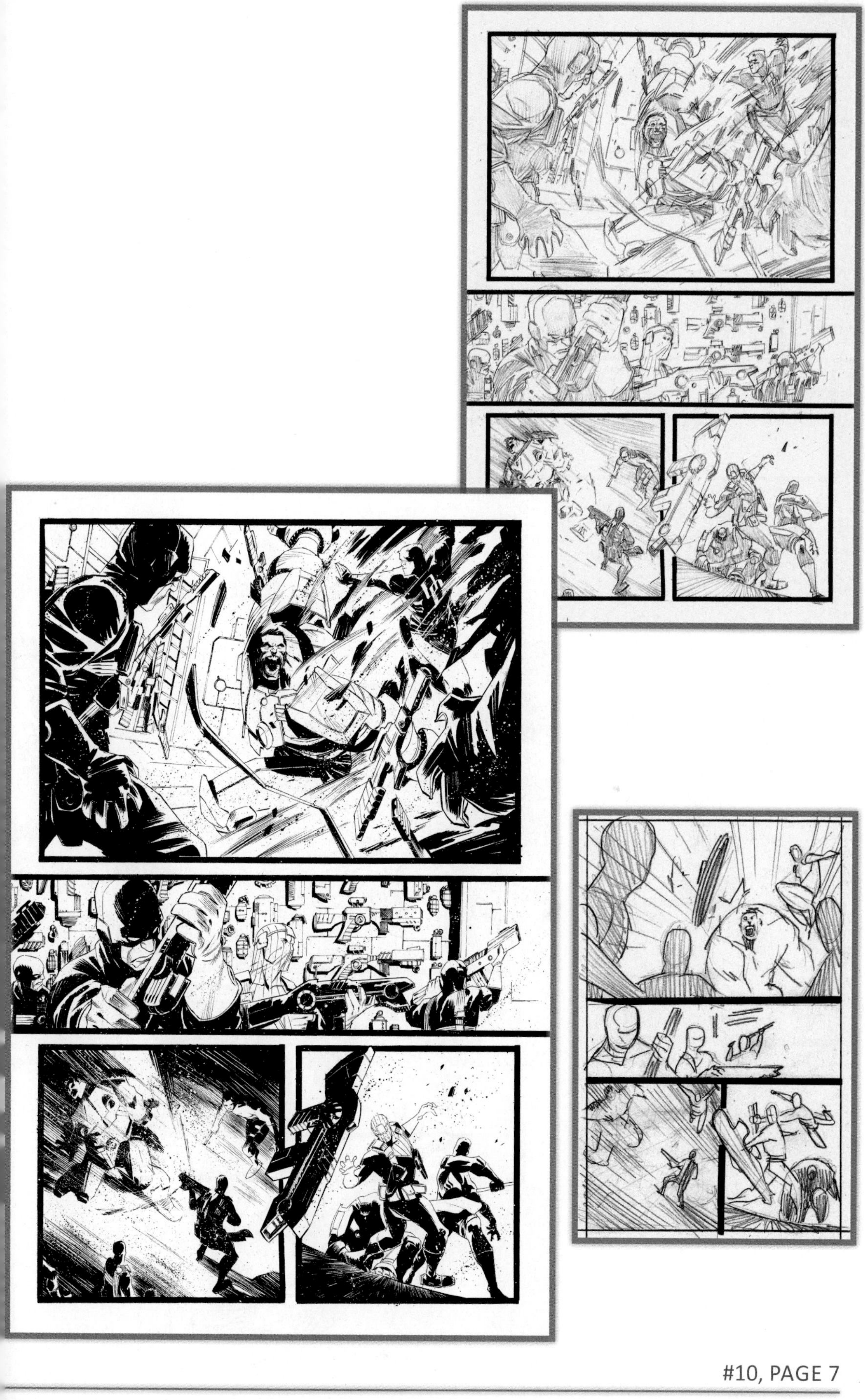

#10, PAGE 7

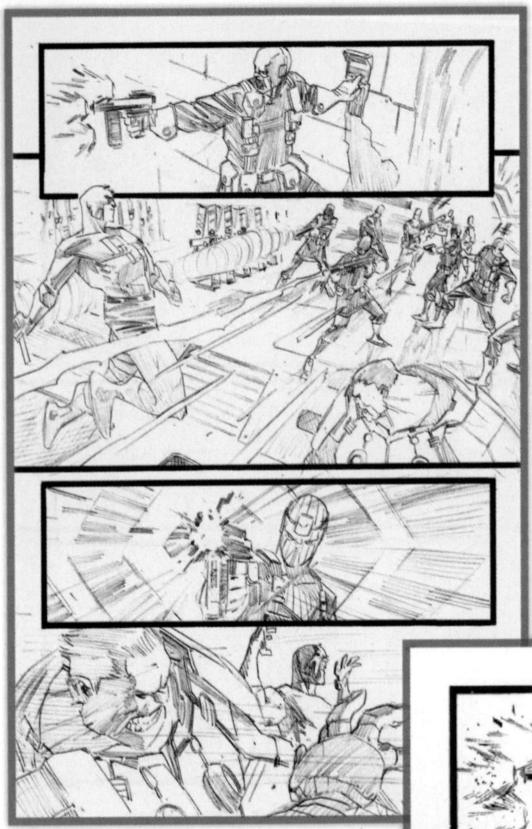

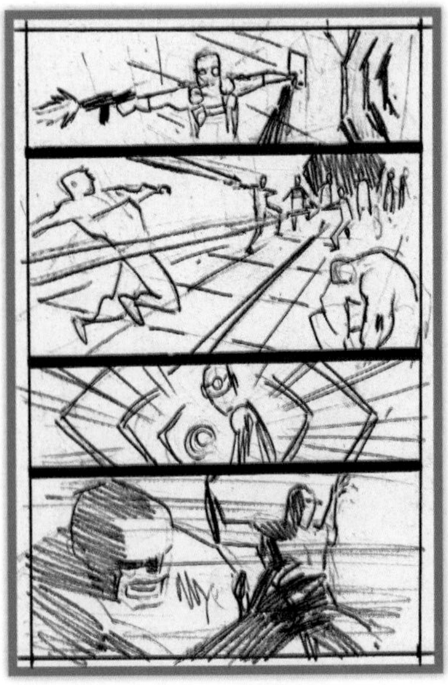

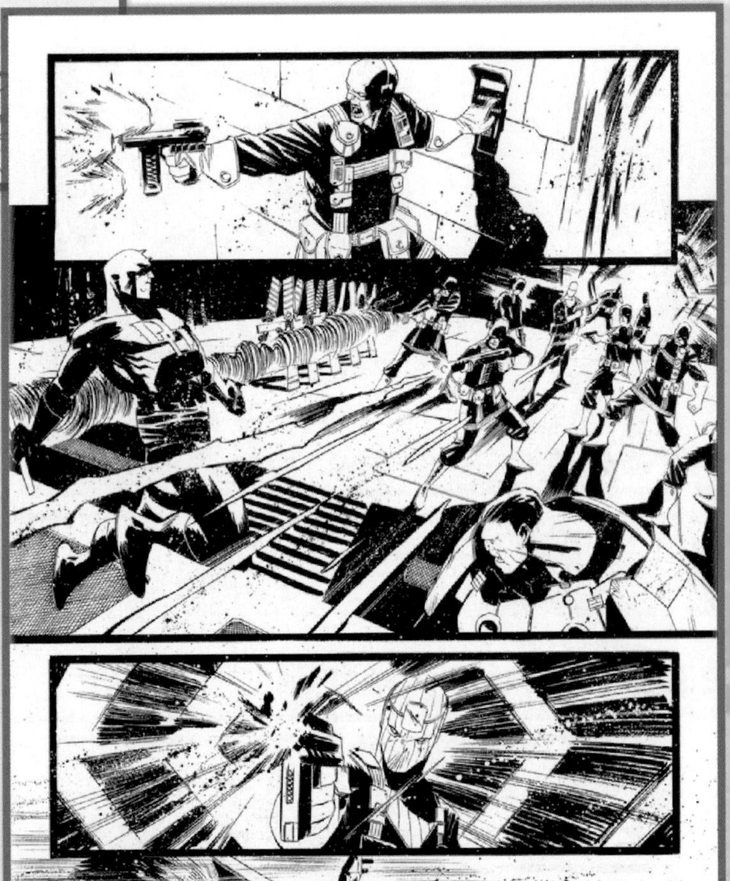

#10, PAGE 8

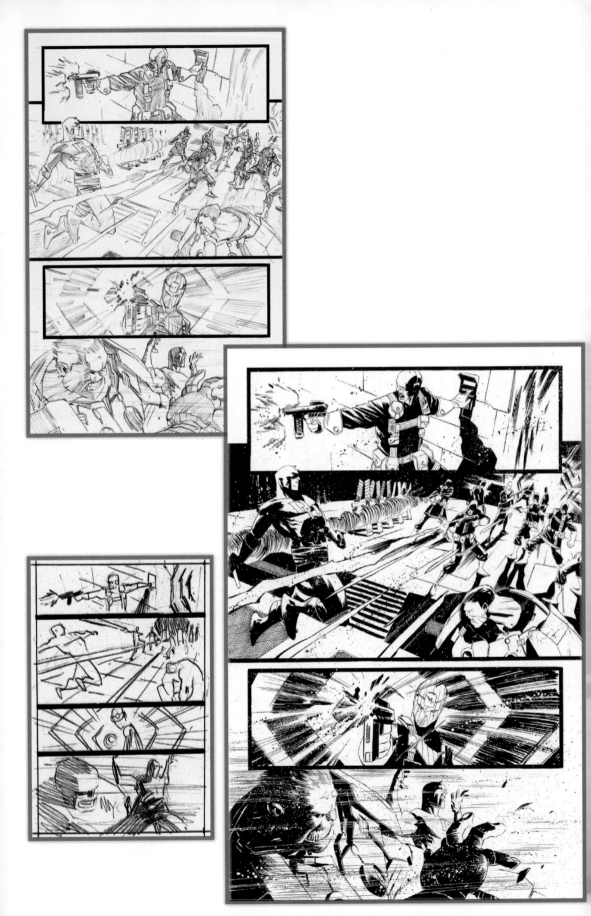

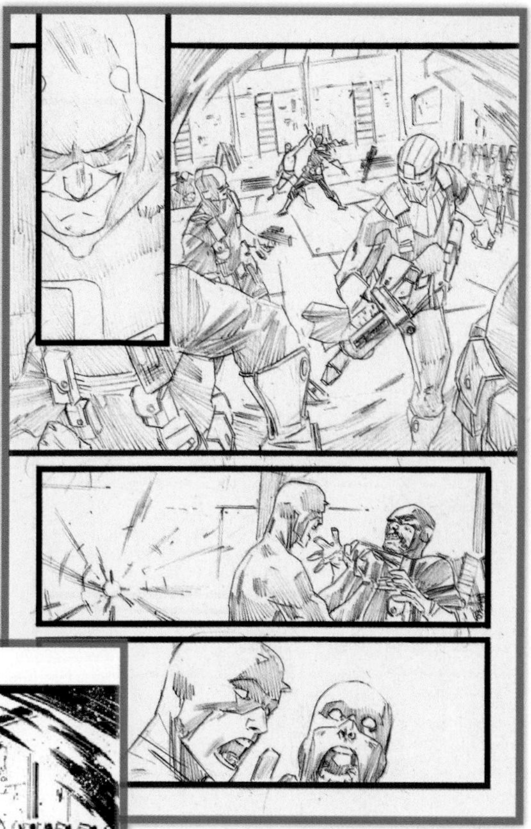

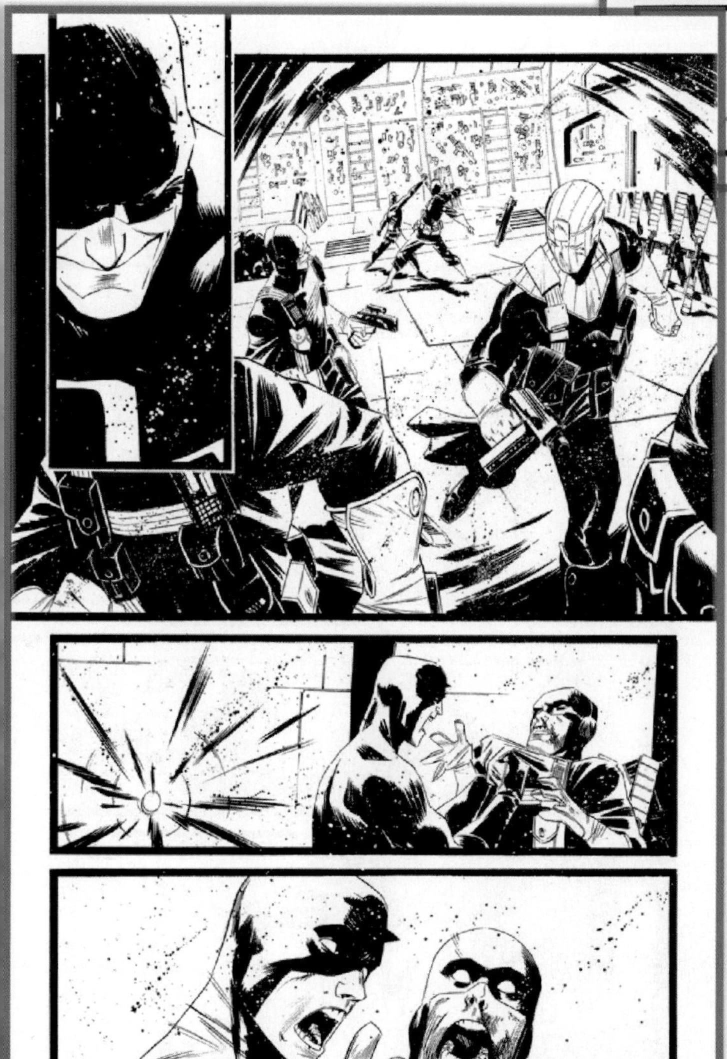

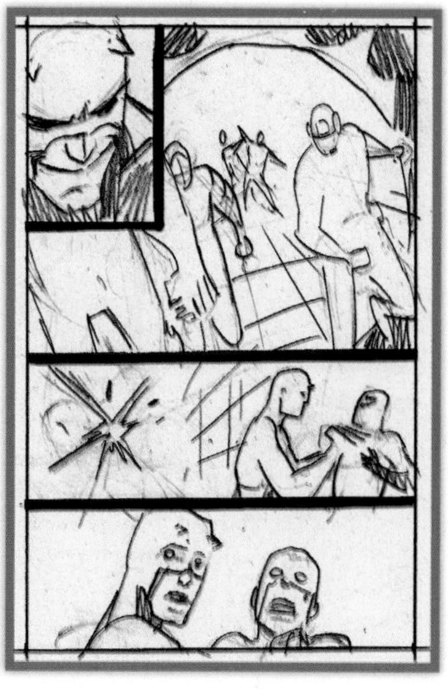

#10, PAGE 9

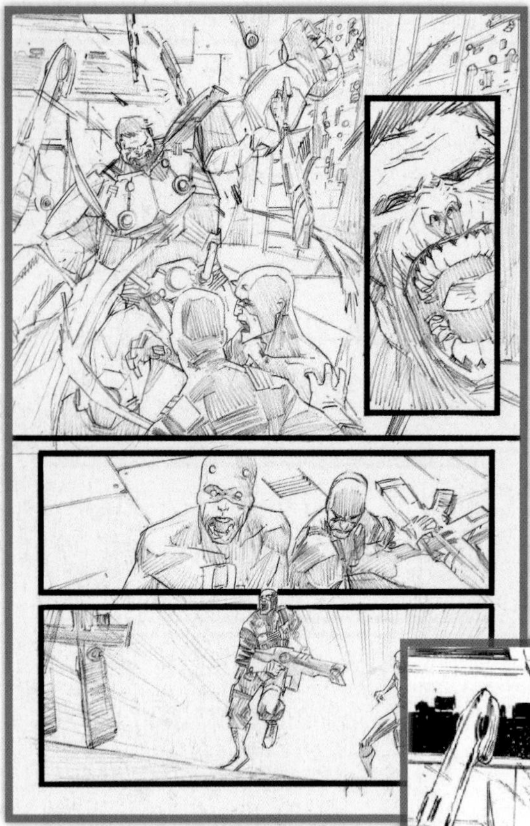

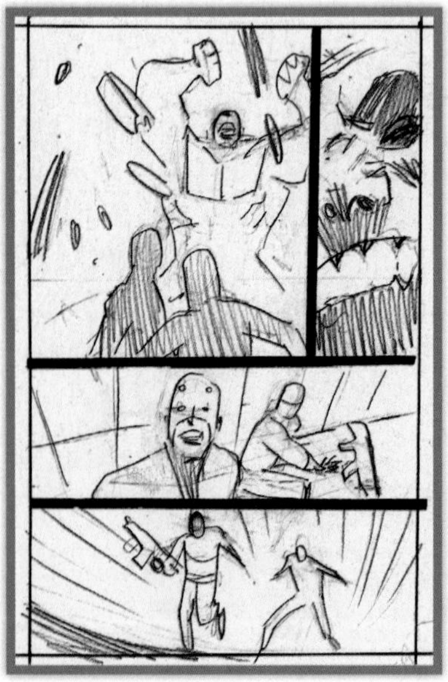

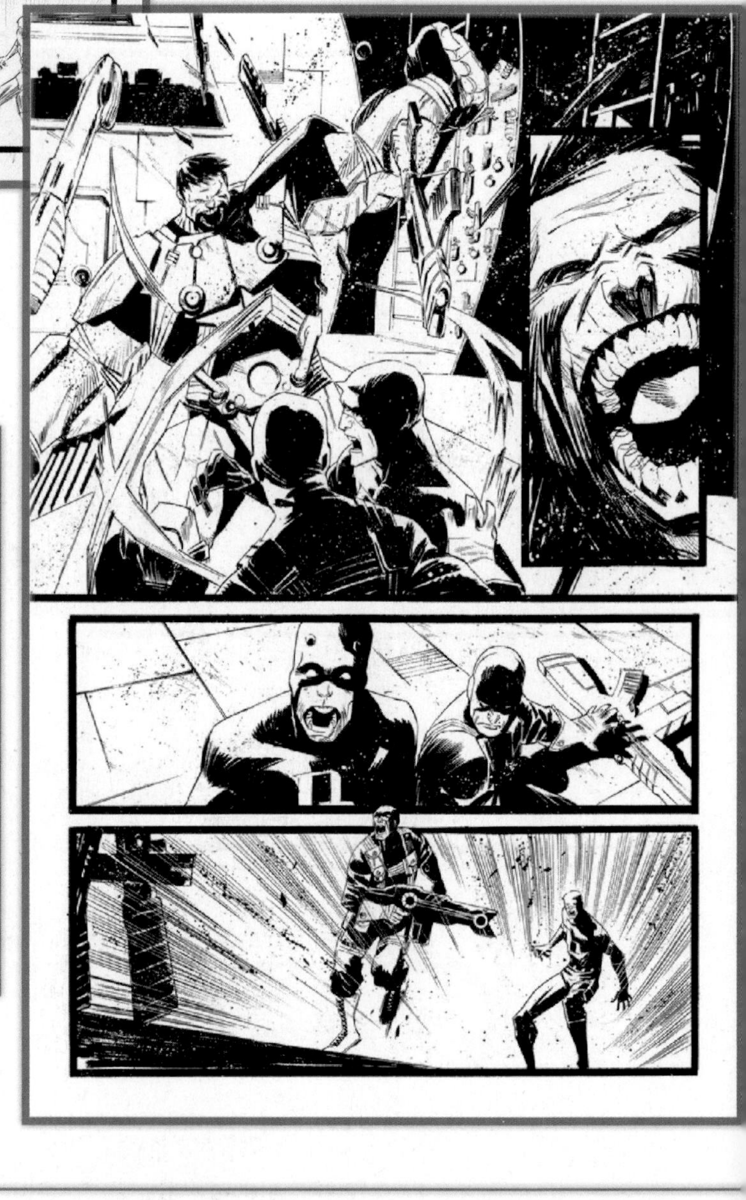

#10, PAGE 10

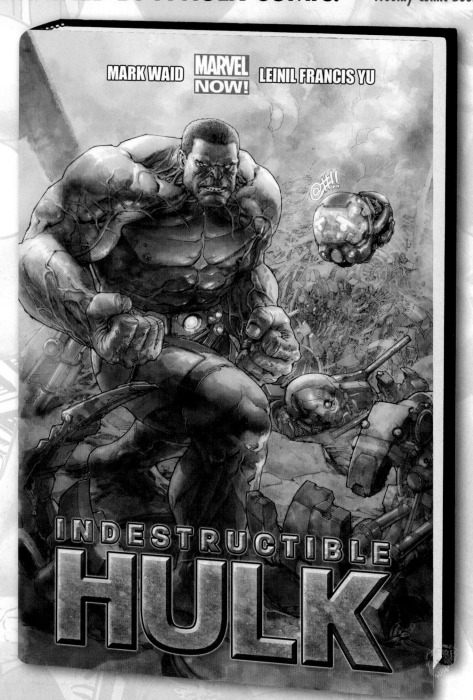

MARVEL AR AUGMENTED REALITY

MARVEL AUGMENTED REALITY (AR) ENHANCES AND CHANGES THE WAY YOU EXPERIENCE COMICS!

TO ACCESS THE FREE MARVEL AR CONTENT IN THIS BOOK*:

1. Locate the AR logo within the comic.
2. Go to Marvel.com/AR in your web browser.
3. Search by series title to find the corresponding AR.
4. Enjoy Marvel AR!

*All AR content that appears in this book has been archived and will be available only at Marvel.com/AR – no longer in the Marvel AR App. Content subject to change and availability.

INDESTRUCTIBLE HULK AR INDEX